Innovative Approaches in the Treatment of Drug Abuse

Recent Titles in
Contributions in Criminology and Penology

Beyond Punishment: A New View on the Rehabilitation of Criminal Offenders
Edgardo Rotman

Police Pursuit Driving: Controlling Responses to Emergency Situations
Geoffrey P. Alpert and Roger G. Dunham

Vigilantism: Political History of Private Power in America
William C. Culberson

Chinese Subculture and Criminality: Non-traditional Crime Groups in America
Ko-lin Chin

A Sword for the Convicted: Representing Indigent Defendants on Appeal
David T. Wasserman

Delinquency in Puerto Rico: The 1970 Birth Cohort Study
Dora Nevares, Marvin E. Wolfgang, and Paul E. Tracy with the collaboration of Steven Aurand

Waging the Battle Against Drunk Driving: Issues, Countermeasures, and Effectiveness
Gerald D. Robin

Policing Western Europe: Politics, Professionalism, and Public Order, 1850–1940
Clive Emsley and Barbara Weinberger, editors

Policing a Socialist Society: The German Democratic Republic
Nancy Travis Wolfe

Domestic Marijuana: A Neglected Industry
Ralph A. Weisheit

Personality and Peer Influence in Juvenile Corrections
Martin Gold and D. Wayne Osgood

Bad Guys and Good Guys: Moral Polarization and Crime
Daniel S. Claster

INNOVATIVE APPROACHES IN THE TREATMENT OF DRUG ABUSE

Program Models and Strategies

Edited by James A. Inciardi,
Frank M. Tims, and Bennett W. Fletcher

CONTRIBUTIONS IN CRIMINOLOGY AND PENOLOGY, NUMBER 39

Greenwood Press
Westport, Connecticut • London

Library of Congress Cataloging-in-Publication Data

Innovative approaches in the treatment of drug abuse : program models and strategies / edited by James A. Inciardi, Frank M. Tims, and Bennett W. Fletcher.
p. cm. — (Contributions in criminology and penology, ISSN 0732-4464 ; no. 39)
Includes index.
ISBN 0-313-28422-9 (alk. paper)
1. Drug abuse—Treatment—United States. I. Inciardi, James A. II. Tims, Frank M. III. Fletcher, Bennett W. IV. Series.
RC564.65.I55 1993
362.29'18'0973—dc20 92-35555

British Library Cataloguing in Publication Data is available.

Library of Congress Catalog Card Number: 92-35555
ISBN: 0-313-28422-9
ISSN: 0732-4464

First published in 1993

Greenwood Press, 88 Post Road West, Westport, CT 06881
An imprint of Greenwood Publishing Group, Inc.

Printed in the United States of America

The paper used in this book complies with the Permanent Paper Standard issued by the National Information Standards Organization (Z39.48-1984).

10 9 8 7 6 5 4 3 2 1

Contents

Part II: Residential Programs

Part III: Case Management Programs

Part IV: Multi-Modality and Other Eclectic Programs

Figures and Tables

FIGURES

TABLES

Improving Treatment: A Program for Systematic Innovation

Bennett W. Fletcher, Frank M. Tims, and James A. Inciardi

In the early 1980s the drug abuse problem in the United States appeared to be under control. While heroin use had been at epidemic rates a decade earlier, the low purity of street heroin—averaging near 4 percent in the late 1970s[1]—enticed few new users. Based on indicators such as admissions to treatment, frequencies of emergency room visits and overdose deaths, and heroin price and purity data, the number of heroin addicts was estimated to decrease from about 525,000 in 1976 to about 420,000 in 1979 (Demaree, Hudiburg, and Fletcher, 1980).[2]

Concern over the illicit use of cocaine remained low throughout the 1960s and 1970s. A perception of cocaine as nonaddictive and relatively benign, coupled with its high cost and low street purity, seemed to limit its abuse potential (Siegel, 1977; Wesson and Smith, 1977). Only about 8 percent of federally funded treatment admissions identified cocaine as their primary drug in 1980 (NIDA, 1981). Intranasal use was the primary route of administration for these admissions, with only about 30 percent injecting cocaine.

This began to change in the early 1980s as the availability of cocaine increased. Already depicted as fashionable among celebrities and young, highly paid professionals, cocaine use was encountered throughout various socioeconomic strata and occupational groups (Clayton, 1985). When a low-cost, smokeable, highly potent, and addictive form of cocaine known as "crack" appeared on the streets, its use quickly reached epidemic proportions, particularly in the lower socioeconomic strata. The greater bioavailability of smoked crack permitted higher concentrations of cocaine to reach the brain, resulting in more intense drug effects. The dependence potential of crack cocaine proved to be very high, and its widespread availability provided dramatic examples of the problems associated with its use. Its appearance was marked by new levels of urban violence as street gangs dealing in cocaine fought for territory. In their preoccupation with obtaining and using crack, addicted women were reported to neglect their children and to exchange sex for drugs. Hospitals in New York City, the District of Columbia, and elsewhere found themselves reluctant custodians of "boarder" babies born to young crack-addicted mothers who abandoned their infants after birth.

Concurrent with the cocaine epidemic, another epidemic was spreading in the population addicted to heroin. Acquired Immune Deficiency Syndrome (AIDS), caused by the Human Immunodeficiency Virus (HIV), was first documented in the United States in homosexual males, but the sharing of contaminated syringes and needles by injection drug users quickly became recognized as another major avenue for spreading HIV. Multiple sexual contacts and partners of infected addicts, including prostitutes and females trading sex for drugs, threatened to provide a vector to spread AIDS in the heterosexual, non-drug-using population. By 1988, 28 percent of AIDS cases were intravenous drug users, and their sexual partners were a rapidly growing risk group.

Treatment programs already labored under severe financial constraints during the 1970s as per-slot funding failed to keep pace with inflation. The Reagan administration introduced a radical change in social and health services program funding with the philosophy of New Federalism in 1981. This philosophy, which sought to reduce the federal role and give states greater discretion in allocating treatment funds, was enacted into law with the Omnibus Budget Reconciliation Act of 1981. This legislation terminated direct federal support of treatment programs and transferred funds directly to states in the form of block grants for alcohol, drug abuse, and mental health treatment. Federal funding of treatment was reduced by some 25 percent to reflect savings in administrative costs. Unable or unwilling to increase state allocations to replace federal administration and monitoring efforts, many states gradually reduced their own levels of treatment funding, with consequent declines in the quality and availability of public drug abuse treatment services.

Although there was a clear need for increased support of drug abuse treatment to combat the growing epidemics of cocaine use and AIDS, there were also widespread misunderstanding and misinformation concerning the nature of drug abuse and the effectiveness of drug abuse treatment. Research showed that treatment could be effective in reducing drug use and criminal behavior (Hubbard et al., 1989; Sells and Simpson, 1980; Tims, Fletcher, and Hubbard, 1991), but changes in patterns of drug use, in characteristics of drug users, and in the organization and structure of the treatment system created uncertainty regarding past findings on the effectiveness of treatment. Anecdotal reports suggested that typical publicly funded, community-based treatment programs developed in the 1960s and 1970s to treat heroin addiction were challenged by new patterns of drug use and were under severe strain from excessive demand, understaffing, and chronic lack of adequate resources and support needed to address such accompanying problems as psychiatric comorbidity and social, educational, and vocational deficits.

The National Institute on Drug Abuse (NIDA) was no longer authorized to collect systematic data to monitor client flow and quality of care after 1981, and was hard pressed to provide satisfactory information on the demand for treatment, the availability of treatment services, and other data needed to guide policy on the federal role in drug abuse treatment. Surveys of the homeless, criminal justice clients, and the general household population provided evidence that the number of publicly funded treatment slots fell far short of the estimated need. The Institute of Medicine estimated that on any given day in 1987/1988, some 5.5 million individuals needed drug treatment (Gerstein and Harwood, 1990: 86), while the public and private treatment capacity in 1987 was estimated at 329,000 clients (Gerstein and Harwood, 1990: 204).

Given this state of affairs, there was an urgent need to expand the availability and improve the effectiveness of treatment services, both to curb cocaine use and to slow the spread of AIDS among injection drug users. Congress provided increased funding for expansion of drug abuse treatment, for research on treatment, and for the development of data systems to monitor treatment demand and utilization. Under Anti-Drug Abuse Acts of 1986 and 1988 and related legislation, federal drug control expenditures increased from $4.1 billion in fiscal year (FY) 1989 to $6.3 billion in FY 1990, and to an estimated $9.5 billion in FY 1991. Over 70 percent of these expenditures were devoted to "supply reduction" activities such as drug-related law enforcement, developing more prison capacity, and drug interdiction efforts. The remainder were allocated to "demand reduction" efforts such as prevention, education, treatment, and treatment research (ONDCP, 1989: 112; ONDCP, 1990: 99).

EXPANDING CAPACITY AND IMPROVING TREATMENT

Faced with cocaine and AIDS epidemics that threatened to overwhelm a weakened treatment system, NIDA developed a program of research demonstrations to improve and expand treatment. This initiative was conceived in 1988 as part of a larger AIDS prevention effort under the premise that more effective drug abuse treatment would reduce risk behaviors that spread HIV infection. The client populations for these studies were defined as those at risk due to (1) intravenous drug use or (2) nonintravenous drug use, which might lead to risk behaviors through sexual activity (e.g., prostitution or exchange of sex for drugs). A second wave of projects was begun the following year to develop and test improved treatments. The focus of this second initiative was broadened to include research on *all* drug abuse treatment client groups, not just those at high risk for HIV. Both treatment improvement initiatives were in support of the objectives of the Department of Health and human Services under the National Drug Control Strategy (ONDCP, 1989).

The research demonstration grant mechanism is most suitable to NIDA's programmatic objectives. In addition to research costs, demonstration grants support research-related treatment costs, thereby providing a means to create new treatment capacity. Increased capacity is of course desirable from several aspects. Through research demonstration grants, more drug-dependent clients may be treated, and many of these will receive research-enhanced drug abuse treatment services. From a research perspective, it helps insure an adequate number of subjects. It also gives the investigator the leverage to insure that the treatment intervention is implemented as designed.

The higher degree of control over treatment is especially important in bringing interventions developed in highly controlled laboratories or clinical research centers into community-based treatment programs. Unlike most university- or medical-school-based treatment programs, which tend to have a strong commitment to research as well as highly qualified treatment and research staff, counselors and other personnel of community-based treatment programs vary widely in training, experience, motivation, and effectiveness. Underfunded public treatment programs often have large client-to-staff ratios, poorly paid counselors, high staff turnover rates, and limited ability to provide more than the most basic services.

These factors tend to make the investigation of innovative treatment interventions more difficult to conduct in community-based treatment programs than in clinical research laboratories. No matter how promising, however, interventions developed in clinical research laboratories are of little use if they cannot be transported to the field. By controlling the funding of treatment services through the mechanism of the research demonstration grant, the investigator can insure that interventions are properly implemented and fairly tested in applied settings.

Fifteen of the projects funded under NIDA treatment improvement research demonstration initiatives are the subject of this volume. These fifteen projects focus on testing applied intervention strategies to improve client recruitment, retention, performance, and treatment outcomes, primarily in community-based treatment programs. A glance at the table of contents reveals that the projects collected herein span a wide range of populations, treatment settings, intervention strategies, and research designs and methodologies. The special value of these studies is that virtually all of them deal with complex, "real-world" issues of implementing and testing innovative treatment approaches in community treatment programs. Clients included as subjects are representative of those entering community-based treatment programs.

Despite the more pronounced challenges of conducting research in applied settings, examination of the research designs will show that treatment strategies are to be tested rigorously and systematically. Use of tightly controlled research designs with random assignment of subjects to treatment interventions is planned in many sites. Sophisticated analytic approaches to behavioral and psychological measurements will help to determine the underlying relationships between client characteristics and predispositions, treatment interventions and services, and external environmental events that impact the client's recovery from drug abuse.

COORDINATION EFFORTS

Concurrently with the funding of treatment research demonstration grants, a contract was developed to help coordinate and monitor these treatment and research initiatives. Because of the legislative interest in treatment capacity, one task under the contract is to collect narrative progress reports and aggregate data from projects to monitor the treatment capacity created and the number of clients treated, and to collect some limited demographic information about subjects in the research projects. The database resulting from this task does not purport to have research utility but is used only in a reporting function. A second objective is to promote the sharing of data across projects to the extent feasible to test alternative explanatory models and to discover limits to the generalizability of observed relationships by using methodologies such as meta-analysis or validity generalization.

The third and most important function of the coordination effort has been to bring investigators in charge of the various research projects together periodically to describe the progress and problems they have encountered in conducting their studies, and to discuss solutions and new directions for investigation. These meetings have served to inform the research field and to facilitate progress and understanding of the drug treatment problems being faced. This and subsequent volumes are a direct result of the research demonstration coordination meetings.

As the reader will appreciate from the chapters, which describe in detail the design and conceptual background of each research project, the grants funded under the research demonstration initiatives have been highly visible and important studies that have improved treatment and expanded treatment capacity nationwide. Because the research demonstration provides the investigator with the ability to pay for study-related treatment costs, the investigator has a tremendous advantage in implementing experimental interventions and in maintaining research control over client selection and assignment, service delivery, and data quality standards and measurement techniques in community-based treatment. Research demonstrations provide the necessary step between developing and testing treatment strategies and protocols in the clinical laboratory and translating these innovations into treatment interventions useful to the field. The following studies, which represent the state of the art in drug abuse treatment evaluation research, will be an outstanding and invaluable resource for our future understanding of what works best, and why, in drug abuse treatment.

As a final note here, this represents the first of three books on the overall treatment demonstration initiative. While this volume focuses on the fifteen *program models and strategies*, a second volume will focus on each program's implementation issues and problems. A third volume will present treatment outcome information.

NOTES

1. Purity is estimated from heroin purchase and seizures by federal, state, and local authorities in the Drug Enforcement Administration's STRIDE street buy program for twenty-four metropolitan areas participating in the Drug Abuse Warning Network (DAWN). Average purity across metropolitan areas was as follows: 1976, 6.7 percent; 1977, 4.5 percent; 1978, 4.2 percent; and 1979, 3.5 percent.

2. R. G. Demaree, A. Hudiburg, and B. W. Fletcher (1980). *Estimates of the Prevalence of Heroin Use in 24 Metropolitan Areas and Nationwide, 1976–1979*. Technical Report prepared under the Drug Abuse Indicator Methodology Project, Contract 271–79–4710. Rockville, MD: National Institute on Drug Abuse.

Estimates for each year were:

1976: 523,000 ± 39,000
1977: 495,000 ± 37,000
1978: 471,000 ± 38,000
1979: 420,000 ± 33,000

REFERENCES

Clayton, R. R. 1985. Cocaine Use in the United States: In a Blizzard or Just Being Snowed? In *Cocaine Use in America: Epidemiologic and Clinical Perspectives*, edited by N. J. Kozel and E. H. Adams, pp. 8–34. NIDA Research Monograph No. 61, DHHS Publication No. (ADM) 87–1414. Washington, DC: U.S. Government Printing Office.

Demaree, R. G., R. A. Hudiburg, and B. W. Fletcher. 1980. *Estimates of the Prevalence of Heroin Use in 24 Metropolitan Areas and Nationwide, 1976–1979*. Technical Report prepared under the Drug Abuse Indicator Methodology Project, Contract 271–79–4710. Rockville, MD: National Institute on Drug Abuse.

Gerstein, D. R., and H. J. Harwood (eds.). 1990. *Treating Drug Problems: A Study of the Evolution, Effectiveness, and Financing of Public and Private Drug Treatment Systems*, vol. 1. Washington, DC: National Academy Press.

Hubbard, R. L., M. E. Marsden, J. V. Rachal, H. J. Harwood, E. R. Cavanaugh, and H. M. Ginzburg. 1989. *Drug Abuse Treatment: A National Study of Effectiveness*. Chapel Hill: University of North Carolina Press.

National Institute on Drug Abuse (NIDA). 1981. *Data from the Client Oriented Data Acquisition Process (CODAP): Annual Data 1980*. Statistical Series E, No. 21, DHHS Publication No. (ADM) 81–1153. Washington, DC: U.S. Government Printing Office.

Office of National Drug Control Policy (ONDCP). 1989. *National Drug Control Strategy*. Washington, DC: U.S. Government Printing Office.

Office of National Drug Control Policy (ONDCP). 1990. *National Drug Control Strategy*. Washington, DC: U.S. Government Printing Office.

Sells, S. B., and D. D. Simpson. 1980. The Case for Drug Abuse Treatment Effectiveness, Based on the DARP Research Program. *British Journal of Addiction*, 75, 117–131.

Siegel, R. K. 1977. Cocaine: Recreational Use and Intoxication. In *Cocaine: 1977*, edited by R. C. Petersen and R. C. Stillman, pp. 119–136. NIDA Research Monograph No. 13, DHEW Publication No. (ADM) 79–741. Washington, DC: U.S. Government Printing Office.

Times, F. M., B. W. Fletcher, and R. L. Hubbard. 1991. Treatment Outcomes for Drug Abuse Clients. In *Improving Drug Abuse Treatment*, edited by R. W. Pickens, C. G. Leukefeld, and C. R. Schuster, pp. 93–113. NIDA Research Monograph No. 106, DHHS Publication No. (ADM) 91–1754. Washington, DC: Department of Health and Human Services.

Wesson, D. R., and D. E. Smith. 1977. Cocaine: Its Use for Central Nervous System Stimulation Including Recreational and Medical Uses. In *Cocaine: 1977*, edited by R. C. Petersen and R. C. Stillman, pp. 137–152. NIDA Research Monograph No. 13, DHEW Publication No. (ADM) 79–741. Washington, DC: U.S. Government Printing Office.

I
METHADONE PROGRAMS

1

Enhanced Methadone Maintenance Treatment: Limiting the Spread of HIV Among High-Risk Los Angeles Narcotics Addicts

M. Douglas Anglin, Mark L. Miller, Kean Mantius, and Christine Grella

Los Angeles County has the largest population of intravenous drug users (IVDUs) outside of New York City; yet its 60,000 to 80,000 seriously dependent IVDUs have sustained relatively low rates of HIV infection compared with those in other areas. HIV seropositivity rates for in-treatment samples of IVDUs were less than 3 percent through 1991 (Longshore and Anglin, 1990, 1991) as compared with approximately 15 percent in San Francisco (Chaisson et al., 1989; Watters et al., 1990) and over 50 percent in New York City and New Jersey (Des Jarlais et al., 1989). These rates for in-treatment samples remained relatively stable through the end of 1992. Furthermore, rates determined from out-of-treatment samples of IVDUs are estimated at no more than 6 to 8 percent (Longshore and Anglin, 1990, 1991).

Although the overall HIV infection rate is low among IVDUs in Los Angeles County, a significant number of the heterosexual AIDS cases are from this group. Of the 1,165 known adult heterosexual cases of clinical AIDS that were reported by October 31, 1991, 384 (33 percent) showed IV drug use as the sole risk factor. These 384 cases represent, however, only 2.8 percent of the 13,537 AIDS cases reported overall. An additional 947 cases (7 percent) were homosexual or bisexual men with a history of IV drug use (Los Angeles County Department of Health Services, 1991). In the case of heterosexual IVDUs, the predominant drug injected is heroin, while for homosexual or bisexual IVDUs, amphetamine predominates. From these data, it is apparent that Los Angeles County contains one of the largest pools of uninfected IVDUs in the nation, a circumstance that warrants close monitoring and aggressive intervention.

HIGH-RISK IVDU GROUPS IN LOS ANGELES COUNTY

Whatever the reasons for the fortuitously low HIV seroprevalence and clinical AIDS rates among Los Angeles IVDUs, self-reports of high-risk behaviors among heroin addicts, the largest local group of IVDUs, portend potentially severe increases if the base rate of HIV infection rises even slightly. Among treatment samples surveyed in the Los Angeles area, approximately 80 percent of IVDUs reported sharing needles with others. Surprisingly, 27 percent of male homosexual[1] IVDUs, 30 percent of male heterosexuals, 42 percent of female homosexuals, and 18 percent of female heterosexuals have reported sharing needles with a known gay or bisexual individual. This is a particularly high-risk activity since in most major cities outside of the New York City area, HIV seroprevalence rates in gay men are greater by several orders of magnitude than the rates among IVDUs. In Los Angeles County, while no rigorous estimate is available, it has been speculated that the seroprevalence rate in gay men may exceed 30 percent.

Studies of treatment samples indicated that the variation of HIV seroprevalence rates within subgroups of the heroin addict population was clearly influenced by sexual activities. Men who reported at least one homosexual experience in the eight years preceding the interview were found to have seroprevalence rates of approximately 13 to 21 percent, as compared to rates of less than 1 percent for exclusively heterosexual or celibate men. Within the former group, black males had the highest rates at 33 to 40 percent, white males ranged from 9 to 29 percent, and none of the relatively few Hispanic males were seropositive.

Although seroprevalence rates in women were very low, averaging less than 2 percent, these rates showed some variation depending on prostitution activities. Women who reported prostitution for drugs or money (63 to 73 percent of all female treatment clients surveyed) showed a seropositivity rate of 2 to 3.5 percent; women who did not report prostitution showed no seropositivity. White prostitutes averaged 4 percent seropositive, black prostitutes 3 percent, and Hispanic prostitutes 1.6 percent (Arnold and Anglin, 1987, 1988). Another study in Los Angeles showed approximately 5 percent of 323 women arrested for prostitution and booked at a central jail facility tested positive for HIV infection (Gill, 1989); 55 percent of these subjects reported recent IV drug use.

Thus, the subgroups of IVDUs in Los Angeles County with the greatest risk of HIV transmission are (1) those IVDUs already identified as HIV-positive, (2) sexually active gay and bisexual men, and (3) sex industry workers. In addition, sexual partners of any members of these groups (and unborn children of pregnant women who may be associated with these groups) are at high secondary risk of infection.

INTERVENTION STRATEGIES TO REDUCE HIV TRANSMISSION

The findings of epidemiological studies of HIV in Los Angeles County have generally provided a direction for strategies to contain the spread of infection.

Although trends toward reduction of some risk behaviors have been reported (Longshore and Anglin, 1990, 1991), overall risk levels remain unacceptably high. A majority of IVDUs now use condoms and clean their needles with bleach at least occasionally, but not consistently. In one study that repeatedly assessed IV-drug-using arrestees, the incidence of needle sharing in the prior twelve months remained stable at about 80 percent of respondents. In the same study, the number of sex partners per IVDU in those twelve months also remained stable: about 65 percent of arrestee IVDUs reported two or more sex partners in this period (Longshore and Anglin, 1991).

A primary means of slowing the spread of HIV infection among IVDUs is to reduce the high-risk behaviors associated with IV drug use, especially needle sharing. A major finding from NIDA's multi-city IVDU quarterly seroprevalence study showed that 25 percent of HIV-positive IVDUs reported sharing needles with known gay or bisexual men, as opposed to only 5 percent of HIV-negative IVDUs (Battjes, Pickens, and Amsel, 1989). These data also showed that few of the men and only 8 percent of heterosexual women reported that they "always" used bleach to clean their equipment when sharing needles with others.

Although prevention and education efforts for the IVDU populations have been well supported by federal agencies, early prevention and education efforts in Los Angeles County were hampered by a conservative Board of Supervisors whose policies prohibited distribution of condoms or bleach by county-supported outreach or treatment efforts. This policy was changed in the spring of 1991, and existing programs added these components to their other efforts. Only a few street outreach programs have been funded, however, with the vast majority of these established after July 1988. Effects of such programs on the transmission rate may have been negligible in any case. Prevention and education programs, as low-cost strategies that can reach a large number of IVDUs, are probably most effective in areas of high-density addict population and a high base rate of HIV infection among IVDUs—conditions that do not prevail in Los Angeles.

An alternative strategy that shows promise in reducing high-risk behaviors relies on the sharply decreased rates of IV drug use that result when narcotics addicts are in methadone maintenance (MM) treatment. For example, Anglin and his colleagues (Anglin and McGlothlin, 1984, 1985; Hser, Anglin, and Booth, 1987; Hser, Anglin, and Chou, 1988) have shown that the percentage of nonincarcerated time engaged in daily narcotics use decreases from about 70 percent (averaging across several studies) when not in MM treatment to about 12 percent when in MM treatment. Further, the percentage of time abstinent from narcotics increases from about 12 percent to about 26 percent.

If the typical IVDU injects about 4 times per day, or 120 times per month (Marmor, Des Jarlais, and Cohen, 1987), and only 2 of these daily occasions, or 60 per month, involve shared equipment, then the typical reduction in shared needles to be achieved by participation in a methadone maintenance program is from 42 (60 $\times$ 70 percent) shared injections to 7 (60 $\times$ 12 percent). Other estimates of the number of injections and shared needles in a day are available, and these vary somewhat by area and population characteristics (Ball and Corty, 1988; Ball, et al., 1988; Hawthorne and Siegel, 1987; Tidone et al., 1987). The overall conclusion, however, is that the typical behavior change observed after entry into methadone treatment includes a dramatic reduction in the number of occasions on which needles are shared among addicts—a reduction in risk behavior that should have a direct impact on the spread of HIV. Thus, a considerable overall containment of HIV infection is possible because of natural behavioral adjustments that occur for both uninfected and infected IVDUs when in methadone maintenance treatment.

Methadone maintenance treatment also places the IVDU in a structure where use of any drug can be detected immediately through frequent urine testing. The detection of drug use provides an opportunity for staff to intervene immediately to make treatment more effective and also to provide additional training in prevention techniques, including use of bleach. Furthermore, through regular voluntary blood tests encouraged by staff, HIV-positive individuals are more likely to be identified; intensive clinical, prevention, education, and hygiene efforts can then be implemented to minimize the likelihood that these individuals will infect another individual, either by IV drug use or through sexual activities.

As a treatment intervention, MM has the advantage of wide appeal, low cost, proven decreases in IV drug use, and long-term retention (Anglin and Fisher, 1987; Brust, 1983; Fisher and Anglin, 1987). With these attributes, methadone maintenance is singularly well suited to help contain the rate of HIV infection among IVDUs and to prevent infection of others through sexual contact with HIV-positive IVDUs.

ENHANCED METHADONE MAINTENANCE AND REDUCTION OF HIV RISK BEHAVIOR

Methadone maintenance has been widely researched as a treatment modality (Hubbard et al., 1983). The side effects of methadone are well known, the results of chronic administration have been identified, and the incidental aspects of dose, counseling adjuncts, and other rehabilitative measures have been reasonably well assessed. For the purpose of HIV containment, the greatest change in drug use behavior for IVDUs occurs simply with admission to methadone maintenance and continues as long as the client is in treatment. The administration of higher doses, with flexible policies in dealing with problematic clients, has also been shown to decrease drug use and improve retention (Senay, Dorus, and Showalter, 1984; Stitzer, Bickel, and Bigelow, 1987).

The basis for the University of California, Los Angeles (UCLA) Enhanced Methadone Maintenance (EMM) Project was to devise a treatment program that provided for the maximum number of overall slots and the most useful enhancements, at a reasonable cost, resulting in an increase in the effectiveness of our efforts to contain the spread of HIV. To design an effective methadone maintenance program for Los Angeles County high-risk IVDUs, we posed two developmental questions: (1) What aspects of existing methadone maintenance programs need improvement and which improvements are feasible? (2) What type of research study should assess such modified interventions? Findings by a number of investigators (Dolan et al., 1985, 1986; Higgins et al., 1986; Kosten et al., 1982; Okpaku, 1986) have demonstrated that relatively low-cost service enhancements to standard methadone maintenance protocols (e.g., group counseling, contingency contracting) can significantly increase compliance with treatment protocols.

A wide variety of enhancements in methadone maintenance—such as contingency contracting (Calsyn and Saxon, 1987; Glosser, 1983; Hall, 1983; Stitzer et al., 1986), dosing variability (Brown et al., 1983; Glosser, 1983; Stitzer, Bickel, and Bigelow, 1987), self-control over dosing (Hebert and Lauterbach, 1983; Preston, Bigelow, and Liebson, 1984; Senay, Dorus, and Showalter, 1984), increased monitoring through random urine testing (D'Amanda, 1983), and ancillary services (Ball and Corty, 1988; Hall, 1983; Rawson et al., 1983; Wermuth, Brummett, and Sorensen, 1987)—have been shown to produce positive effects for some types of addicts at some point in their addiction careers.

The desired treatment protocol also needed to be flexible enough to encompass the needs of the heterogeneous groups of addicts contained within our target population, including those dual-diagnosed with alcohol problems (Bickel, Marion, and Lowinson, 1987; Corty and Ball, 1987; Roszell, Calsyn, and Chaney, 1986), those multiply diagnosed with comorbidities of psychiatric illness (Brizer et al., 1985; Corty and Ball, 1987; Kleber, 1983; Madden, Ong, and Singer, 1987; McLellan et al., 1984; Roszell, Calsyn, and Chaney, 1986), and the socially deviant (Ben-Yehuda, 1984; Cohen, 1986; Shaffer et al., 1988). Additionally, the treatment approach needed to be able to accommodate the heterogeneity of narcotics addicts in terms of gender, ethnicity, sexual orientation, socioeconomic status, and lifestyle.

We hypothesized that by utilizing available methadone maintenance treatment, with enhancements designed to retain clients in treatment and promote responsible injection hygiene and sexual activities, we could have some impact on the spread of HIV in Los Angeles County. We believed that the most useful strategy to contain local HIV infection would be to utilize a treatment modality as a vehicle for intensive AIDS prevention and education for those who were either already seropositive and at risk of infecting others, or at extremely high risk of infection and subsequent transmission to others (Niven, 1987; Veatch, 1987).

AN OVERVIEW OF THE INTERVENTION AND TARGET POPULATION

Because of the heterogeneity of IVDUs, the best application of our intervention to achieve the goal of HIV containment was a case management approach. The goal of case management is to determine the specific mix of enhancements that is likely to produce maximum improvement for a given client. This approach is similar to psychiatric case management for the chronic mentally ill, in which treatment plans are based on an assessment of the client's problems, needs, and resources and are regularly reviewed and adapted to changing circumstances in any of these areas. We implemented an individual case management model, with specific enhancements added to traditional methadone maintenance, as decided upon in case conferences with the client. The "menu" of possible enhancements for an individual includes contingency contracting evaluated by means of objective urine test results, as well as a variety of supplemental services, including group education and counseling sessions; assistance with food, shelter, transportation, and medical needs; and rewards such as movie tickets and restaurant coupons.

Outcomes of the enhanced methadone maintenance program will be compared with outcomes of a control program in which clients receive only the standard state-mandated methadone maintenance program. Enhanced treatment is expected to produce improved outcomes in terms of increased program retention, diminished drug use, diminished high-risk behavior, and increased mental and physical well-being.

Target Population

The population for participation in the EMM study are: (1) IVDUs who are already identified as HIV-positive; (2) male IVDUs with histories of homosexual activities (including "heterosexual" hustlers) within the five years preceding intake; (3) female IVDUs who engage in prostitution; and (4) IVDUs who are sex partners of individuals in the first three groups.

Although the category of sex partners includes partners of people who are *not* in treatment, we have a special interest in recruiting partners of clients already enrolled in treatment for two reasons. First, sexual partners of targeted IVDUs are themselves at high risk for HIV infection (Geis, Fuller, and Rush, 1986). Second, the treatment goals of treatment retention, reduced drug use, and safer sexual activities are more likely to be achieved if both IVDU partners are in treatment (Anglin, Hser, and Booth, 1987). Both partners are assigned to the same treatment condition.

In addition to the above criteria, study participants must meet the current California criteria for methadone maintenance admissions (under emergency regulations established to provide easier access in the AIDS era), which are: (1) documented history of at least one year of narcotics addiction; (2) minimum age of eighteen years; (3) certification of fitness for methadone treatment by a physician, based on physical examination, medical history, and indicated laboratory findings; (4) evidence of current narcotic dependence; or (5) documentation of treatment within the prior six months (for previous methadone maintenance or methadone detoxification clients). We require that clients be out of treatment for ninety days before admission to the UCLA-subsidized treatment. This exclusionary criterion serves two purposes: (1) we are actually bringing additional IVDUs into treatment, not simply providing a low-cost alternative to those already enrolled; and (2) local fee-for-service clinics do not perceive the project as encroaching on their client base.

Client Recruitment

Subjects are recruited by means of general outreach efforts as well as methods specific to each target group. Globally, a specialized brochure was developed announcing the availability of the subsidized treatment slots in the EMM Project, and direct contacts were made with supervisory personnel of service agencies working with our target groups. Repeated telephone contacts have often been made as necessary to recruit individual subjects through counselors, and clients already in our program have been hired as outreach workers for short periods of time. More specific recruitment efforts are described below.

Seropositive IVDUs are recruited by contacting all Los Angeles County methadone facilities, the County Alcohol and Drug Programs Administration, the AIDS ward at the County/University of Southern California (USC) Hospital, and other referral sources to publicize the availability of subsidized treatment slots for narcotics-addicted IVDUs who have tested positive for HIV.

Gay and bisexual male IVDUs are recruited through Los Angeles County counseling programs for gay and bisexual men. We also recruit through other community outreach programs and gay organizations, as well as through fliers and brochures. Within this target group, male hustlers are especially sought because they are at multiple risk of contracting and transmitting HIV, either through IV drug use or unprotected sex acts. Findings from Waldorf's 1987 study involving interviews with 178 hustlers in San Francisco found that 26 percent had injected heroin in the year prior to interview, and approximately 10 percent were daily users of heroin (Waldorf et al., 1990). Over 70 percent of injectors reported sharing needles. Those infected bisexual or heterosexual hustlers who continue to engage in IV drug use and unprotected sex could also be a major factor in introducing the virus to groups with low current risk.

Sex industry worker IVDUs are recruited through agencies that offer counseling services to (female) prostitutes or by street outreach efforts. An additional population of prostitutes comes from the Drug Use Forecasting (DUF) Program conducted in Los Angeles by DARC staff. Of the approximately 175 women arrestees interviewed each quarter, 44 percent are charged with prostitution; 42 percent of the prostitutes report a history of IV drug use, and approximately 75 percent of this group are dependent on narcotics.

Finally, two additional methods of recruitment have been used. First, EMM staff members have met with outreach workers in AIDS prevention and education to describe our program and discuss its eligibility requirements. Second, people already enrolled in our project act as informal unpaid outreach workers and recruit by word of mouth.

REGULAR AND ENHANCED METHADONE MAINTENANCE PROTOCOLS

Upon admission to the EMM Project, clients are randomly assigned to either the standard or enhanced treatment condition. In both conditions clients are assessed; long- and short-term treatment plans are developed and reviewed quarterly and annually. After two years of treatment, justifications are required by the state from the clinic and client for further MM treatment. The clinic staff includes a clinic director and a medical director, with medical coverage provided by a physician's assistant.

Because it is typical of most protocols available in California, the standard program will be described briefly. We will devote considerable space to the enhanced protocol since the innovative aspects of our enhanced methadone maintenance lie in the case management approach and the types of ancillary services provided.

Standard Methadone Program

One counselor is provided for every forty clients in the standard methadone program. Clients in the standard methadone program receive program elements that meet minimal state requirements, as described below:

1. Intake and annual medical examinations are provided.
2. Take-home doses are obtained in four stages, with a minimum of ninety days at each stage. Maximum take-homes allowed after two years of acceptable performance are three doses, with a minimum of two clinic visits per week.
3. Clients are tested for drug use monthly, with pregnant addicts tested weekly. A refusal to submit to a urine test is counted as a positive test.
4. Two hours of counseling (in two sessions) are required each month, with additional counseling, typically on a crisis intervention basis, provided upon request.
5. A violation of clinic rules may result in a disciplinary detoxification of no less than fifteen days and no more than sixty days.

Enhanced Methadone Program

The enhanced program adds components to the standard MM program that have been shown in controlled studies to improve patient retention, reduce illicit drug use, and promote prosocial behavior. The specific interventions included in this enhanced program are not evaluated in a controlled clinical trial. Rather, the interventions are chosen so as to create a more flexible, responsive, and clinically oriented therapeutic model. Because treatment retention has been shown to correlate with positive treatment outcome, and because the longer a client stays in treatment, the less opportunity he or she will have to contract or transmit the HIV virus, a major goal of the project is to increase treatment retention. The components of the enhanced program are selected to retain clients in treatment and to shape, facilitate, and reinforce behavior expected to reduce the risk of HIV transmission.

Counselor and Case Manager Training. The key to the creation of the proper therapeutic context is the selection and hiring of counselors who can be trained to deliver a type of service that will be relevant to the needs of the subjects and will prioritize issues to maximize treatment effectiveness (McLellan et al., 1988).

In recruiting and selecting the case managers, the clinical management team looks for people who are experienced in the case management approach and also are familiar with the target groups and their specialized needs. We also recruit a diverse range of case managers in terms of sex, ethnicity, and sexual orientation. Case managers receive in-service training in relevant topics, such as medical, cultural, and legal issues in heroin addiction; treatment and contingency contracting goals for MM; strategies for eliminating illicit drug use; strategies for eliminating alcohol use; establishing a therapeutic attitude; maintaining a nonjudgmental attitude; problem solving; employment problems; how to discuss positive urine tests; counseling on the dangers of needle sharing, the use of bleach, and the use of condoms; the value of methadone dose adjustment; and strategies for evaluating and intervening with the use of cocaine, amphetamine, and PCP. Case managers are urged to attend conferences, lectures, and workshops and to bring back new material to the group for continuing education.

Intensive First-Month Contact. The overall goal of the first month's treatment is to orient the client to the program and establish a strong positive working relationship between the client and the treatment team. The new client meets with a case manager on the first day of dosing. Clients are told in this interview that the program is not intended to burden them with extra "required counseling," but is designed to help them in a way that will improve their health, reduce the risk of contracting or transmitting AIDS, and provide them with opportunities for employment and psychological and social benefits.

Unfortunately, a significant number of subjects are not stabilized by the end of the first month. With these clients, treatment staff continue to focus on eliminating IV drug use and high-risk sexual behaviors. Ideally, the first month's contact with the client supplies detailed knowledge that makes it possible to design strategies to address these problem areas in subsequent months.

Contingency Contracting. At the beginning of the second month, an initial contingency contract is established during a case management conference for all clients in the enhanced program. Contingency contracts are modified by the case manager as appropriate. Programs that provide incentives contingent upon the delivery of opiate-free urine samples have proven to be highly effective in reducing illicit drug use, increasing program retention rates, and decreasing symptom complaints (Bigelow, Stitzer, and Liebson, 1984; Higgins et al., 1986; Iguchi et al., 1988; Stitzer and Bigelow, 1984).

In our contingency contracting procedure, clients who test clean are given rewards, such as food coupons at local restaurants. Alternatively, dirty tests lead to a graduated series of punishments (from verbal reprimands and reduced rewards to—as a last resort—detoxification). The contract is specific and simple so that the client knows exactly what is expected, what rewards will accrue if he or she continues to test drug-free, and which earned privileges will be withdrawn if certain patterns of dirty urine tests or other contract-prohibited behaviors are obtained.

Enhanced Program Services. The services offered in the enhanced MM program are coordinated by the case manager and are provided to the client in addition to the normal methadone maintenance program services mandated by the state. Case managers in the enhanced condition have thirty-five clients, compared with a caseload of forty-five for counselors offering the standard methadone treatment. Enhanced program services include, but are not limited to, the services described in the following paragraphs.

1. Case Management. The first and most notable program enhancement is case management. During the client's first few weeks in the program, case managers immediately identify critical survival needs and refer clients to self-help groups and other crucial services relevant to our client population. Where necessary, case managers act as advocates for the clients in obtaining needed social services. (Releases are always obtained before case managers communicate with anyone on behalf of a client.) Case managers maintain a supply of donated clothing for clients, who are also assisted with bus coupons and money to buy bus passes during the first few weeks of their involvement with the UCLA program.

At every opportunity, the case manager inquires about high-risk and safer sexual practices. Condoms are freely available, and their use is strongly encouraged.[2] Case managers provide information about sexually transmitted diseases, and referrals for medical treatment are made as needed. In particular, sex workers are praised for asking for condoms. HIV and women's groups (described more fully below) discuss relevant issues to promote safer sexual activities. Clients see videos that deal with various sex and health issues, and HIV testing is strongly encouraged. These prevention and education approaches are used to help clients develop healthy, self-preserving attitudes and reduce high-risk behaviors.

2. Crisis Management. One of the more important enhancements is the role of the case managers in handling clients' crises. Clients will on occasion lose their homes or their welfare checks, experience medical emergencies or legal entanglements, become victims or perpetrators of battering, or face other crises. The case manager calls on a variety of resources to manage these and other crises.

Crisis management in the era of AIDS presents special difficulties. Case managers frequently find themselves spending large amounts of time advocating for their HIV-positive clients with other agencies and institutions to get them the assistance they need. The HIV-positive client also experiences family problems, requiring the case manager to assist with family counseling and education.

3. On-Site Psychiatric Consultation. The EMM Project has secured the services of Dr. Richard Ciasca, a psychiatrist experienced with methadone maintenance, for four to six hours per week to conduct psychiatric evaluations, prescribe medication as needed, assist with dual-diagnosis referrals and hospitalizations, and be available to clients and case managers for consultation.

4. Incentives. On occasion, case managers meet and select a subset of clients who either have tested clean from their admission date or show visible progress in decreasing their use during the previous three months, and who have shown themselves to be responsible and willing to work toward recovery. A "Reward Meeting" is held, where restaurant coupons are given to those who attend. Other incentives, such as movie passes and alarm clocks, are also available; additional incentives will be added in the future.

5. Additional Monitoring by Urinalysis. Current California regulations require one urine test per month, screening for methadone and its primary metabolite, as well as for morphine, codeine, amphetamine, methamphetamine, phenobarbital, and secobarbital. If analysis is farmed out to a private laboratory, turnaround time can be excruciatingly slow (at least two weeks, often three to four weeks). Feedback after such a long lag time has little or no motivational impact. In the event of a "dirty" test, the client can usually explain away the test result. In addition, some drug tests are not used because they are extremely expensive.

In the enhanced program, our strategy has been to purchase an on-site Abbott ADX urinalysis machine so that we can test clients more frequently and have results available immediately. With this machine we can conduct our own tests, get quick results, and provide rapid feedback to clients on their behavior across a wide range of drugs. Our experience has been that such quick, focused feedback makes it much more difficult for the client to be evasive, minimizes conflict, and has a more powerful effect on the client's behavior.

We attempt to test clients weekly, with no fewer than two tests per month. We are currently screening for cocaine, opiates, and benzodiazepines. (The standard MM program maintains the state-mandated schedule.) Feedback on the test results is used by case managers as a criterion in contingency contracting and as a means of breaking through client denial.

When test results are available quickly, the staff can immediately address the conditions that produced a drug use episode. If the client tests positive for narcotics, amphetamines, or cocaine, or if the client reports IV drug use, the client and case manager meet to discuss options. The client is reminded about the dangers of high-risk sexual and needle-using activities and about the potential damage to the immune system from using multiple drugs along with methadone.

6. Cocaine Group. Early examination of EMM urinalysis results revealed a high percentage of cocaine use among the clients. Twenty daily cocaine users were identified by their case managers and assigned to participate in a cocaine

abusers' group. Since the group started in May of 1991, attendance has averaged seven. Resistant clients have been put on behavioral contracts.

Dr. Richard Rawson and other staff of the Matrix Institute have been engaged to facilitate the cocaine groups, with case managers serving as cofacilitators. Eventually, case managers will facilitate these groups independently after this specialized "internship" with an expert in dealing with cocaine abuse.

7. AIDS Education and Prevention Group. This group meets once a week for four weeks and is repeated as often as needed so that everyone can attend. Clients learn about HIV and how it is transmitted.

Those being tested for HIV receive a pre- and posttest counseling component. Since some issues are thought to be gender-specific, the group divides into men's and women's groups for some of the meeting time.

8. Women's Group. A Women's Group, designed to support victims of violence and abuse, aims to help group members build self-confidence and self-esteem. The incidence of child abuse, sexual abuse, and domestic violence among female addicts is very high; often women feel unsafe exploring these experiences in mixed-sex groups. Women who are addicted face additional self-esteem and self-confidence problems in light of society's disapproval of addicted women, which can be harsher than that directed toward addicted men.

The group meets for an hour and a half once a week for six weeks, and is limited to ten participants. The women practice expressing their feelings, building their self-esteem, and receiving feedback and support from the other women.

9. Future Enhancements. As this project evolves we will identify other enhancements that can and should be added. We are already considering more flexible dosing and accelerated take-homes, so that dosing can be better tailored to the individual needs of the client and so that more powerful motivators for change can be brought to bear on the client's behavior. We are also developing stress management courses (breathing techniques, visualization, biofeedback, etc.) to teach our clients to cope with life stresses.

We intend to use preliminary data analysis of client characteristics as the basis for designing services that directly address client needs. The task of maintaining the distinction between the two treatment conditions will be particularly challenging since all services have been consolidated into one site.

CONCLUSION

Limiting the spread of HIV within the IVDU population in Los Angeles requires a rapid and well-conceived response. The UCLA/Matrix EMM Project was designed to capitalize on the flexibility that methadone maintenance offers for developing interventions for the IVDU population. By utilizing a treatment modality with a long research history and proven effectiveness in reducing needle usage, the Enhanced Methadone Maintenance Project will be able to examine the effectiveness of an array of services designed to maximize program retention and reduce high-risk behaviors for HIV infection. Enhanced methadone maintenance provides the opportunity to combine both treatment and prevention interventions for the population that will determine the course of HIV transmission in the years to come.

ACKNOWLEDGMENTS

This research report was prepared under support from NIDA grant DA06250. Dr. Anglin is also supported by research scientist development award DA 00146 from NIDA. Special thanks are due to staff at the Enhanced Methadone Maintenance Project and at the UCLA Drug Abuse Research Center for manuscript preparation.

NOTES

1. The term "homosexual" is being used to indicate sexual behavior with a person of the same gender, and not necessarily a homosexual or bisexual orientation.

2. Condoms are openly displayed and available to clients in the standard condition as well.

REFERENCES

Anglin, M. D., and D. G. Fisher. 1987. Survival Analysis in Drug Program Evaluation: Part II. Partitioning Treatment Effects. *International Journal of the Addictions*, 22(4), 377–387.

Anglin, M. D., Y. Hser, and M. W. Booth. 1987. Sex Differences in Addict Careers: Treatment. *American Journal of Drug and Alcohol Abuse*, 13(3), 253–280.

Anglin, M. D., and W. H. McGlothlin. 1984. Outcome of Narcotic Addict Treatment in California. In *Drug Abuse Treatment Evaluation: Strategies, Progress, and Prospects*, edited by F. M. Tims and J. P. Ludford, pp. 106–128. NIDA Research Monograph No. 51, DHHS Publication No. (ADM) 84–1349. Rockville, MD: National Institute on Drug Abuse.

Anglin, M. D., and W. H. McGlothlin. 1985. Methadone Maintenance in California: A Decade's Experience. In *The Yearbook of Substance Use and Abuse*, vol. 3, edited by L. Brill and C. Winick, pp. 219–280. New York: Human Sciences Press.

Arnold, J. E., and M. D. Anglin. 1987. Report of an AIDS Seroprevalence Study of Intravenous Drug Users in Residential Drug Treatment Facilities in Los Angeles County. Unpublished manuscript. UCLA.

Arnold, J. E., and M. D. Anglin. 1988. Preliminary Report of an AIDS Seroprevalence Study of Intravenous Drug Users in Methadone Maintenance and Methadone Detoxification Facilities in Los Angeles County. Unpublished manuscript. UCLA.

Ball, J. C., and E. Corty. 1988. Basic issues Pertaining to the Effectiveness of Methadone Maintenance Treatment. In *Compulsory Treatment of Drug Abuse: Research and Clinical Practice*, edited by C. G. Leukefeld and F. M. Tims, pp. 178–191. NIDA Research Monograph No. 86, DHHS Publication No. (ADM) 88–1578. Rockville, MD: National institute on Drug Abuse.

Ball, J. C., W. R. Lange, C. P. Myers, and S. R. Friedman. 1988. Reducing the Risk of AIDS through Methadone Maintenance Treatment. *Journal of Health and Social Behavior*, 29, 214–226.

Battjes, R. J., R. W. Pickens, and Z. Amsel. 1989. Introduction of HIV Infection among Intravenous Drug Abusers in Low Prevalence Areas. *Journal of Acquired Immune Deficiency Syndrome*, 2, 533–539.

Ben-Yehuda, N. 1984. A Clinical Sociology Approach to Treatment of Deviants: The Case of Drug Addicts. *Drug and Alcohol Dependence*, 13, 267–282.

Bickel, W. K., I. Marion, and J. H. Lowinson. 1987. The Treatment of Alcoholic Methadone Patients: A Review. *Journal of Substance Abuse Treatment*, 4, 15–19.

Bigelow, G. E., M. L. Stitzer, and I. A. Liebson. 1984. The Role of Behavioral Contingency Management in Drug Abuse Treatment. In *Behavioral Intervention Techniques in Drug Abuse Treatment*, edited by J. Grabowski, M. L. Stitzer, J. E. Henningfield, pp. 36–52. NIDA Research Monograph No. 46, DHHS Publication No. (ADM) 84–1282. Washington, DC: U.S. Government Printing Office.

Brizer, D. A., N. Hartman, J. Sweeny, and R. B. Millman. 1985. Effect of Methadone Plus Neuroleptics on Treatment-Resistant Chronic Paranoid Schizophrenics. *American Journal of Psychiatry*, 142, 1106–1107.

Brown, B. S., J. K. Watters, A. S. Ingelhart, and C. Atkins. 1983. Methadone Maintenance Dosage Levels and Program Retention. *American Journal of Drug and Alcohol Abuse*, 9, 129–139.

Brust, J. C. 1983. The Nonimpact of Opiate Research on Opiate Abuse. *Neurology*, 33 (10), 1327–1331.

Calsyn, D. A., and A. J. Saxon. 1987. A System for Uniform Application of Contingencies for Illicit Drug Use. *Journal of Substance Abuse Treatment*, 4, 41–47.

Chaisson, R. E., P. Bacchetti, D. Osmond, B. Brodie, M. A. Sande, and A. R. Moss. 1989. Cocaine Use and HIV Infection in Intravenous Drug Users in San Francisco. *Journal of the American Medical Association*, 261, 561–565.

Cohen, A. 1986. A Psychosocial Typology of Drug Addicts and Implications for Treatment. *International Journal of the Addictions*, 21, 147–154.

Corty, E., and J. C. Ball. 1987. Admissions to Methadone Maintenance: Comparisons Between Programs and Implications for Treatment. *Journal of Substance Abuse Treatment*, 4, 181–187.

D'Amanda, C. 1983. Program Policies and Procedures Associated with Treatment Outcome. In *Research on the Treatment of Narcotic Addiction: State of the Art*, edited by J. R. Cooper, F. Altman, B. S. Brown, and D. Czechowicz, pp. 637–679. NIDA Treatment Research Monograph Series, DHHS Publication No. 83–1281. Rockville, MD: National Institute on Drug Abuse.

Des Jarlais, D., S. R. Friedman, D. M. Norick, J. L. Sotheran, P. Thomas, S. R. Yancovitz, D. Mildvan, J. Weber, M. J. Kreek, R. Maslansky, S. Bartelone, T. Spira, and M. Marmor. HIV–1 Infection Among Intravenous Drug Users in Manhattan, New York City, from 1977 through 1987. *Journal of the American Medical Association*, 261(7), 1008–1012.

Dolan, M. P., J. L. Black, W. E. Penk, R. Robinowitz, and H. A. DeFord. 1985. Contracting for Treatment Termination to Reduce Illicit Drug Use among Methadone Maintenance Treatment Failures. *Journal of Consulting and Clinical Psychology*, 53, 549–551.

Dolan, M. P., J. L. Black, W. E. Penk, R. Robinowitz, and H. A. DeFord. 1986.

Predicting the Outcome of Contingency Contracting for Drug Abuse. *Behavior Therapy*, 17, 470–474.

Fisher, D. G., and M. D. Anglin. 1987. Survival Analysis in Drug Program Evaluation: Part I. Overall Program Effectiveness. *International Journal of the Addictions*, 22(2), 115–134.

Geis, S. B., R. L. Fuller, and J. Rush. 1986. Lovers of AIDS Victims: Psychological Stresses and Counseling Needs. *Death Studies*, 10, 43–53.

Gill, S. 1989. Personal communication. University of Southern California.

Glosser, D. S. 1983. The Use of a Token Economy to Reduce Illicit Drug Use among Methadone Maintenance Clients. *Addictive Behaviors*, 8, 93–104.

Hall, S. M. 1983. Methadone Treatment: A Review of the Research Findings. In *Research on the Treatment of Narcotic Addiction: State of the Art*, edited by J. R. Cooper, F. Altman, B. S. Brown, and D. Czechowicz, pp. 575–632. NIDA Research Monograph Series, DHHS Publication No. 83–1281. Rockville, MD: National Institute on Drug Abuse.

Hawthorne, W., and L. Siegel. 1987. Should There Be HIV Testing in Clinical Dependency Treatment Programs? *Advances in Alcohol and Substance Abuse*, 7, 15–19.

Hebert, S. W., and E. C. Lauterbach. 1983. Methadone Maintenance in the Small Community Drug Abuse Clinic. *International Journal of the Addictions*, 18, 863–874.

Higgins, S. T., M. L. Stitzer, G. E. Bigelow, and I. A. Liebson. 1986. Contingent Methadone Delivery: Effects on Illicit-Opiate Use. *Drug and Alcohol Dependence*, 17, 311–322.

Hser, Y., M. D. Anglin, and M. W. Booth. 1987. Sex Differences in Addict Careers: Addiction. *American Journal of Drug and Alcohol Abuse*, 13(3), 231–251.

Hser, Y., M. D. Anglin, and C. P. Chou. 1988. Evaluation of Drug Abuse Treatment: A Repeated Measures Design Assessing Methadone Maintenance. *Evaluation Review*, 12(5), 547–570.

Hubbard, R. L., et al. 1983. An Overview of Client Characteristics, Treatment Services, and During-Treatment Outcomes for Outpatient Methadone Clinics in the Treatment Outcome Prospective Study (TOPS). In *Research on the Treatment of Narcotic Addiction: State of the Art*, edited by J. R. Cooper, F. Altman, B. S. Brown, and D. Czechowicz, pp. 714–751. NIDA Research Monograph Series, DHHS Publication No. 83–1281. Rockville, MD: National Institute on Drug Abuse.

Iguchi, M. Y., M. L. Stitzer, G. E. Bigelow, and I. A. Liebson. 1988. Contingency Management in Methadone Maintenance: Effects of Reinforcing and Aversive Consequences on Illicit Polydrug Use. *Drug and Alcohol Dependence*, 22, 1–7.

Kleber, H. D. 1983. Concomitant Use of Methadone with Other Psychoactive Drugs in the Treatment of Opiate Addicts with Other DSM-III Diagnoses. In *Research on the Treatment of Narcotic Addiction: State of the Art*, edited by J. R. Cooper, F. Altman, B. S. Brown, and D. Czechowicz, pp. 19–148. NIDA Research Monograph Series, DHHS Publication No. 83–1281. Rockville, MD: National Institute on Drug Abuse.

Kosten, T. R., B. M. Astrachan, C. E. Riordan, and H. D. Kleber. 1982. The Organization of a Methadone Maintenance Program. *Journal of Drug Issues*, 12, 333–342.

Longshore, D., and M. D. Anglin. 1990. *HIV Transmission and Risk Behavior among*

Drug Users in Los Angeles County. Los Angeles: L.A. County AIDS Program Office.

Longshore, D., and M. D. Anglin. 1991. *HIV Transmission and Risk Behavior Among Drug Users in Los Angeles County*. Los Angeles: L.A. County AIDS Program Office.

Los Angeles County Department of Health Services. 1991. *AIDS Epidemiology Program: AIDS Report for October 1991*. Los Angeles: L.A. County.

Madden, C., B. Ong, and G. Singer. 1987. Mood State of Heroin-Dependent Persons Undergoing Methadone Detoxification. *International Journal of the Addictions*, 22, 93–102.

Marmor, M., D. C. Des Jarlais, H. Cohen, S. R. Friedman, S. T. Beatrice, N. Dubin, W. el-Sadr, D. Mildvan, S. Yancovitz, and U. Mathur. 1987. Risk Factors for Infection with Human Immunodeficiency Virus among Intravenous Drug Abusers in New York City. *AIDS*, 1, 39–44.

McLellan, A. T., A. R. Childress, J. Griffith, and G. E. Woody. 1984. The Psychiatrically Severe Drug Abuse Patient: Methadone Maintenance or Therapeutic Community? *American Journal of Drug and Alcohol Abuse*, 10, 77–95.

McLellan, A. T., L. Luborsky, G. E. Woody, and L. Goebl. 1988. Counselor Differences in Methadone Treatment. In *Proceedings of Committee on Problems of Drug Dependence*, edited by L. S. Harris, pp. 242–250. NIDA Research Monograph No. 81, DHHS Publication No. (ADM) 88–1564. Rockville, MD: National Institute on Drug Abuse.

Niven, R. G. 1987. The Impact of AIDS on the Chemical Dependency Field. *Advances in Alcohol and Substance Abuse*, 7, 3–14.

Okpaku, S. O. 1986. Psychoanalytically Oriented Psychotherapy of Substance Abuse (with Observations on the Penn–VA study). *Advances in Alcohol and Substance Abuse*, 6, 17–33.

Preston, K. L., G. E. Bigelow, and I. A. Liebson. 1984. *Self-Administration of Clonidine and Oxazepam by Methadone Detoxification Patients*. In *Problems of Drug Dependence 1983*, pp. 192–198. 45th Annual Scientific Meeting of the Committee on Problems of Drug Dependence, Inc. Behavioral Pharmacology (1983, Lexington, KY). NIDA Research Monograph No. 49, DHHS Publication No. (ADM) 84–1316. Rockville, MD: Department of Health and Human Services.

Rawson, R. A., A. J. Mann, F. S. Tennant, and D. Clabough. 1983. Efficacy of Psychotherapeutic Counselling During 21-Day Ambulatory Heroin Detoxification. *Drug and Alcohol Dependence*, 12, 197–200.

Roszell, D. K., D. A. Calsyn, and E. F. Chaney. 1986. Alcohol Use and Psychopathology in Opioid Addicts on Methadone Maintenance. *American Journal of Drug and Alcohol Abuse*, 12, 269–278.

Senay, E. C., W. Dorus, and C. Showalter. 1984. Methadone Detoxification: Self versus Physician Regulation. *American Journal of Drug and Alcohol Abuse*, 10, 361–374.

Shaffer, J. W., D. N. Nurco, T. E. Hanlon, T. W. Kinlock, K. R. Duszynski, and P. Stephenson. 1988. MMPI–168 Profiles of Male Narcotic Addicts by Ethnic Group and City. *Journal of Clinical Psychology*, 44(2), 292–298.

Stitzer, M. L., W. K. Bickel, and G. E. Bigelow. 1987. Altered Dose Incentive Procedures: Effects on Polydrug Use among Methadone Maintenance Patients. In *Problems of Drug Dependence 1986*, pp. 162–167. 48th Annual Scientific Meeting of the Committee on Problems of Drug Dependence (1986, Tahoe City, CA). NIDA Research Monograph No. 76, DHHS Publication No. (ADM) 87–1508. Rockville, MD: Department of Health and Human Services.

Stitzer, M. L., W. K. Bickel, G. E. Bigelow, and I. A. Liebson. 1986. Effect of Methadone Dose Contingencies on Urinalysis Test Results of Polydrug-Abusing Methadone-Maintenance Patients. *Drug and Alcohol Dependence*, 18, 341–348.

Stitzer, M. L., and G. E. Bigelow. 1984. Contingent Methadone Take-Home Privileges: Effects on Compliance with Fee Payment Schedules. *Drug and Alcohol Dependence*, 13, 395–399.

Tidone, L., F. Sileo, A. Guglio, and G. C. Borra. 1987. AIDS in Italy. *American Journal of Drug and Alcohol Abuse*, 13, 485–486.

Veatch, C. L. 1987. The Response of State Agencies to AIDS, Addiction, and Alcoholism. *Advances in Alcohol and Substance Abuse*, 7, 117–142.

Waldorf, D., S. Murphy, D. Lauderbach, C. Reinarman, and T. Marotta. 1990. Needle Sharing among Male Prostitutes: Preliminary Findings of the Prospero Project. *Journal of Drug Issues*, 20, 309–334.

Watters, J. K., Y. T. Cheng, M. Segal, J. Lorvick, P. Case, and J. Carlson. 1990. Epidemiology and Prevention of HIV in Heterosexual Intravenous Drug Users in San Francisco 1986–1989. In *AIDS in the Nineties: From Science to Policy*, vol. 2, p. 116. International Conference on AIDS (June 1990, San Francisco).

Wermuth, L., S. Brummett, and J. L. Sorensen. 1987. Bridges and Barriers to Recovery: Clinical Observations from an Opiate Recovery Project. *Journal of Substance Abuse Treatment*, 4, 189–196.

2

Improving Retention on Methadone Maintenance

James F. Maddux

While maintained on methadone, opioid-dependent persons reduce their illicit opioid use and related criminal activity and increase their legitimate employment (Senay, 1985; Platt, 1986; Hubbard et al., 1989; Ball and Ross, 1991). Furthermore, improvement continues with increasing time on methadone maintenance (Hargreaves, 1983; Kreek, 1991). Retention in treatment became more urgent in the 1980s with the recognition that Acquired Immunological Deficiency Syndrome (AIDS) is spread through sharing of injection equipment (Cooper, 1989).

In this chapter I review variations in reported retention rates and factors that may affect retention. I describe our current attempt to conduct four treatment innovations designed to improve retention on methadone maintenance: (1) elimination of treatment fees, (2) patient-regulated methadone dose, (3) optional counseling, and (4) rapid admission. We call these changes ''innovations'' although similar treatment conditions have existed previously. The effects of the innovations on retention are being evaluated in an experimental research design.

Wide variation in rates of retention on methadone maintenance has been reported. In the early years of methadone maintenance, high rates of retention for 1 year or longer were generally reported. Gearing (1974) reported that 89 percent of 1,230 patients admitted to methadone maintenance in New York City during the years 1964 to 1968 were retained in treatment for 1 year or longer. Babst, Ellis, and Schmeidler (1976) reported that 78 percent of 1,008 male patients, also in New York City, admitted to methadone maintenance during the years 1965 through 1969 were retained in treatment for 2 years. In San Antonio, Texas, Maddus and McDonald (1973) reported that 74 percent of 100 patients admitted in 1970 were retained for 1 year. In Toronto, however, in an exception to these reports, Krakowski and Smart (1974) reported that only 43 percent of 90 patients whose admissions started in 1970 were retained for 1 year.

In subsequent years lower retention rates were generally reported. Using data sent to the Drug Abuse Reporting Program (DARP) from 52 drug abuse treatment agencies in the United States, Sells and colleagues (1978) reported that 60 percent, 51 percent, and 40 percent, respectively, of 3 cohorts of patients admitted to methadone maintenance in 1969–1971, 1971–1972, and 1972–1973 were retained for 1 year. Ling and colleagues (1976) reported that 47 percent of a cohort of 288 patients admitted to methadone maintenance in 1973 and 1974 at twelve Veterans Administration hospitals were retained for ten months. By the end of the 1970s, retention rates had diminished even more. Hubbard and associates (1989) reported that only 34 percent of 2,698 patients admitted to 17 methadone maintenance clinics in 1979 and 1980 were retained for more than 1 year. Ball and Ross (1991) reported that only 38 percent of 126 patients admitted to methadone maintenance in 1985 in 3 northeastern cities were retained for 1 year.

While a historical decrease in retention apparently occurred, wide variations in contemporary programs have also been reported. In the Veterans Administration study, cited above, 47 percent of all subjects were retained for ten months, but the percentage retained for ten months among the twelve hospitals varied greatly, from 18 percent to 77 percent (Hargreaves, 1983). Among twenty-one methadone maintenance programs studied by the U.S. General Accounting Office (1990) the percentages of patients retained for six months varied from 42 percent to 83 percent.

VARIABLES RELATED TO RETENTION

The historical and contemporary variations in retention on methadone maintenance presumably arise from variables in the patients, in the communities, and in the programs.

McLellan (1983) reviewed 113 studies reported from 1971 to 1983 that attempted to evaluate the relation of patient characteristics to retention and other outcomes. He found that age, race, marital status, employment, and other patient variables were related to retention, but the best combination of these variables probably accounted for only 25 percent to 45 percent of the variance in retention.

Community variables influence the patients directly and indirectly through their effects on the program. Hawkins (1983) defined five views of "community" and identified variables in each which might affect treatment outcomes. No studies have reported on the relation of community variables to retention on methadone maintenance.

Several publications during the 1980s identified program variables of probable importance and reviewed studies of the relation of program variables to outcomes (Cooper et al., 1983; Onken and Blaine, 1990; Pickens, Leukefeld, and Schuster,

1991; Hubbard et al., 1989; Ball and Ross, 1991). Controlled studies of the effects of methadone dose, contingency management, and psychotherapy were reported. Only the factor of dose, however, was studied in relation to retention.

While the number of program variables that could be studied seems almost unlimited, some seem more likely than others to affect retention on methadone maintenance. Included among these are the four variables we are attempting to evaluate. Additional variables, or sets of variables, that may be related to retention are geographic accessibility, retention policy, the level of services offered, take-home policy, and urine monitoring procedures.

BACKGROUND OF THE FOUR INNOVATIONS

Fees for Treatment

Many private methadone maintenance programs are supported entirely by fees paid by patients, and many publicly supported programs charge fees. In 1987, 73 percent of 4,227 drug abuse treatment units reporting to the National Drug and Alcoholism Treatment Unit Survey obtained part of their funding from client fees (Butynski, 1991). Treatment fees help to finance the programs, but fee collection may also be justified by the assumption that payment of a fee improves the effectiveness of treatment. It has been assumed that payment of a fee improves the effectiveness of psychotherapy (Menninger, 1958), but a positive association of fee payment with psychotherapy outcome has not been demonstrated (Orlinsky and Howard, 1986). Several reports suggest that required treatment fees do not improve methadone maintenance treatment but often impair it by causing premature termination of treatment.

Price and others (1991) reported that 13 percent of patients discharged in 1987 and 1988 from methadone maintenance programs in mental health centers left treatment because they failed to pay for treatment or exhausted insurance coverage. This is probably a minimum estimate because some of those who left treatment "voluntarily" may have done so because of difficulty in paying the treatment fees.

Rosenbaum and associates (Rosenbaum, Murphy, and Beck, 1987; Murphy and Rosenbaum, 1988; Rosenbaum, Irwin, and Murphy, 1989) described the consequences of a new program policy in Alameda County, California, of limiting methadone maintenance treatment in a funded treatment slot to two years. When the new policy was established, all patients who had been in a funded slot for two years had to begin paying $160 per month. This amount was later increased to $200. The investigators followed 143 patients affected by the policy for two and a half years. Most were adversely affected. A small group, 6 percent of the sample, were able to detoxify and continue a conventional lifestyle. A larger group, 25 percent of the sample, were marginal patients who were not improving. Most of this group were detoxified, and they returned to the heroin life. The largest group, 69 percent of the sample, were stabilized patients. They were hardest hit by the pay requirement. Most, including those who were working, had difficulty paying the $200 per month. Many within this group who were detoxified returned to active heroin use.

Anglin and colleagues (1989) reported the consequences of the closure of a publicly financed methadone maintenance program in San Diego. Private fee-for-service programs were available to which patients could transfer. The investigators interviewed 331 patients approximately 2 years after their treatment was terminated. Only a minority (40 percent) transferred to private programs. Compared to the subjects who transferred, the subjects who did not transfer reported more illicit narcotic use, more property crime, more drug dealing, and more incarceration.

The findings of these three studies concur in supporting the hypothesis that, for a large number of patients, required treatment fees lead to premature termination of treatment and reduced retention on methadone maintenance.

A required treatment fee may also inhibit entry into methadone maintenance. In a project conducted in New Jersey, outreach workers offered coupons to drug users for thirty days of free treatment in one methadone maintenance program and referred others to two programs that charged fees. A preliminary report showed that 90 percent of those referred with coupons entered treatment, but only 33 percent and 28 percent of those referred to two clinics without coupons entered treatment (Johnson, Record, and Young, 1991).

Patient-Regulated Methadone Dose

Hargreaves (1983) reviewed twenty-three studies published from 1970 to 1981 on the relation of methadone dose to treatment outcomes, mainly retention in treatment and illicit opioid use. Most of the studies had methodological problems, and Hargreaves thought that causal inferences could be drawn from only six of the studies. Here I briefly review five of these studies; the sixth study did not report retention as an outcome.

Jaffe (1971) randomly assigned sixty-three patients at admission to two groups, one whose mean dose was approximately 100 milligrams (mg) and one whose mean dose was approximately 36 mg. The percentage retained at fourteen weeks was slightly higher for the high dose group (58 percent) than it was for the low dose group (50 percent), but the difference was not statistically significant.

Garbutt and Goldstein (1972) randomly assigned 180 patients at admission to three groups that received doses of 30 mg, 50 mg, and 100 mg. The percentages retained for 53 weeks were 45 percent of the 30 mg group, 55 percent of the 50 mg group, and 35 percent of the 100 mg group. The high dose group had the lowest retention rate, but the differences were not statistically significant.

Goldstein and Judson (1973) randomly assigned 120 patients at admission to 3 groups that, after stabilization on 80 mg, had their doses gradually differentiated to 40 mg, 80 mg, and 160 mg. The period of observation from admission was 27 weeks, but the period the patients spent on the differentiated doses was only

10 weeks. The percentages retained for 27 weeks were 60 percent of the 40 mg group, 75 percent of the 80 mg group, and 73 percent of the 160 mg group. The two higher dose groups had somewhat higher retention rates than the 40 mg group, but the differences were not statistically significant.

Berry and Kuhn (1973) paired fifty-two patients that had been in treatment for a mean of ten months and were stabilized on a daily dose of 100 mg of methadone. One of each pair had a gradual reduction in dose to 50 mg. The other member of the pair remained at the dose level of 100 mg. At the end of the five-month dose reduction period, 69 percent of the 100 mg group and 65 percent of the 50 mg group remained in treatment. This small difference was not statistically significant. The findings suggest that a dose of 100 mg can be gradually reduced to 50 mg without adverse effect on retention.

In the previously cited multi-clinic study conducted at twelve Veterans Administration hospitals (Ling et al., 1976), patients were randomly assigned to two dose levels of methadone—50 mg (N = 146) and 100 mg (N = 142). All subjects were followed for ten months after admission, or for shorter periods if they remained in treatment less than ten months. The percentage retained for ten months was higher in the 100 mg group (52 percent) than in the 50 mg group (42 percent), but the difference was not statistically significant. This modest difference in retention attributable to methadone dose stands in contrast to the marked differences in retention ranging from 18 percent to 77 percent, among the programs at the twelve hospitals.

Three of these five dose-retention studies found nonsignificant trends toward increased retention with higher doses, and two did not. The findings of the dose-retention studies suggest that while many patients will continue in treatment on methadone doses of less than 50 mg, some patients need higher doses.

Requests from patients for dose changes, especially increases, are usually evaluated by the counselor and the physician, and the negotiation may not lead to a decision satisfactory to the patient. Permitting the patients, within limits, to regulate their methadone doses eliminates a source of controversy between patients and staff, and it allows the patients to find subjectively suitable doses. It may also reduce illicit drug use and improve retention.

Several studies have shown that patients do not markedly increase their methadone doses when allowed, within limits, to regulate their doses (Goldstein, Hansteen, and Harris, 1975; Resnick, Butler, and Washton, 1982; Havassy and Hargreaves, 1981).

Optional Counseling

In addition to the level of services provided (Childress, McLellan, and Woody, 1991), the level of treatment structure (Woody, 1983) may also affect treatment outcomes. Structure includes the rules and requirements for treatment participation and for patient performance, with the sanctions for obtaining compliance. A low level of structure means few rules and few requirements for patient performance. A high level of structure means more rules, mandatory counseling sessions, and more requirements for patient performance. The two types of methadone maintenance programs described by Cole and James (1975)—adaptive and change-oriented—seem distinguished, in part, by level of structure. The adaptive program seems less structured, and the change-oriented program more structured.

Because patients who do not meet program requirements are discharged, a high level of structure should obtain better performance than a low level of structure, but at the cost of decreased retention. Four studies have reported data related to the hypothesis that level of structure is inversely related to retention.

Jaffe (1971) reported the retention of patients admitted to a program unit with a policy of "high level expectation." The staff had little tolerance for alcoholism, continued use of illicit drugs, and failure to obtain legitimate employment. Only 54 percent of sixty-three patients were retained in treatment for fourteen weeks after admission. Higher rates of retention were obtained in other less demanding units of this program. The findings tend to support the hypothesis that level of structure is inversely related to retention.

McGlothlin and Anglin (1981) reported a 6- to 7-year followup study of 347 patients admitted to methadone maintenance programs with different retention policies. Two programs had a high-dose, long retention policy, in which involuntary termination was used as a last resort. The third program had a low dose, two-year retention policy, with fairly strict terminations for program violations. While the program descriptions were limited, the third program seemed more highly structured than the other two programs. Retention was longer in the less structured programs (means of 4.3 and 3.2 years) than in the more structured program (mean of 2.2 years). This study also suggests that structure is inversely related to retention, but the effect of structure was confounded with that of methadone dose and the two-year retention policy.

Joe and Simpson (1975) reported 1-year retention rates in the DARP methadone maintenance programs by type of program. Less than half (40 percent) of 2,868 patients admitted to adaptive programs but over half (54 percent) of 2,113 patients admitted to change-oriented programs were retained in treatment for 1 year. This finding appears inconsistent with the hypothesis that level of structure is inversely related to retention, but the effect of structure was confounded by that of methadone dose.

McCarthy and Borders (1985) randomly assigned sixty-nine patients at admission to structured and unstructured treatment groups. The structured group had limits set on illicit drug use, which, if exceeded, resulted in withdrawal from methadone. The unstructured group had no limits set on illicit drug use. At the end of one year, 53 percent of the structured group but only 30 percent of the unstructured group remained in treatment. These findings also appear inconsistent with the hypothesis that level of structure is inversely related to retention.

The findings of these four studies seem ambiguous. Two tend to support the hypothesis that level of structure is inversely related to retention, and two do not. Possibly the structure variable contains component variables that have inconsistent effects, and possibly different levels of structure have divergent effects.

In many programs, counseling serves as the primary mechanism for maintaining the treatment structure. The counselor explains the rules and procedures to the patient, monitors the patient's performance, and participates in the use of sanctions to obtain patient compliance. Counseling is often mandatory and scheduled. To conduct a study of level of structure that we considered feasible, we chose to evaluate the effects on retention of optional counseling versus mandatory counseling.

Rapid Admission

Waiting lists for methadone maintenance mean that opioid users cannot promptly obtain treatment. Some cannot tolerate the waiting period and disappear from the waiting list. Furthermore, long waiting periods may deter some opioid users from applying for treatment. In 1989 the number of persons on waiting lists for alcohol and drug abuse treatment in 44 states and the District of Columbia was 66,766 (Sisk, Hatziandreu, and Hughes, 1990). The average estimated waiting period for outpatient treatment was 22 days. Waiting lists are deplored not only because they signify insufficient treatment for drug abusers, but also because untreated illicit drug injectors continue to spread AIDS. The Presidential Commission on the Human Immunodeficiency Virus Epidemic recommended "treatment-on-demand" for intravenous drug users (Presidential Commission, 1988). A committee on AIDS research of the National Research Council recommended "treatment on request" for intravenous drug users (Turner, Miller, and Moses, 1989). A committee on substance abuse of the National Research Council asserted that public coverage of drug treatment should provide for "timely admission" of individuals who cannot pay for it (Gerstein and Harwood, 1990).

Studies of attrition (or, conversely, retention) during the period from application to admission to methadone maintenance have not been reported. We are evaluating the difference in pretreatment retention between rapid admission (within one day) and slow admission (fourteen days). While we expect that rapid admission will be associated with increased pretreatment retention, it could reduce retention and rehabilitation during treatment. The waiting period may serve to screen out the more impulsive and erratic patients who would perform poorly in treatment. Consequently, we are also evaluating the effects on treatment retention and rehabilitation of the two admission conditions.

CONDUCTING THE INNOVATIONS

The four innovations and their evaluations are being conducted as a collaborative project of the University of Texas Health Science Center (HSC) and the

Center for Health Care Services (CHCS), both located in San Antonio. The latter agency is a community mental health center which serves a county population of approximately 1,185,400 persons. The Substance Abuse Program of the CHCS was established in 1970 and has operated continuously to the present time. Methadone maintenance has always been the major component of the program. In November 1989, 386 patients, excluding project patients, were maintained on methadone in 2 geographically separate treatment units. The methadone patients have always been predominantly young, Mexican American, male adults. The project began in September 1989 and will end in August 1994.

Before the grant application was submitted, the HSC investigators and the CHCS program executives spent some twenty hours in face-to-face and telephone conferences to plan the innovations and their evaluation. After the grant was awarded but before the start of the project, conferences were held with caseworkers, physicians, nurses, and others to explain the innovations, to describe the roles of clinical and research staff, and to respond to questions and comments. The staff members were given written ''Research Guides,'' plus one-page summaries of the procedures for physicians, caseworkers, and nurses. During the project, the research staff have had daily interactions with the clinical staff in which information is exchanged about the innovations and the data collection. In addition, the investigators have several group conferences each year with the clinical staff to review the progress of the innovations and their evaluation and to discuss any problems in maintaining the innovations. The four innovations have been introduced and maintained with only minor problems. The project benefited from excellent continuing collaboration between the research staff and the clinical staff.

The innovations have been conducted as prospective clinical experiments. Clients need to meet the following criteria for enrollment: (1) be eligible for methadone maintenance, (2) be aged 18 or over, (3) not be pregnant (4) have used intravenous drugs during at least 21 of the past 30 days, (5) not have been in treatment during the past 30 days, and (6) not be enrolled in a preceding study of this project. Nearly all eligible patients wanted to enroll because they would obtain treatment at reduced cost or no cost for 1 year. The project was funded to pay for the cost of treatment. After informed written consent was obtained, the patient was enrolled and then randomly assigned to an experimental (innovative) or control (standard) treatment condition. From September 1989 to November 1991, 638 subjects were enrolled in the project. In December 1991, 286 remained in treatment.

The treatment service for all subjects were equivalent, with the exception of the treatment innovations. The treatment innovation for each subject was provided for one year following admission, after which time the subject could continue in standard methadone maintenance treatment. The four innovations were introduced sequentially, rather than simultaneously, because the complexity of procedures might have impaired the integrity of the innovations or the validity of the evaluations.

All caseworkers, physicians, and nurses served both experimental and control subjects. In some of the innovations, optional counseling, for example, two caseworkers could have been selected to serve the optional counseling caseload. While this would have simplified the introduction, maintenance, and monitoring of the innovation, it would have complicated interpretation of the outcome data because some of the differences in outcomes might have resulted from differences in the caseworkers.

The special features of the innovations are as follows.

Elimination of Treatment Fees

The fee study had one eligibility criterion in addition to those listed above: the person must be qualified to pay $2.50 per day. This excluded persons receiving welfare payments or disability payments; these persons pay reduced fees. Subjects assigned to the experimental group paid no fees. Subjects assigned to the control group paid $2.50 per day. In instances of hardship, fees were temporarily deferred, in accordance with CHCS policy. The assigned treatment condition was maintained for one year.

Patient-Regulated Methadone Dose

During the first two weeks of treatment, the physician attempted to stabilize the patient on a methadone dose that relieved withdrawal symptoms. Thereafter the experimental subjects regulated their own doses. Once a week they could request an increase or decrease not to exceed 10 mg. The maximum dose allowed was 100 mg. Physicians could advise the subject about his or her methadone dose, but the subject decided. At the end of the one-year treatment period, the experimental subjects and control subjects could continue in treatment, but the former experimental subjects no longer regulated their doses.

Optional Counseling

During the first month of treatment, the caseworker saw the experimental subject one to three times to orient him or her to the program, to explain procedures and requirements, to identify any personal or social problems that distressed the subject, and to offer counseling. A treatment plan for one year, subject to change if needed, was prepared. Thereafter the caseworker saw the subject only on request of the subject, except in unusual circumstances. The caseworker did not call the subject in for confrontation about problems such as positive urine tests or unemployment. The subject could, however, ask the caseworker for help with these problems. In unusual circumstances the caseworker saw the subject without request. These circumstances included serious adverse behavior such as physical violence or a medical emergency. After the first month, the physician also saw the subject only on request, except in unusual circumstances. The control subjects, assigned to standard treatment, were required to attend two counseling sessions per month. After one year of treatment, all subjects could continue in treatment, but those assigned to optional counseling were changed to standard mandatory counseling.

Rapid Admission

At the Screening and Evaluation Unit of the CHCS all persons seeking assistance for a mental health, mental retardation, or substance abuse problem are seen promptly for a brief initial interview to identify the problem and to initiate the admission process, if service at the CHCS seems appropriate. This is followed by a screening interview. In the standard procedure, persons with probable opioid dependence who express interest in methadone maintenance are given appointments for an admission social assessment, laboratory analyses of blood and urine, electrocardiogram, and medical examination. Two weeks or more often elapse from application for treatment to the first methadone dose.

In the rapid admission study, subjects who appeared eligible at the brief initial interview were invited to enroll in the study. After enrollment they were randomly assigned to rapid admission (within one day after application) or slow admission (fourteen days after application). For the rapid admission subjects, the social and clinical assessments were not curtailed; they were compressed into a twenty-four-hour period. Subjects who failed to keep their appointments were rescheduled as soon as possible, but they were allowed only thirty days from enrollment to complete the admission evaluations. If more than thirty days elapsed, a subject could not be admitted to treatment as a research subject. After admission to treatment, subjects received standard treatment but did not pay treatment fees for one year.

CONCLUSION

Four treatment innovations designed to improve retention on methadone maintenance have been introduced and maintained in one substance abuse treatment program. The evaluation procedures and outcomes will be reported in subsequent publications.

ACKNOWLEDGMENTS

This study was supported by Public Health Service grant number DA06128 from the National Institute on Drug Abuse. D. P. Desmond and K. N. Vogtsberger reviewed the manuscript and provided helpful comments.

REFERENCES

Anglin, M. D., G. R. Speckart, M. W. Booth, and T. M. Ryan. 1989. Consequences and Costs of Shutting Off Methadone. *Addictive Behaviors*, 14, 307–326.

Babst, D. V., R. Ellis, and J. Schmeidler. 1976. Testing Predictive Efficiency of Patient Classifications for Methadone Maintenance Clients. *British Journal of Addiction*, 71, 359–367.

Ball, J. C., and A. Ross. 1991. *The Effectiveness of Methadone Maintenance Treatment: Patients, Programs, Services, and Outcome*. New York: Springer-Verlag.

Berry, G. J., and K. L. Kuhn. 1973. Dose-related Response to Methadone: Reduction of Maintenance Dose. In *Proceedings of the Fifth National Conference on Methadone Treatment*, pp. 972–979. New York: National Association for the Prevention of Addiction to Narcotics.

Butynski, W. 1991. Drug Treatment Services: Funding and Admissions. In *Improving Drug Abuse Treatment*, edited by R. W. Pickens, C. G. Leukefeld, and C. R. Schuster, pp. 20–52. NIDA Research Monograph No. 106, DHHS Publication No. (ADM) 91–1754. Rockville, MD: U.S. Department of Health and Human Services.

Childress, A. R., A. T. McLellan, and G. E. Woody. 1991. Are There Minimum Conditions Necessary for Methadone Maintenance to Reduce Intravenous Drug Use and AIDS Risk Behaviors? In *Improving Drug Abuse Treatment*, edited by R. W. Pickens, C. G. Leukefeld, and C. R. Schuster, pp. 167–177. NIDA Research Monograph No. 106, DHHS Publication No. (ADM) 19–1754. Rockville, MD: U.S. Department of Health and Human Services.

Cole, S. G., and L. R. James. 1975. A Revised Treatment Typology Based on the DARP. *American Journal of Drug and Alcohol Abuse*, 2, 37–49.

Cooper, J. R. 1989. Methadone Treatment and Acquired Immunodeficiency Syndrome. *Journal of the American Medical Association*, 262, 1664–1668.

Cooper, J. R., F. Altman, B. S. Brown, and D. Czechowicz (eds.). 1983. *Research on the Treatment of Narcotic Addiction: State of the Art*. NIDA Treatment Research Monograph Series, DHHS Publication No. (ADM) 83–1281. Rockville, MD: National Institute on Drug Abuse.

Garbutt, G. D., and A. Goldstein. 1972. Blind Comparison of Three Methadone Maintenance Dosages in 180 Patients. In *Proceedings of the Fourth National Conference on Methadone Treatment*, pp. 411–414. New York: National Association for the Prevention of Addiction to Narcotics.

Gearing, F. G. 1974. Methadone Maintenance Treatment Five Years Later—Where Are They Now? *American Journal of Public Health Supplement*, 64, 44–50.

Gerstein, D. R., and H. J. Harwood (eds.). 1990. *Treating Drug Problems*. Washington, DC: National Academy Press.

Goldstein, A., R. W. Hansteen, and W. H. Harris. 1975. Control of Methadone Dosage by Patients. *Journal of the American Medical Association*, 234, 734–737.

Goldstein, A., and B. A. Judson. 1973. Efficacy and Side Effects of Three Widely Different Methadone Doses. In *Proceedings of the Fifth National Conference on Methadone Treatment*, pp. 21–44. New York: National Association for the Prevention of Addiction to Narcotics.

Hargreaves, W. A. 1983. Methadone Dosage and Duration for Maintenance Treatment. In *Research on the Treatment of Narcotic Addiction*, edited by J. R. Cooper, F. Altman, B. S. Brown, and D. Czechowicz, pp. 19–79. NIDA Treatment Research Monograph Series, DHHS Publication No. (ADM) 83–1281. Rockville, MD: U.S. Department of Health and Human Services.

Havassy, B. E., and W. A. Hargreaves. 1981. Allowing Methadone Clients Control Over Dosage: A 48-Week Controlled Trial. *Addictive Behaviors*, 6, 283–288.

Hawkins, J. D. 1983. Community Characteristics Associated with Treatment Outcome. In *Research on the Treatment of Narcotic Addiction*, edited by J. R. Cooper, F.Altman, B. S. Brown, and D. Czechowicz, pp. 680–700. NIDA Treatment Research Monograph Series, DHHS Publication No. (ADM) 83–1281. Rockville, MD: U.S. Department of Health and Human Services.

Hubbard, R. L., M. E. Marsden, J. V. Rachal, H. J. Harwood, E. R. Cavanaugh, and H. M. Ginzburg. 1989. *Drug Abuse Treatment: A National Study of Effectiveness*. Chapel Hill: University of North Carolina Press.

Jaffe, J. H. 1971. Further Experience with Methadone in the Treatment of Narcotic Users. In *Methadone Maintenance*, edited by S. Einstein, pp. 29–40. New York: Marcel Dekker.

Joe, G. W., and D. D. Simpson. 1975. Retention in Treatment of Drug Users: 1971–1972 DARP Admissions. *American Journal of Drug and Alcohol Abuse*, 2(1), 63–71.

Johnson, J., N. Record, and P. Young. 1991. Drug Treatment Programs Conduct Effective Outreach and Behavior Change Interventions. *NADR Network* (newsletter of the NOVA Research Company, Bethesda, MD), Summer, 1–5.

Krakowski, J., and R. G. Smart. 1974. Social and Psychological Characteristics of Heroin Addicts Dropping Out of Methadone Treatment. *Canadian Psychiatric Association Journal*, 19, 41–47.

Kreek, M. J. 1991. Using Methadone Effectively: Achieving Goals by Application of Laboratory, Clinical, and Evaluation Research and by Development of Innovative Programs. In *Improving Drug Abuse Treatment*, edited by R. W. Pickens, C. G. Leukefeld, and C. R. Schuster, pp. 245–266. NIDA Research Monograph No. 106, DHHS Publication No. (ADM) 91–1754. Rockville, MD: U.S. Department of Health and Human Services.

Ling, W., V. C. Charuvastra, S. C. Kaim, C. F. Klett. 1976. Methadyl Acetate and Methadone as Maintenance Treatments for Heroin Addicts. *Archives of General Psychiatry*, 33, 709–720.

Maddux, J. F., and L. K. McDonald. 1973. Status of 100 San Antonio Addicts One Year After Admission to Methadone Maintenance. *Drug Forum*, 2, 239–252.

McCarthy, J. J., and O. T. Borders. 1985. Limit Setting on Drug Abuse in Methadone Maintenance Patients. *American Journal of Psychiatry*, 142, 1419–1423.

McGlothlin, W. H., and M. D. Anglin. 1981. Long-Term Followup of Clients of High- and Low-Dose Methadone Programs. *Archives of General Psychiatry*, 38, 1055–1063.

McLellan, A. T. 1983. Patient Characteristics Associated with Outcome. In *Research in the Treatment of Narcotic Addiction*, edited by J. R. Cooper, F. Altman, B. S. Brown, and D. Czechowicz, pp. 500–529. NIDA Treatment Research Monograph Series, DHHS Publication No. (ADM) 83–1281. Rockville, MD: U.S. Department of Health and Human Services.

Menninger, K. 1958. *Theory of Psychoanalytic Technique*. New York: Basic Books.

Murphy, S., and M. Rosenbaum. 1988. Money for Methadone II: Unintended Consequences of Limited-Duration Methadone Maintenance. *Journal of Psychoactive Drugs*, 20, 397–402.

Onken, L. S., and J. D. Blaine (eds.). 1990. *Psychotherapy and Counseling in the*

Treatment of Drug Abuse. NIDA Research Monograph No. 104, DHHS Publication No. (ADM) 91–1722. Rockville, MD: U.S. Department of Health and Human Services.

Orlinsky, D. E., and K. I. Howard. 1986. Process and Outcomes in Psychotherapy. In *Handbook of Psychotherapy and Behavior Changes*, 3rd edition, edited by S. L. Garfield and A. E. Bergin, pp. 311–381. New York: Wiley and Sons.

Pickens, R. W., C. G. Leukefeld, and C. R. Schuster (eds.). 1991. *Improving Drug Abuse Treatment*. NIDA Research Monograph No. 106, DHHS Publication No. (ADM) 91–1754. Rockville, MD: U.S. Department of Health and Human Services.

Platt, J. J. 1986. *Heroin Addiction: Theory, Research, and Treatment*, 2nd edition. Malabar, FL: Krieger.

Presidential Commission on the Human Immunodeficiency Virus Epidemic. 1988. *Report of the Presidential Commission on the Human Immunodeficiency Virus Epidemic*. Washington, DC: U.S. Government Printing Office.

Price, R. H., A. C. Burke, T. A. D'Aunno, D. M. Klingen, W. C. McCaughrin, J. A. Rafferty, and T. E. Vaughn. 1991. Outpatient Drug Abuse Treatment Services, 1988: Results of a National Survey. In *Improving Drug Abuse Treatment*, edited by R. W. Pickens, C. G. Leukefeld, and C. R. Schuster, pp. 63–91. NIDA Research Monograph No. 106, DHHS Publication No. (ADM) 91–1754. Rockville, MD: U.S. Department of Health and Human Services.

Resnick, R. B., P. Butler, and A. M. Washton. 1982. Patient Self-Adjustment of Methadone Maintenance Dose. In *Problems of Drug Dependence 1981*, edited by L. S. Harris, pp. 327–330. NIDA Research Monograph No. 41, Rockville, MD: U.S. Department of Health and Human Services.

Rosenbaum, M., J. Irwin, and S. Murphy. 1989. De Facto Destabilization as Policy: The Impact of Short-Term Methadone Maintenance. *Contemporary Drug Problems*, 15, 491–517.

Rosenbaum, M., S. Murphy, and J. Beck. 1987. Money for Methadone: Preliminary Findings from a Study of Alameda County's New Maintenance Policy. *Journal of Psychoactive Drugs*, 19, 13–19.

Sells, S. B., R. G. Demaree, D. D. Simpson, and G. W. Joe. 1978. Evaluation of Present Treatment Modalities. *Annals of the New York Academy of Sciences*, 311, 270–281.

Senay, E. C. 1985. Methadone Maintenance Treatment. *International Journal of the Addictions*, 20, 803–821.

Sisk, J. E., E. J. Hatziandreu, and R. Hughes. 1990. *The Effectiveness of Drug Abuse Treatment: Implications for Controlling AIDS/HIV Infection*. Background Paper, OTA-BP-H–73. Washington, DC: Office of Technology Assessment, Congress of the United States.

Turner, C. F., R. G. Miller, L. E. Moses (eds.). 1989. *AIDS: Sexual Behavior and Intravenous Drug Use*. Washington, DC: National Academy Press.

U.S. General Accounting Office. 1990. *Methadone Maintenance*. GAO/HRD–90–104. Washington, DC: U.S. General Accounting Office.

Woody, G. E. 1983. Treatment Characteristics Associated with Outcome. In *Research in the Treatment of Narcotic Addiction*, edited by J. R. Cooper, F. Altman, B. S. Brown, and D. Czechowicz, pp. 541–564. NIDA Treatment Research Monograph Series, DHHS Publication No. (ADM) 83–1281. Rockville, MD: U.S. Department of Health and Human Services.

3

Enhancing Drug Abuse Treatment by Mobile Health Service

Joseph V. Brady

A major impediment to the expansion of treatment services for drug abusers is identifying sites where new programs can be offered. Inner-city treatment programs, especially those non-hospital-based outpatient facilities for reducing intravenous (IV) drug abuse and the spread of AIDS, are saturated. More money will not necessarily permit these programs to deliver more services. Yet it is becoming exceedingly difficult to find additional locations to deliver these services to drug users who are being pressured to seek treatment by stepped-up law enforcement activity or newly initiated outreach programs aimed at reducing IV drug abuse and the spread of AIDS. Neighborhood and community organizations are increasingly less tolerant of indigenous "drug programs" despite the likelihood that those who would benefit from the programs are individuals who live in the very communities that oppose the establishment of new clinic facilities.

In the city of Baltimore, Maryland, where a mobile health service approach to the treatment of drug abuse has been undertaken, it is estimated that there are between 30,000 and 40,000 intravenous drug abusers, some 25,000 cocaine abusers, and 70,000 alcohol-dependent individuals. There is, of course, substantial overlap across these populations, and the problem is further complicated by the fact that between 30 percent and 40 percent of the AIDS victims in Baltimore report drug use as a risk factor. Based on a population of 750,000 (swelling to well over a million during the work day), it is estimated that 1 in 10 Baltimoreans has a substance abuse problem, but less than 1 in 20 of the substance abusers can be accommodated by the existing treatment system. In recent years, for example, less than 5,000 treatment slots have been available to serve this burgeoning substance-abusing population.

The approach described in this initial report is based on the now confirmed fact that, in general, communities find it less objectionable to have such treatment services offered from mobile health units. By temporarily parking such units a few hours each day at agreed upon locations (e.g., church parking lots, city-owned facilities, etc.) and limiting the time at each location by appropriate scheduling (e.g., avoiding school passage times), community concerns have been satisfied so as to make the approach feasible. In addition, the mobile units have been designed to deliver selected additional medical services to the community, (such as blood pressure screening and diabetic evaluations) to insure that they are legitimately viewed as health units.

Quite apart from the issue of feasibility as a means of responding to community concerns, mobile units offer the possibility of testing certain factors associated with success in treatment. It is now generally accepted that for opioid dependence, at least, time spent in treatment is an important variable in determining outcome (Simpson and Sells, 1982; Ban and Antes, 1981; De Leon, 1985; Anglin, Hser, and Booth, 1987; Fisher and Anglin, 1982; Hubbard et al., 1989). Patients who spend fewer than ninety days in treatment appear to fare considerably less well on most outcome measures than those who stay longer. Furthermore, in some studies (e.g., McLellan et al., 1985) patients remaining fewer than ninety days appear to be worse off at followup than they were at entry into treatment. A number of investigations are exploring ways to increase length of time patients remain in treatment in various modalities. In outpatient programs, key variables appear to be staff skills, leadership, program morale, staff training, and, for those programs using methadone, the dose of methadone (see Alleson, Hubbard, and Rachal, 1985; Ball et al., 1986, 1988).

Another variable that probably plays a role but has never been systematically evaluated is the *response effort* of remaining in treatment. Response effort refers to the overall costs to the individual of complying with the program requirements. In addition to any out-of-pocket monetary costs, response-effort costs include time required to get to and from the site of treatment, waiting time at the program, and time spent in actual treatment. Moreover, the savings in travel time may reduce opportunities for drug-related diversions that might occur on the way to more distant treatment sites. Although this reduction may well have direct benefits, the time invested must also be seen as time taken from other perhaps even more rewarding pursuits. Other costs include any side effects of medication involved in the treatment and the distress that comes of examining one's own current shortcomings and past failures and misdeeds. Taken together, the costs of treatment from the patient's perspective may be quite high even when the treatment cost measured in monetary terms is negligible. Furthermore, these costs are, at least in the early stages, competing with the memories of drug-induced euphoria and/or anxiolytic effects.

The mobile health service initiative described has the objective of bringing drug abuse treatment into close proximity of the patient's home to reduce travel time and dependence upon transportation without increasing risk of diversion.

BACKGROUND

There is but one brief report in the literature describing the use of mobile units in drug abuse treatment. This account of the methadone by bus project in Amsterdam (Buning et al., 1990) summarizes the development of a mobile methadone treatment program in response to the needs of a population of heroin users in Amsterdam from the former Dutch colony of Suriname. Faced with the familiar difficulty of having a stable clinic building accepted by the neighborhoods, two mobile bus-like clinics were commissioned to cruise the city, stopping at six different locations daily. Based on "harm-reduction" principles (i.e., in the absence of a "cure" for hard drug use, attempts should be made to at least minimize the harm caused to the individual and the environment), liquid methadone was dispensed and consumed on the spot, and clean needles and condoms were made available. A central methadone registration required of all Amsterdam programs prevented double prescriptions, and clients could graduate to higher threshold methadone as soon as they refrained from the use of illegal drugs. In the absence of a counseling component, however, the reported outcomes from contacts with many thousands of drug abusers suggest that relatively few of the Amsterdam methadone bus clients "graduated" to the more stable, "higher threshold" programs.

There has been a more recent development in the use of mobile methadone dispensing units by drug abuse treatment programs in Boston, Massachusetts. The service provider, the Habit Management Institute, uses two converted Winnebago mobile homes to transport and dispense the medication in the Brockton, Lakeville, and Quincy suburbs of the city. Although there have been no published descriptions of the program, personal communication and on-site inspection have revealed at least some of the procedural details. The vehicles travel to three and four locations each day, remain for approximately two hours at each location, and serve approximately fifty patients. The mobile units function solely as medication dispensaries, provide no counseling or other services, and are available only to patients with a previously determined commitment to treatment who would otherwise be required to travel some distance to obtain their daily medication. Patients must be identified with picture ID cards before admission to the mobile unit, and noncompliant or unresponsive patients are referred back to more stable, comprehensive treatment programs. There are, however, no data available on the extent to which the mobile units have effectively enhanced recruitment and retention of the indicated treatment populations.

DESCRIPTION OF THE PROGRAM

Two separate inner-city regional divisions in eastern and northwestern Baltimore were selected as sites for this demonstration drug abuse treatment project. The selection was based on the ranking of these communities among the geographic localities with the highest number of individuals admitted to treatment

Figure 3.1
Mobile Health Service Treatment Program Medication Dispensing Van

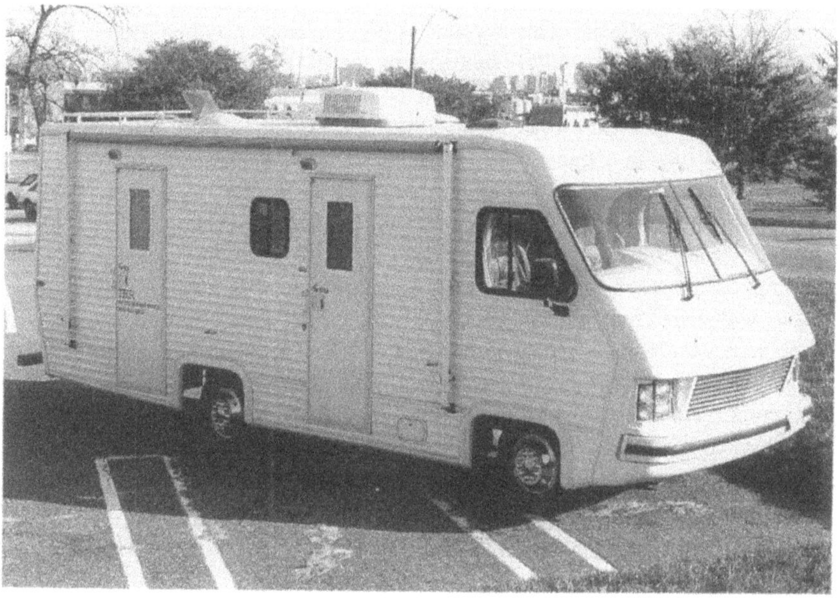

for substance abuse problems in the city. Over a period of a year beginning in October 1990, an extended series of personal contacts and organized meetings with key persons involved in community activities and health service delivery served to insure an essential degree of local community knowledge and to support the goals and objectives of the project and the mobile health service procedures. Selection of the sites for temporary parking of the vehicles was determined only after extensive consultation and agreement with the City of Baltimore Planning and Zoning Department, local legislators, health providers, and other community leaders. The assistance of the clergy and church groups proved to be invaluable in this sensitive process. As a result, several sites were identified in both the eastern and northwestern Baltimore localities, and the project vehicles were introduced to the community during "open house" visitations at each site.

During this extended community outreach period, the design and construction of medication vans and counseling trailers were undertaken with the assistance of a local supplier of recreational vehicles. Figure 3.1 shows one of the two twenty-five-foot Newport Motor Homes that were custom modified to serve as mobile medication dispensing units. In addition to a secure nurses' station with medication safe and dispensing window, each vehicle is equipped with a lavatory, a small patient waiting area, and an elaborate security alarm system. Figure 3.2 shows one of the two thirty-one-foot Newmar Travel Trailers that were custom modified to serve as counseling and general medical service units. Each trailer

Figure 3.2
Mobile Health Service Treatment Program Combination Counseling and General Medical Service Facility

contains two private individual counseling and examination areas separated by a larger centralized group meeting/waiting area, all with appropriate furnishings for seating and note-taking as required. A backup unit is provided by a nineteen-foot Coachman Motor Home, custom modified in a manner similar to the two Newport Motor Homes to serve as a mobile medication dispensing unit when necessary.

A home base for the Mobile Health Service has been established at the Bayview Campus of the Johns Hopkins University Francis Scott Key Medical Center in Baltimore. In addition, a facility for initial screening and medical examination has been provided at the Rapid Medical Intake Program of the Baltimore City Addict Referral and Counseling Center for evaluating and enrolling patients. In keeping with the proposed demonstration research design, one medication van and trailer unit is located at the same centralized site in the eastern division of the city six days a week. The second medication van and trailer circulate among three or four different locations in the northwestern region during the course of each week. After a performance baseline has been established under these conditions over a twelve- to eighteen-month period, the eastern regional division units will circulate among three or four locations in that division during the course of each week, and the northwestern regional division units will be located at one centralized site throughout the week.

Several weeks before enrolling the first patients into treatment, the trailer units alone were used to introduce the mobile health service in accordance with the site location schedules for the eastern and northwestern region. Without the accompanying medication vans, project personnel on the trailers responded to community inquiries about the program, explained the nature of the services that were to be provided, and distributed printed material on prevention measures, referral sources, and other health-related information. In addition, the nursing staff on the trailers offered screening tests for hypertension (blood pressure measures) and diabetes (blood glucose determinations) to interested individuals. During this period as well, staff training was undertaken to insure proficiency in the use of intake evaluation forms and the data management system for maintaining program records and generating necessary reports. The substance abuse data management system utilizes laptop computers on the mobile treatment units, with the database refreshed daily by downloading from the central computer at the Francis Scott Key Medical Center.

Admissions criteria for the treatment program require candidate participants to have a verifiable one-year history of opioid abuse and dependence and to be a minimum of eighteen years old. Following the initial screening interview, the Individual Assessment Profile and medical examination, including urinalysis and other laboratory tests, are completed. Upon acceptance into the program and completion of the informed consent procedure, a picture ID is prepared for each patient, and assignment to the mobile health treatment unit is determined by zip code. A written order by the staff physician establishes the initial methadone dose for each patient, and entry into the computerized data management system provides the necessary information to the nursing staff on the medication vans. Medication (methadone) is dispensed via soluble diskettes by authorized mobile health service staff upon verification of the patient's identity.

Urine specimens are obtained from each patient at least once per week, and results are returned to staff within forty-eight hours. Upon acceptance into the treatment program and completion of two additional assessment instruments (Beck Depression Scale and Symptom Checklist–SCL90), each client is assigned a counselor. Collaboration between the counselor and client provides the basis for establishing an individualized treatment plan including the development of both short- and long-range goals that are behaviorally defined and specific. Each individualized treatment plan is based on the requirement that the patient ingest the established dose of methadone once a day for the duration of participation in the treatment research demonstration program. In addition, the client is expected to participate in counseling sessions at the mobile trailer once a week, minimum. The weekly counseling sessions serve to identify specific objectives and assign specific tasks to enable the client to successfully attain the established treatment goals. The counseling sessions also permit periodic review and revision of the individualized treatment plan as necessary and appropriate.

The primary goal of the treatment is to maintain effective functioning rather than require detoxification, and complete withdrawal from medication is not encouraged for the twelve- to eighteen-month course of the study. In keeping with this objective, a flexible approach to medication dosage is taken with encouragement to maintain doses between 60 mg and 80 mg whenever possible. All the empirical evidence indicates that patients are least likely to use intravenous opiates or drop out of treatment at those doses (Ball and Ross, 1991). With regard to the management of noncompliant and misbehaving patients, the emphasis on treatment retention as a major objective of the program dictates a reasonable degree of tolerance of periodic, but not continuous, drug and/or alcohol consumption. And while this "high threshold" program does not expect to make "model patients" out of its clientele, it is necessarily intolerant of belligerent and aggressive behaviors in the interest of staff safety and the integrity of the mobile health service. Finally, the avowed aim of the counseling component of the mobile health service treatment program is behavior change as it relates specifically to drug-seeking and drug-taking. And while the "high tolerance" philosophy of the treatment approach subscribes to a procedure that offers and encourages counseling, participation in drug abuse counseling is not an absolute requirement.

RESEARCH EVALUATION

Both process and outcome studies are being conducted to evaluate the feasibility, implementation, and results of the interventions on drug abuse and related measures in the geographically defined areas of the indicated urban setting. The continuing process evaluation provides an ongoing account of all the necessary steps required to initiate this complex undertaking. All internal staff meetings and discussions as well as all meetings with external individuals and groups are documented in a standardized written format and communicated to the research evaluation team in an expeditious manner. Essential baseline data against which to evaluate outcome measures have also been incorporated into the Individual Assessment Profile and other client information forms and records completed on each patient at intake and throughout the course of treatment (McGlothlin, 1977).

REFERENCES

Alleson, M., R. Hubbard, and J. V. Rachal. 1985. *Treatment Process in Methadone, Residential and Outpatient Drug Free Programs*. NIDA Treatment Research Monograph, DHHS Publication No. (AM) 85–1388. Washington, DC: U.S. Government Printing Office.

Anglin, M. D., J. Hser, and M. W. Booth. 1987. Sex Differences in Addict Careers: Treatment. *American Journal of Drug and Alcohol Abuse*, 13(3), 253–280.

Ball, J. C. E. Corty, P. Petroski, and A. Comasello. 1986. Medical Services Provided to 2,394 Patients at Methadone Programs in Three States. *Journal of Substance Abuse Treatment*, 3, 203–209.

Ball, J. C., W. R. Lange, C. P. Myers, and S. R. Friedman. 1988. Reducing the Risk of AIDS through Methadone Maintenance Treatment. *Journal of Health and Social Behavior*, 29, 214–226.

Ball, J. C., and A. Ross. 1991. *The Effectiveness of Methadone Maintenance Treatment: Patients, Programs, Services, and Outcome*. New York: Springer-Verlag.

Ban, H., and D. Antes. 1981. *Factors Related to Recovery and Relapse in Followup*. Final Report of Project Activities Under NIDA Grant H81-DAO 1864.

Buning, E. C., G.H.A. Van Brussel, and G. Van Santen. 1990. The "Methadone by Bus" Project in Amsterdam. *British Journal of Addiction*, 85, 1247–1250.

De Leon, G. 1985. The Therapeutic Community: Status and Evolution. *International Journal of the Addictions*, 20(6, 7), 823–844.

Fisher, D. G., and M. D. Anglin. 1982. Survival Analysis in Drug Program Evaluation. Part 1. Overall Program Effectiveness. *International Journal of the Addictions*, 22(2), 115–134.

Hubbard, R. L., M. E. Marsden, J. V. Rachal, H. J. Harwood, E. R. Cavanaugh, and H. M. Ginzburg. 1989. *Drug Abuse Treatment: A National Study of Effectiveness*. Chapel Hill: University of North Carolina Press.

McGlothlin, W. H. 1977. *An Evaluation of a Follow-up of Admissions to the California Civil Addicts Program*. NIDA Monograph, Services Research Branch. Washington, DC: U.S. Government Printing Office.

McLellan, A. T., L. Luborshy, J. Cacciola, J. Griffith, P. McGahan, and C. P. O'Brien. 1985. *Guide to the Addiction Severity Index: Background, Administration, and Field Testing Results*. NIDA Treatment Research Report. Rockville, MD: National Institute on Drug Abuse.

Simpson, D. D., and S. B. Sells, 1982. Effectiveness of Treatment for Drug Abuse: An Overview of the DARP Research Program. *Advances in Alcohol and Substance Abuse Treatment*, 2(1), 729–742.

II

RESIDENTIAL PROGRAMS

4

Four Residential Drug Treatment Programs: Project IMPACT

Benjamin F. Lewis, Jane McCusker, Rita Hindin, Ray Frost, and Frances Garfield

Project IMPACT is a collaborative effort to evaluate the outcomes of two different models of residential, drug-free treatment: a classical therapeutic community (TC) and a modified therapeutic community in which programs of relapse prevention and health education (RP/HE) have been embedded. Within each model, shorter and longer programs have been developed, comprising six- and twelve-month versions of the TC and three- and six-month versions of the RP/HE programs. The main aims of the project are to compare the effectiveness of the four programs in achieving long-term outcomes of abstinence from drugs, reductions in concomitant social problems, and reductions in HIV-risky behaviors. In this chapter we provide an overview of (1) the rationale underlying development of the four treatment programs, (2) the implementation of the programs, and (3) the evaluation design.

RATIONALE

Project IMPACT concerns itself with three aspects of residential drug treatment: the different approaches to treatment of the two treatment models, TC and RP; the effects of program duration; and the potential for AIDS prevention. The rationale for our focus on these aspects is elaborated in the following sections.

Approaches to Treatment

There are many approaches to the treatment of drug addiction, based in part on different models of the etiology of addictive behaviors and the etiology of factors involved in changing these behaviors. Brickman, Rabinowitz, and Karuga (1982) proposed four general models of addiction, based on the extent to which addicted individuals are held personally responsible for the development of their addiction and for changing their behavior. In the *moral* model, individuals are held responsible for both the development of and the solution to their problem. In the *medical* model, individuals are believed to be responsible for neither the problem nor its solution, and they are given treatment for both. In the *enlightenment* model, individuals are considered responsible for their problems but unwilling or unable to provide solutions, and they are believed to require discipline. In the *compensatory* models, individuals are seen as not responsible for their problem but for its solution, for which they need to be empowered.

While moral and medical models have dominated treatment and posttreatment environments, increasingly there has been an evolving biopsychosocial model of addictive behaviors that views addiction as a complex and progressive behavior pattern with component processes (Donovan, 1988). Treatment episodes, and to a lesser extent self-generated abstinence, are attempts to initiate behavior change. Relapse involves a failure to maintain behavioral change. Traditional approaches to the treatment of drug abusers may be effective in initiating change in behaviors but may be less effective or ineffective in sustaining behavioral change over time.

Using Brickman's scheme, the two models upon which our treatment programs are based are the enlightenment and compensatory models (see Table 4.1). The TC is based on an enlightenment model: it provides a highly structured community setting within which change becomes possible through the relinquishment of personal control to a "higher power" or collective group entity (Marlatt, 1988). The principles of the RP/HE program, on the other hand, are based on the compensatory model. Individuals are encouraged to accept responsibility for changing their behavior and are taught skills that help to accomplish this.

It is unrealistic to assume that either of these approaches achieves better results for all outcomes of interest or for all clients. Rather, our rationale for comparing the two models is to understand which outcomes, both behavioral and psychosocial, are differentially affected by the programs and which clients within which program are likely to fare better. For example, one might hypothesize that the relapse prevention program would have a more beneficial effect on self-efficacy or the confidence to abstain from using drugs in high-risk situations. However, this program may be less effective for clients with poorer cognitive status or clients who are not ready to take responsibility for change. Some of these individuals may be in the "precontemplation" or "contemplation" stages of behavior change, using the classification of Prochaska and DiClemente (1983). Thus, we hope that this research provides useful data for the more effective matching of clients to treatments (Marlatt, 1988).

Therapeutic Community (TC). Current drug abuse treatment programs are part of a generation of programs that originated in the 1950s and began to flourish in the 1960s and 1970s. The first treatment modality that began to fill the void

Table 4.1
Major Contrasting Characteristics of Therapeutic Community (TC) and Relapse Prevention/Health Education (RP/HE) Treatment

Characteristic	TC	RP/HE
Etiologic Hypotheses	Character defect	Learned behaviors for which the client is not held responsible
Treatment Focus	'Restructuring' the individual. Creating community	Behavior modification
Primary Focus for Individual Character-ological Development	Self-esteem	Self-efficacy
Treatment Goals	Abstinence Lifestyle change	Ability to prevent occasional lapses becoming full relapses to previous level of use. Abstinence
Treatment Nature	Learning experiences through the group	Training in skills implementation, decision-making awareness, cognitive reframing practice

that existed prior to the late 1950s is the prototype of the current TC and provided treatment from the premise that drug addiction derived from fundamental defects in character and maturation. In 1958, Synanon, the first TC, reported encouraging results; other early TCs (Phoenix House, Gateway, and Daytop Village) also reported positive results, and their numbers increased (Hubbard et al., 1989).

The TC has been described as: (1) an explicitly designed concept with its own model and methods (De Leon, 1984); (2) a self-help, mutual-help dynamic rehabilitative community (De Leon and Ziegenfuss, 1986); and (3) a socioeducational institution (Jones, 1953). The TC method derives from the assumptions that the causes of substance abuse are deficits, both social and psychological, in the individual and that "working on the whole individual" is required. Total abstinence from drugs is the major expected outcome from TC treatment.

Specifically, rehabilitation is done at two interrelated levels. The first is social: the recovering substance abuser is a "member" of a highly hierarchical community in the TC. Upon entry into treatment a new member has few or no responsibilities and is regarded as untrustworthy. With time, trust and responsibility are earned as he or she progresses successfully through a structured program of incremental instruction and exhibits the several behavioral characteristics that are necessary for a drug-free lifestyle. These responsibilities include: taking responsibility, improved social skills, helping oneself, trusting others, helping peers, reinforcing honesty, and making a commitment to abstain from drugs.

The second level of rehabilitation is in the psychosocial domain. The aim of TC treatment is to change the negative patterns of behavior, thinking, and feeling that underlie drug abuse. Some of the therapeutic tools used to achieve this aim include: separating the residents from past sources of negative influences, confronting behaviors, beliefs, and attitudes associated with drug abuse; enforcing responsibility; utilizing mutual and self-help techniques; and crediting privilege and increased status within the TC community to longevity and achievement in areas of personal growth (De Leon, 1986).

Relapse Prevention/Health Education (RP/HE). It has been recognized for a long time that drug addiction is a chronic condition that may be characterized by alternating periods of abstinence and return to drug use over time. Recovery from drug addiction can mean a number of things: cure of addiction, "abstinence" from drug use, or remission of the drug-dependent state (Wesson, Havassy, and Smith, 1986). Theories of recovery include "maturation out" (Winick, 1962), "natural recovery" (Waldorf, 1983), and the Twelve-Step concept of "being in recovery," which views addiction as a lifelong incurable disease where abstinence from substance use is an active, continuing, lifelong process.

The other side of the recovery coin is relapse. There are numerous theories of relapse addressing both occurrence and prevention. These approaches have implications for the way relapse is defined and understood. Genetic and metabolic theories (Schuckit and Duby, 1982; Dole and Nyswander, 1967; Goldstein, 1978;

Ho, Wen, and Ling, 1980), which are predicated on predisposing vulnerability, are used to support the medical model of drug dependence, which, in turn, has implications for explaining how relapse occurs and may be prevented. Similarly, those who view addiction as a manifestation of underlying psychopathological processes may focus treatment on the resolution of the pathology. Continued use, or relapse, is evidence of unresolved underlying issues.

Enlightenment theories such as the conditioning theory (Wikler, 1973; Ludwig and Wikler, 1974; Sideroff and Jarvik, 1980) and social learning theory (Bandura, 1977a; Marlatt and Gordon, 1980, 1985) acknowledge the role of classical and operant conditioning and attempt to focus on cognitive-mediated processes in the acquisition, maintenance, and modification of behavior. Each theory also carries with it specific belief systems and operational activities that both derive from and interact with treatment modality and goals of treatment. For example, in a medical model where zero tolerance is the prevailing value, any posttreatment drug use may be seen as relapse. Alternatively, with a methadone maintenance client, where reduction in illicit drug use is the goal, resumption of frequent or daily use may be the measure of relapse (Wesson, Havassy, and Smith, 1986).

Relapse prevention as a theory (or theories) can be the focus of treatment or an adjunct to the treatment of various addictions (Marlatt and Gordon, 1980; Marlatt, 1985). Characteristics of the addictive experience in this theory include:

1. a basis in both physiology and "learned expectations";
2. the contribution of physical and psychological states to the experience;
3. the role of conditioning so that not only the addictive behavior but a wide variety of other changes become stimuli;
4. the "paradox of control," namely that the addictive behavior, which in some sense is the individual's effort to assert control, is out of his or her control;
5. the high rates of relapse after a period of abstinence; and
6. the ability of certain situations or behaviors to trigger relapse.

Applied to this view of addiction is the social learning theory, specifically Bandura's theory of self-efficacy, which provides a useful framework for the development of the RP/HE psychoeducational approach for the treatment of drug abusers. This theory suggests that even the most powerful methods of initiating and achieving behavioral changes may not be the most effective techniques for producing generalization and maintenance of treatment effects, with resultant relapse (Bandura, 1977a).

Specifically, it is hypothesized that drug abuse behaviors become established because they are followed by some form of immediate gratification (Marlatt and Gordon, 1985; Wesson, Havassy, and Smith, 1986) that represents a maladaptive response to stress (Chaney and Roszell, 1985). RP emphasizes cognitive-mediated processes of behavior change. In RP/HE theory, relapse does not lead to inevitable failure; rather RP theory acknowledges the frequent occurrence of slips or lapses and teaches the drug abuser to anticipate triggers to use (Childress, Fureman, and Fureman, 1989). In RP, addicts are trained to increase their ability to cope with high-risk thinking and/or high-risk situations through improving self-efficacy utilizing a variety of skills, techniques, and activities and to believe in the effectiveness of these acquired skills (Marlatt and Gordon, 1985). In addition, because of the belief that a lapse or relapse can provide important lessons about high-risk situations, relapse need not equate to treatment failure.

Specifically, in Project IMPACT's RP/HE model, clients are taught and encouraged to practice: (1) the identification of individual cues, triggers, and mood states that prompt drug use; (2) the behavioral coping skills that must be implemented in the place of drug use; and (3) the avoidance of high-risk situations for drug use. This education is reinforced by an understanding of the consequences associated with the decisions that are made with respect to drug use—namely personal, societal, interpersonal, legal, and economic consequences.

A purported advantage of the RP/HE modality, relative to TC treatment, is its recognition of the potential for drug relapse. Specifically, it has been hypothesized that the TC client who has internalized the goal of complete abstinence may not be equipped with the cognitive skills necessary to cope with the unanticipated high-risk situation that results in lapse and that the internalization of the belief that any lapse is a failure promotes full relapse. A counterargument is that the skills mastery developed in RP/HE programs is not a viable substitute for the changing of an individual's behavioral characteristics as is accomplished in TC treatment.

Program Duration

Program duration is of interest because of the public health imperative to treat more individuals and the biases in previous research on the effects of treatment duration. A number of prior studies document the association of longer duration in treatment with better outcomes (Bale, 1979; Simpson, 1981; De Leon and Schwartz, 1984; Hubbard et al., 1989; Lewis and Ross, forthcoming). For example, Hubbard and colleagues (1988) conclude that retention in treatment for at least six months is necessary for treatment to have the greatest effect on abstinence rates. However, this conclusion is drawn from observational data, in which there is the potential for selection bias. For example, clients who are more motivated to change their behavior may be retained longer in treatment, and their better outcomes may be explained by motivation rather than actual retention. Perhaps these clients might do equally well in shorter programs. It is also possible that certain clients may drop out of treatment early, discouraged by the length of time before "graduation" can take place. Successful completion of a shorter program by a larger proportion of clients might actually increase the self-esteem of completers sufficiently to provide the motivation to continue the recovery process either on their own or with the help of certain after-care services.

In conclusion, planned duration of treatment has not been adequately examined. A unique contribution of Project IMPACT is the ability to disentangle selection bias from planned duration by using a design in which clients are randomly allocated to shorter or longer versions of their treatment program.

Potential for AIDS Prevention

The role of residential drug abuse treatment in modifying HIV risk behaviors is also of considerable interest (DesJarlais and Friedman, 1986; Sorensen, forthcoming; McCusker and Sorensen, forthcoming). Beyond reducing drug use, many treatment environments have implemented programs that promote reduction in needle sharing, increased utilization of paraphernalia-disinfecting procedures, and, to a lesser extent, increased employment of protective sexual behaviors. In previous work we have evaluated alternative AIDS educational interventions for clients admitted to a short-term inpatient drug detoxification and rehabilitation program (McCusker et al., 1992). The results indicate the potential for such interventions to enhance the effectiveness of drug treatment in reducing the incidence of relapse (McCusker et al., 1991). In addition, an evaluation from this same project of the effects of HIV status upon behavior change suggests that counseling and testing in the context of drug abuse treatment can further enhance appropriate drug and sexual behavior change (McCusker and Lewis, 1990).

These findings are exciting as they suggest that incorporation of HIV/AIDS interventions into drug treatment will further enhance the potential of drug abuse treatment in AIDS prevention. In Project IMPACT, AIDS interventions are integral components of both treatment programs, adapted to suit the specific treatment program context. The assessment of HIV risk behaviors at baseline and at followup provides important information on the effects of residential drug abuse treatment upon HIV risk behavior.

IMPLEMENTATION

Project IMPACT is being carried out at two sites: a residential drug abuse treatment program in central Massachusetts, where the RP/HE program is being implemented, and a residential program in Rhode Island where a traditional TC program is operating.

Both sites provide residential drug-free treatment services to male and female clients, eighteen years old and over. While some clients may be referred to treatment by the criminal justice system or by family members, admissions are essentially voluntary.

Both sites have had parallel experiences in organizational development as TCs and have had close working relationships with each other over a period of more than twenty years, some predicated on program graduates from each being employed at the other. While fostering a healthy sense of competition, the longstanding relationships between the sites have also fostered a sense of collaboration.

The TC site has been operated as a therapeutic community for over twenty years. As such, its planned duration for each client is over a year. It adheres to the basic TC philosophy and structure described earlier in this chapter (see also Table 4.2).

Formerly, the RP/HE treatment site operated as a long-term therapeutic community. Over a three-year period preceding this study it gradually shortened its planned duration from two years to one year to six months. Over the same time period, and aware of high relapse rates among its TC program graduates, the program introduced a time-limited module of relapse prevention training for readmissions. This program operated within the structure of the TC and consisted of a series of group meetings focused on learning relapse prevention principles, identifying personal triggers to drug use, and planning after-care. Retention in this ninety-day relapse program was quite good, with approximately 85 percent staying to completion. With this positive "booster" and increased retention for its former TC clients as a rationale, the program expanded the relapse prevention instruction to all clients and later augmented this exposure within the context of the TC by developing a health education program consisting of HIV education, relaxation training, substance abuse education, and STD prevention (see Table 4.3).

In the early implementation phase, the conversion of the former TC into an RP program was not without its problems. The same was true of the development in the traditional TC of a six-month program duration.

In the RP program, historic client expectations of treatment, considerable staff ambivalence and trepidation about shifting the focus and methods of treatment, and lack of sufficient time for staff to "process" the rapid and radical changes they had experienced in the recent past and were currently experiencing in the program may initially have resulted in cosmetic changes in language and content only. The critical context of treatment—the milieu—with shared staff and client needs for safety and structure, may have mitigated against an essential shift in treatment emphasis. Initial discomfort with drug cue exposure was also magnified by staff feeling that they did not have enough time or structure to "process out" feelings. In addition, program staff were initially uncomfortable because the entire clinical program was perceived as a research project and because of disequilibrium experienced with the infusion of research interviewers and instruments.

Also initially, the implications of random assignment were experienced in part as challenging clinical judgment regarding matching client needs with treatment duration. Integrating both a new treatment focus and a large research study of the program presented many concerns and challenges for staff and modifications in initial design for the research team. In fact, one of the concerns at the outset of the study was that the RP/HE program was merely an enhancement of the TC. This was a departure from the original design, which contemplated an

Table 4.2

Major Programmatic Features of the Therapeutic Community (TC) Programs; Comparison with the Relapse Prevention/Health Education (RP/HE) Programs

Program Feature	TC Content	RP/HE Content
Creating Community		
-Special Language/ Vocabulary	Extensive	Limited
-Subject-to-Subject Confrontation & Encounter Groups	Yes	No
-Rules for Daily Living	Extensive	Limited
-Organized Teaching of Values	Yes	No
Hierarchical Structure		
-Formal Stages of Personal Autonomy	Yes	No
-Role Status	Heavily Emphasized	No
-Work	As a Hierarchy	In crews
Other		
-Sanctions for Misbehavior	Wider Range	Lesser Range
-Psychotherapy	Psychodynamically oriented group and individual therapy (emphasis on returning with problems to the group)	Limited and focused individual therapy

Table 4.3
Relapse Prevention Program Components

Component	Number of Weeks or Sessions: Three Month Intervention	Six Month Intervention
Admission	1 week	1 week
Orientation	1-4 weeks	1-4 weeks
Core Group Sessions:		
Overview	1 session	2 sessions
Cravings, external events, antecedents	3 sessions	6 sessions
Skills	7 sessions	14 sessions
Lifestyle balance	2 sessions	4 sessions
Relapse Planning	4 sessions	8 sessions
Aftercare Planning	4 sessions	4 sessions
TOTAL number of sessions	21 sessions	42 sessions
HIV Education	4 sessions	4 sessions
Stress Management Education	4 sessions	4 sessions
Substance Abuse Education	1-2 weeks	1-2 weeks
Safe Sex Education	1-2 weeks	1-2 weeks
Other Health Education, including Parenting	1-2 weeks	1-2 weeks
HIV Education Booster	1 session	1 session
Vocational Counseling	5 weeks	5 weeks

Table 4.4
Therapeutic Community Program Stages

Stages	Number of Months: Six Month Intervention	Number of Months: Twelve Month Intervention
Orientation	2 weeks	2 weeks
First Stage	2 & 1/2 months	5 - 5 & 1/2 months
Transition	2 - (3) weeks	2 - (3) weeks
Second Stage	2 & 1/2 months	5 & 1/2 - 6 months

essential change in treatment philosophy and substantive aspects of treatment, such as the use of individual counseling to support and individualize an RP/HE program focus.

Even though the RP/HE emphasis introduced some conflicts, this program was able to develop a program protocol more easily than the TC program because much of what the program required could be imported from other applications. In the traditional TC, where an oral history predominated, there were many challenges to the development of a program protocol. Prototypical TC philosophy, methods, and activities needed to be looked at and then the experience of this particular TC observed and measured against a historical template for TCs. Defining the shorter, six-month TC program called for critical decisions regarding simply halving the twelve-month program or modifying it so that it was a shorter, but coherent process. For example, reentry, or the working-out/living-out phase of the program, was sacrificed because it was simply not feasible (see Table 4.4).

Two consultants, G. Allan Marlatt (relapse prevention) and George De Leon (therapeutic community), experts in their respective fields, were engaged to review program protocols, observe program activities, and interview staff. Their input and "blessing" that key elements of the two different approaches were reflected in what they read and saw were important to validate the major differences between the two programs and to get the study moving. The challenges continue to be to identify those elements that are similar in the programs (use of structure, for example), to try to understand the program rationale for continuing to function in a certain way, and to document the occurrence of such phenomena.

Process evaluation activities are being conducted to monitor the consistency and integrity of each of the four interventions over the life of the project. Structures have been developed for ongoing feedback to research/program staff on the appropriate delivery of the program protocols and identification of specific intreatment data that may be appropriate for incorporation into outcome analyses. Process evaluation includes identification, observation, document-review, and data-gathering activities designed to document that:

1. All interventions are conducted in a manner consistent with the organizations' standards for the quality and appropriateness of client care and treatment.
2. The program's service delivery can be distinguished as relapse prevention/health education or therapeutic community models.
3. The interventions are consistently delivered according to protocols and in their entirety to all subjects.
4. There is no difference in the quality of individual client care related to the client's participation or refusal to participate in Project IMPACT.
5. Useful and appropriate program data on participants and the program as a whole are identified for use in outcome evaluation.
6. Changes or variations in program components, protocols, or other significant intreatment variables over the period of the study are documented.

EVALUATION DESIGN

The evaluation design of Project IMPACT comprises observational and experimental components. It can best be thought of as two concurrent, randomized, controlled trials, in which duration of treatment program is randomly assigned within each treatment modality.

At each site, all clients admitted are randomly allocated to the shorter or longer version of the program, regardless of their agreement to participate in the research. The few exceptions are those clients whose duration of treatment has been mandated.

The location of the two collaborating treatment programs in adjacent states makes random assignment to treatment modality impractical. Thus, in our comparison of the two treatment modalities, TC and RP/HE, selection bias can be controlled only in the analysis. However, such comparisons are facilitated by the use of standardized data collection methods. The inclusion of a six-month version of each program allows us to control for planned treatment duration in our analyses. Nevertheless, preliminary data indicate that there are substantial differences between the two sites in methods or referral and in certain client characteristics at baseline, which precludes us from drawing definitive conclusions about the relative effectiveness of the two treatment modalities.

The primary study outcomes are assessed at followup, approximately eighteen months after admission, and include measures of time to first lapse, degree of relapse, addiction severity and related social problems, and HIV risk behaviors. Additional followup is carried out to measure behavior during the months immediately following discharge from treatment. In addition to behavioral outcomes, selected intermediate outcome variables assess the effects of treatment on program retention and completion and on a range of psychosocial variables including self-esteem, self-efficacy, and stage of behavior change.

CONCLUSION

Project IMPACT is an ambitious endeavor involving the collaboration of treatment programs and researchers. Major achievements to date include the modification of a therapeutic community to incorporate principles of relapse prevention, the development of treatment protocols for both short- and long-term versions of the two programs, and the implementation of a randomized design by both programs.

REFERENCES

Bale, R. N. 1979. Outcome Research in Therapeutic Communities for Drug Abuse: A Critical Review 1963–1975. *International Journal of the Addictions*, 14(8), 1053–1074.

Bandura, A. 1977a. Self-Efficacy: Toward a Unifying Theory of Behavioral Change. *Psychology Review*, 84, 191–215.

Bandura, A. 1977b. *Social Learning Theory*. Englewood Cliffs, NJ: Prentice-Hall.

Bandura, A. 1988. Perceived Self-Efficacy: Exercise of Control Through Self-Belief. In *Annual Series of European Research in Behavior Therapy*, vol. 2, edited by J. P. Dauwalder, M. Perrez, and V. Hobi, pp. 27–59. Lisse, the Netherlands: Swets and Zeitlinger.

Brickman, P., V. C. Rabinowitz, and J. Karuga. 1982. Models of Helping and Coping. *American Psychologist*, 37, 368–384.

Catalano, R. F., and J. D. Hawkins. 1985. Project Skills: Preliminary Results from a Theoretically Based Aftercare Experiment. In *Progress in the Development of Cost-Effective Treatment for Drug Abusers*, edited by R. S. Ashery, pp. 157–181. NIDA Research Monograph No. 58, DHHS Publication No. (ADM) 88–1401. Washington, DC: Department of Health and Human Services.

Chaney, E. F., and D. K. Roszell. 1985. Coping in Opiate Addicts Maintained on Methadone. In *Coping and Substance Use*, edited by S. Shiffman and T. A. Wills, pp. 267–293. San Diego: Academic Press.

Childress, A. R., B. B. Fureman, and I. Fureman. 1989. *Extinction Procedures for Opiate and Cocaine Dependence: A Clinical Guide*. Philadelphia: Department of Psychiatry, Philadelphia VA Medical Center, and the University of Pennsylvania, Center for Studies in Addiction.

De Leon, G. 1984. *The Therapeutic Community: Study of Effectiveness*. NIDA Treatment Research Monograph Series, DHHS Publication No. (ADM) 84–1286. Rockville, MD: National Institute on Drug Abuse.

De Leon, G. 1986. The Therapeutic Community for Substance Abuse: Perspective and Approach. In *Therapeutic Communities for Addictions: Readings in Theory, Research and Practice*, edited by G. De Leon and J. T. Ziegenfuss, pp. 5–18. Springfield, IL: Charles C. Thomas.

De Leon, G., and S. Schwartz. 1984. The Therapeutic Community: What Are the Retention Rates? *American Journal of Drug and Alcohol Abuse*, 10, 267–284.

De Leon, G., and J. T. Ziegenfuss (eds.). 1986. *Therapeutic Communities for Addictions: Readings in Theory, Research, and Practice*. Springfield, IL: Charles C. Thomas.

DesJarlais, D. C., and S. R. Friedman. 1986. AIDS and Therapeutic Communities: Policy Implications. In *Bridging Services*, edited by A. Acampora and E. Nebelkopf, pp. 74–79. San Francisco: Walden House, Inc.

Dole, V. P., and M. E. Nyswander. 1967. Heroin Addiction: A Metabolic Disease. *Archives of Internal Medicine*, 120, 19–24.

Donovan, D. D. 1988. Assessment of Addictive Behaviors: Implications of an Emerging Biopsychosocial Model. In *Assessment of Addictive Behaviors*, edited by D. Donovan and G. A. Marlatt, pp. 3–48. New York: Guilford Press.

Goldstein, A. 1978. Endorphins: Physiology and Clinical Implications. *New York Academy of Science*, 311, 49–58.

Ho, W.K.K., H. L. Wen, and N. Ling. 1980. Beta-Endorphin-like Immunoactivity in the Plasma of Heroin Addicts and Normal Subjects. *Neuropharmacology*, 19, 117–120.

Hubbard, R. L., M. E. Marsden, E. Cavanaugh, J. V. Rachal, and H. M. Ginzburg. 1988. Role of Drug-Abuse Treatment in Limiting the Spread of AIDS. *Review of Infectious Diseases*, 10, 377–384.

Hubbard, R. L., M. E. Marsden, J. V. Rachal, H. J. Harwood, E. R. Cavanaugh, and H. M. Ginzburg. 1989. *Drug Abuse Treatment: A National Study of Effectiveness*. Chapel Hill: University of North Carolina Press.

Hubbard, R. L., J. V. Rachal, S. G. Craddock, and E. R. Cavanaugh. 1984. Treatment Outcome Prospective Study (TOPS): Client Characteristics and Behaviors Before, During and After Treatment. In *Drug Abuse Treatment Evaluation: Strategies, Progress, and Prospects*, edited by F. M. Tims and J. P. Lunford, pp. 42–68. NIDA Research Monograph No. 51, DHHS Publication No. 84–1349. Rockville, MD: National Institute on Drug Abuse.

Joe, G. W., B. K. Singh, W. Lehman, D. D. Simpson, and S. B. Sells. 1980. Differences in Client Posttreatment Outcomes Among Drug Abuse Treatment Programs. Institute of Behavioral Research, Texas Christian University, IRB Report 80–12.

Jones, M. 1953. *The Therapeutic Community*. New York: Basic Books.

Lewis, B. F., and R. Ross. Forthcoming. Retention in Therapeutic Communities: Challenges for the 90's. In NIDA Monograph on Research in Therapeutic Communities, edited by F. Tims.

Ludwig, A. M., and A. Wikler. 1974. "Craving" and Relapse to Drink. *O. J. Stud. Alcohol*, 35, 108–130.

Marlatt, G. A. 1985. Coping and Substance Abuse: Implications for Research, Prevention and Treatment. In *Coping and Substance Abuse*, edited by S. Shiffman and T. A. Wills, pp. 367–386. New York: Academic Press.

Marlatt, G. A. 1988. Matching Clients to Treatment: Treatment Models and Stages of Change. In *Assessment of Addictive Behaviors*, edited by D. D. Donovan and G. A. Marlatt. New York: Guilford Press.

Marlatt, G. A., and J. R. Gordon. 1980. Determinants of Relapse: Implications for the Maintenance of Behavior Change. In *Behavioral Medicine: Changing Health Lifestyles*, edited by P. A. Davidson and S. M. Davidson, pp. 410–452. New York: Brunner/Mazel.

Marlatt, G. A., and J. R. Gordon (eds.). 1985. *Relapse Prevention: Maintenance Strategies in the Treatment of Addictive Behaviors*. New York: Guilford Press.

McCusker, J., and B. F. Lewis. 1990. *Correlates and Outcomes of HIV Antibody Testing in Drug Abusers*. 118th Annual Meeting of American Public Health Association (September 30–October 4, New York).

McCusker, J., and J. Sorensen. Forthcoming. HIV and Therapeutic Communities. In NIDA Monograph on Research in Therapeutic Communities, edited by F. Tims.

McCusker, J., A. M. Stoddard, J. Zapka, C. Bigelow, M. Zorn, C. Morrison, and B. F. Lewis. 1991. *Behavioral Outcomes of AIDS Educational Interventions for Drug Users in Treatment*. VII International Conference on AIDS (June 16–21, Florence, Italy).

McCusker, J., A. M. Stoddard, J. A. Zapka, C. S. Morrison, M. Zorn, and B. F. Lewis. 1992. AIDS Education for Drug Abusers: Evaluation of Short-Term Effectiveness. *American Journal of Public Health*, 82(4), 533–540.

Prochaska, J. O., and C. C. DiClemente. 1983. Stages and Processes of Self-Change of Smoking: Towards a More Integrative Model of Behavior Change. *Journal of Consultant Clinical Psychology*, 51, 390–395.

Schuckit, M. A., and J. Duby. 1982. Alcohol-Related Flushing and the Risk for Alcoholism in Sons of Alcoholics. *Journal of Clinical Psychiatry*, 43(10), 415–418.

Sells, S. B., D. D. Simpson, G. Joe, R. Demaree, L. Savage, and M. A. Lloyd. 1976. A National Follow-up Study to Evaluate the Effectiveness of Drug Abuse Treatment: A Report of Cohort 1 of the DARP 5 Years Later. *American Journal of Drug and Alcohol Abuse*, 3(4), 545–556.

Sideroff, S. I., and M. E. Jarvik. 1980. Conditional Responses to a Videotape Showing Heroin-Related Stimuli. *International Journal of Addiction*, 15(4), 529–536.

Simpson, D. D. 1981. Treatment for Drug Abuse: Follow-up Outcomes and Length of Time Spent. *Archives of General Psychiatry*, 38(8), 875–880.

Simpson, D. D., L. J. Savage, M. R. Lloyd, and S. B. Sells. 1978. *Evaluation of Drug Abuse Treatments Based on First Year Follow-up*. NIDA Services Research Monograph Series DHEW Publication No. (ADM) 78–701. Washington, DC: U.S. Government Printing Office.

Sorensen, J. L. Forthcoming. Preventing HIV Transmission in Drug Treatment Programs: What Works? *Advances in Alcohol Substance Abuse Treatment*.

Waldorf, D. 1983. National Recovery from Opiate Addiction: Some Social-Psychological Processes of Untreated Recovery. *Journal of Drug Issues*, 13, 237–281.

Wesson, D. R., B. E. Havassy, and D. E. Smith. 1986. Theories of Relapse and Recovery and Their Implications for Drug Abuse Treatment. In *Relapse and Recovery in Drug Abuse*, edited by F. M. Tims and C. C. Leukefeld, pp. 5–19. NIDA Research Monograph No. 72, DHHS Publication No. (ADM) 86–1473. Washington, DC: U.S. Government Printing Office.

Wikler, A. 1973. Dynamics of Drug Dependence: Implications of a Conditioning Theory for Research and Treatment. In *Opiate Addictions: Origins and Treatment*, edited by S. Fisher and A. Freedman, pp. 7–21. Washington, DC: Winston and Sons.

Winick, C. 1962. Maturing Out of Narcotic Addiction. *Bulletin of Narcotics*, 14(1), 1–7.

5

CREST Outreach Center: A Work Release Iteration of the TC Model

Dorothy Lockwood and James A. Inciardi

Therapeutic communities, more commonly known as TCs by practitioners in the drug field, have existed for decades, and the premises on which they are based have been evident for centuries (De Leon, 1986: 6). Although therapeutic communities were first developed for the mentally ill, it was not until the 1960s that models for drug abusers began to appear. The first was Synanon in 1958, followed by Daytop Village in the early 1960s. In the decades hence, the therapeutic community movement spread, with the TC model continually developing and evolving.

Briefly described, the therapeutic community is a total treatment environment structured in a family-type setting. The primary clinical staff of the TC are typically former substance abusers—"recovering addicts"—who themselves were habilitated or rehabilitated in therapeutic communities. The treatment perspective of the TC is that drug abuse is a disorder of the whole person—that the problem is the *person* and not the drug, that addiction is a *symptom* and not the essence of the disorder. In the TC's view of recovery, the primary goal is to change the negative patterns of behavior, thinking, and feeling that predispose the person to use drugs. As such, the overall goal is a responsible, drug-free lifestyle (see De Leon, 1986; Yablonsky, 1989).

Recovery through the TC process depends on positive and negative pressures to change, and this is brought about through a self-help process in which relationships of mutual responsibility to every resident in the program are built. or, as the noted TC researcher George De Leon once described it: "The essential dynamic in the TC is mutual self-help. Thus, the day-to-day activities are conducted by the residents themselves. In their jobs, groups, meetings, recreation, personal, and social time, it is residents who continually transmit to each other the main messages and expectations of the community'' (De Leon, 1985: 825).

In addition to individual and group counseling, the TC process has a system of explicit rewards that reinforce the value of earned achievement. As such, privileges are *earned*. In addition, TCs have their own specific rules and regulations that guide the behavior of residents and the management of their facilities. Their purposes are to maintain the safety and health of the community and to train and teach residents through the use of discipline. TC rules and regulations are numerous, the most conspicuous of which are total prohibitions against violence, theft, and drug use. Violation of these cardinal rules typically results in immediate expulsion from a TC.

During the 1980s the focus of therapeutic community expansion and evolution in the United States became correctional systems and prison populations. Through Project Reform, a Bureau of Justice Assistance initiative, six states, including Delaware, were selected for planning grants. Through this initiative, Delaware established The KEY, a prison-based therapeutic community for inmates with histories of drug abuse (Inciardi et al., 1992; Hooper and Wald, 1990). The KEY has grown and developed into a complete inprison TC. It provides primary treatment for seventy men at any given time, with the length of stay ranging from nine to twenty-four months.

Unfortunately, the state of Delaware failed to make provisions for continued therapeutic community treatment beyond the prison walls for those graduating from The KEY and returning to the free community. In addition, neither Project Reform nor the state of Delaware provided comparable TC treatment for women. In fact, drug abuse treatment for women offenders is almost nonexistent in Delaware.

As the state and the administrators of The KEY began to contemplate these issues, the Delaware Department of Correction, like most state prison systems, continued to experience population increases, principally because of the growing numbers of drug offenders. Work release populations in the state were also expanding. (Work release is an alternative to total incarceration whereby inmates are permitted to work for pay in the free community but must spend their nonworking hours back at the institution or a correctional ''halfway house.'') As such, the need for additional drug treatment slots for offenders in both prison and the community became readily evident.

Considering these factors, the Center for Drug and Alcohol Studies at the University of Delaware proposed a therapeutic community for drug-abusing offenders to be implemented at the point of work release. Therapeutic communities have been found to be a successful treatment modality for drug offenders, with graduates remaining crime free and drug free longer than other prison releases, including TC dropouts (Rouse, 1991; Wexler, Falkin, and Lipton, 1990; Field, 1989; Holland, 1978). However, most therapeutic communities for offenders are in prison settings, leaving the question of the efficacy and feasibility of a work release TC unanswered.

This program established in Delaware, known as CREST Outreach Center, represents the nation's first work release therapeutic community. Through the research design, the project will assess several aspects of a work release TC treatment. It will identify factors associated with relapse and recidivism among both regular work release and TC work release clients. It will provide information on the clinical efficacy of a work release TC as both a primary and after-care treatment initiative. It will also examine relapse, recidivism, and program success among women offenders.

Perhaps most important, this project will provide insights into the TC treatment process. The therapeutic community is a dynamic and fluid environment. Although the daily routine is structured, the interactions among clients and staff are spontaneous. And it is from these interactions that change emanates. As such, the first step in understanding the TC treatment process is to understand the specifics of the TC model implemented at CREST.

THE CREST TREATMENT PHILOSOPHY

The treatment philosophy at CREST Outreach Center is similar to that of most other modern therapeutic communities. It is based on the notion that substance abuse and addiction are symptoms of a wider behavioral disorder and that, in order to discontinue drug use, all aspects of an addict's life must be reevaluated and changed where appropriate. As such, the treatment regimen at CREST focuses on changing negative behaviors, attitudes, and feelings, with the aim of making global changes in lifestyle.

CREST operates in an autonomous atmosphere, separated from Delaware's conventional state work release facility (Plummer Center). CREST and Plummer Center are located adjacent to one another, in the city of Wilmington. Separation is particularly important when establishing a therapeutic community for correctional clients. The general prison population tends to support and encourage negative lifestyles, including criminal activity and drug use (Inciardi et al., 1992; Field, 1989; Levinson, 1980). And although CREST is not a prison-based TC, separation and autonomy from Plummer Center are essential in order to create the sense of community and self-sufficiency characteristic of TCs (Sugarman, 1986). In addition, it removes residents from the dehabilitating influences of traditional correctional environments.

CREST incorporates the rational authority model introduced more than three decades ago by Charles Deidrick at Synanon. This model includes an authority figure and a chain of command that must be followed through an established hierarchy and set of rules. The history of therapeutic communities is marked by instances of leaders overstepping the bounds of authority and destroying programs (Bratter, Bratter, and Heimberg, 1986; Weppner, 1983). To avoid this, CREST is dependent not only on a strong authority figure, but also on staff and client accountability, self-reliance, openness, and honesty (Hooper and Wald, 1990). This model is based on the premise that no one at CREST is above reproach.

Staff, including the director, attend and participate in groups and can be confronted about their behaviors.

Clients at CREST are organized in a hierarchical system of status rankings, a mechanism to incorporate the role modeling and reward systems characteristic of TCs (De Leon, 1986). Each resident has a job function in this hierarchy, and work assignments have both practical and rehabilitative functions. They are the means by which the day-to-day operational tasks of the program are accomplished, and they are clinical tools for teaching responsibility and cooperation. At times clients may be transferred from one job to another to facilitate the experiential learning process integral to the TC modality, or they are put in positions of lower status to evaluate how well they can deal with change.

Treatment at CREST relies more heavily on direct action and participation as learning tools rather than on traditional, passive means of education. Therapy is an ongoing and evolving process, for such experiential learning is fundamental to the TC treatment process (Kerr, 1986). The climate for experiential learning is established in a therapeutic community by clear and concise rules, rewards for prosocial behavior, and confrontation of negative behaviors and attitudes.

All clients entering CREST become intimate with the "program manual," a document which asserts the rules of the house and the consequences of breaking those rules. The program rules and the clients' understanding of them are essential for successful operation of any therapeutic community. TC clients, particularly those in the criminal justice system, respond best to clear rules that are consistently enforced (Field, 1989; De Leon, 1986). CREST also operates on the reward/punishment scheme common to most therapeutic communities (Winick, 1990: Field, 1989; De Leon, 1986). Privileges for appropriate and positive behavior, particularly increased responsibility, are awarded. Privileges and rewards include additional community furloughs, better job assignments, higher status, and the potential for paid employment as a counselor trainee in the program after graduation.

Inappropriate behavior is confronted immediately. This confrontation is integral to the treatment process and often involves the entire community. Addressing asocial behavior in such a direct and intense manner is considered part of the habilitation process (Sugarman, 1986). Not only does this approach teach individuals appropriate work behavior and community responsibility, it also teaches all members how to interact with others in the community. It must be stressed, however, that confrontation at CREST is typically *not* the immoderate and brutal verbal assaults characteristic of TCs in years past. Moderation is more often the manner and method.

THE CREST TREATMENT PROCESS

CREST Outreach Center is structured in a five-phase system over a six-month period. The first phase is a two-week orientation process consisting of client assessment and evaluation. During this period, residents become familiar with program rules, procedures, and expectations. The second phase accentuates involvement in morning meetings, community jobs, and group and individual therapy. Confrontation and nurturing are the experiential learning interests of this phase. Role modeling and supervision of other clients are the focus of the third phase, a period lasting about five weeks. Phase four is a two-week transition stage during which a client begins to move from the therapeutic community environment to the outside free community. Clients prepare for transition by participating in job-seeking seminars, resumé preparation, mock interviews, and presentation-of-self exercises. Reentry begins with phase five, when clients obtain and maintain employment outside the TC. During the seven weeks of this final phase, clients continue to live at CREST. However, they begin to look for appropriate housing and initiate the recovery stage of their treatment.

For the majority of clients, CREST serves as their "primary" treatment. That is, CREST represents their first treatment experience since the onset of their incarceration. For the remainder, about a fourth of the client population, CREST is "secondary" treatment. For this latter group, CREST is a transitional program of graduates of The KEY, the inprison TC described earlier. Not surprisingly, these clients are expected to progress through CREST more rapidly, having already spent a year or more in a therapeutic community modality.

Daily activities mark the routine schedule at CREST. These include morning meetings, encounter groups, group therapy, individual counseling, seminars, and evening meetings (De Leon, 1986). Time to complete job functions is also arranged. Special seminars and other presentations are scheduled as necessary, as are special outings. As residents at CREST complete the more intensive stages of treatment—phases one through four—and begin working in the community, their TC activities are tailored to their work schedule.

As noted earlier, the entire treatment process is designed for a six-month length of stay. Length of stay in a therapeutic community has been found to be one of the major factors associated with program success. Some of the first TCs promoted lengthy stays, from eighteen to twenty-four months (De Leon, 1986; Holland, 1978), but nine- to twelve-month periods of treatment have become more common in recent years (Rouse, 1991; Wexler, Falkin, and Lipton, 1990; Field, 1989).

The program design at CREST balances the length of treatment with the period of time remaining on residents' sentences. It is essential that the treatment program and client sentence length are compatible for two reasons. First, because all CREST clients are under the custody of the Department of Correction, they must be released at the end of their sentence. Second, some studies suggest that staying too long in a therapeutic community can produce negative effects on a client. Residents that are not permitted to cycle out of the TC in conjunction with their progress through treatment begin to regress (Wexler et al., 1988).

Beyond CREST's six-month period of treatment, however, provisions have been made for continued after-care. This has become a primary concern of all therapeutic communities (De Leon, 1990–1991). As with the Alcoholics Anonymous model, TCs recognize that recovery is a lifetime commitment and a continuous process. Thus, the final phase at CREST involves establishing a recovery plan, such as participation in Alcoholics Anonymous (AA) and/or Narcotics Anonymous (NA) and individual outpatient counseling. CREST graduates are expected to donate one day a month to CREST by participating in TC activities and serving as role models for other residents. Weekend retreats for graduates and residents are another aspect of the recovery process.

CREST CLIENTS

Since all CREST clients are on work release status, they are under the custody of the Delaware Department of Correction. This situation results in a number of special considerations related to the contradictory priorities of correctional and treatment staff. Correctional staff are primarily concerned with custody and security. They tend to distrust inmates and are not supportive of a therapeutic community environment in which residents are active participants in administering the program (Inciardi et al., 1992; Jones, 1980). By contrast, a primary aim of the TC clinical staff is to enable clients to assume increased responsibility for their own actions as well as the operations of the program (Field, 1989; De Leon, 1986).

CREST operates completely separate from the adjacent Department of Correction work release program. Many therapeutic communities for offenders have correctional officers trained in the TC model, successfully satisfying both treatment and correctional needs (Inciardi et al., 1992; Jones, 1980). Due to state budget restraints, however, the Department of Correction was unable to provide such coverage at CREST. Therefore, security issues are dealt with primarily by CREST personnel. What has resulted, therefore, is a correctional facility being operated by university personnel.

Therapeutic communities depend on the flexibility of recruiting clients as well as discharging unsuitable ones (Sugarman, 1986). Like other treatment modalities, TCs are not appropriate for everyone. Motivation and readiness for treatment are particularly important for the intense regimen provided in a TC (Field, 1989; De Leon and Jainchill, 1986). In addition, coerced and compulsory treatment has been found successful for offenders (De Leon, 1988; Leukefeld and Tims, 1988). However, participation in CREST must be voluntary, as required not only by our research protocol, but also by federal protections of prisoners as research subjects. This requirement adds a caveat to the client selection process. Since prison sentences cannot be changed in order to participate in CREST or shortened as a result of participating in CREST, clients must be "work release eligible" under Department of Correction guidelines. Furthermore, since inmates serving mandatory sentences are ineligible for work release, they are not part of the potential client pool. As a result, potential CREST residents are identified by research staff from two pools of inmates: those approved for work release by the Department of Correction and those who must serve part of their sentence in a drug treatment program as ordered by the sentencing court. Thus, all CREST clients come *directly from prison*—both men and women from the state's five prisons. They have a diversity of criminal backgrounds, drug abuse histories, and problems at intake.

CREST STAFF

The structure, process, and success of any therapeutic community are dependent largely on staff composition and skill. Traditionally, TC staff has been comprised of recovering addicts, particularly those who have completed TC treatment. Recovering addicts provide appropriate role models and an understanding of TC dynamics (Wexler et al. 1988). For therapeutic community clients with criminal justice involvement, it is also beneficial to have exaddict, exoffender staff who have remained drug free and crime free for several years. Such personnel are essential for addressing the manipulative behaviors found in offender populations.

Recent research on therapeutic communities reflects increased involvement by nonoffender/nonrecovering "professional" staff. This includes clinicians with bachelor's and master's degrees with orientations toward traditional mental health models of treatment (Carroll and Sobel, 1986). The superiority of one model over the other—professional staff model versus recovering addict staff model—has been argued (Jones, 1980), with a combination of the two typically preferred. Within this context, the CREST staffing pattern consists of professionals, recovering addicts, and TC graduates. It is racially diverse and has a few more women than men counselors. The clinical director and three counselors are graduates of other TCs; two staff members pursue master's degrees; and two have experience in outpatient counseling. CREST also provides stipends for clients who have progressed through the program and are interested in careers in counseling. At any given time there are two or three clients being paid as part-time staff, acquiring hands-on training applicable for future employment outside CREST. This combination balances the diverse needs of the clients, especially in the transition from prison to the community.

POSTSCRIPT

Prisons continue to be warehouses for criminal offenders, and, with the pressures of overcrowding in recent years, it would appear that correctional institutions have become warehouses with revolving doors. Drug-abusing offenders enter prison with little or no employment experience, long histories of drug abuse, low educational attainment, and myriad other problems. Typically, they leave with the same profile, having gained no education, skills, or treatment. Frequently, offenders return to the community only to reinitiate drug use and criminal activity. With the increased efforts to apprehend and punish drug offenders, these problems have been exacerbated.

In order to interrupt this cycle, intense treatment must be provided. It should be long-term and comprehensive, addressing all aspects of an offender's lifestyle. For many drug abusers, treatment strives for habilitation rather than rehabilitation. Whereas *rehabilitation* emphasizes the return to a way of life previously known and perhaps forgotten or rejected, *habilitation* involves the client's initial socialization into a productive and responsible way of life (Inciardi and Scarpitti, 1992). Habilitation has always been the purpose of therapeutic communities for substance abuse.

CREST Outreach Center is a traditional therapeutic community model administered in a work release setting. It aims to reduce recidivism and relapse by offenders with histories of drug abuse. More important, CREST intends to change the negative patterns of behavior and thinking of its clients through a habilitative process, based on learning, growing, and healing in a family/communal setting through rewards, sanctions, and confrontation. Progress through treatment is marked by increased responsibility for one's own actions as well as increased responsibility and status in the TC. At CREST, residents learn to work cooperatively and to communicate productively, enabling them to function more positively in the free community.

ACKNOWLEDGMENT

This research was supported by grant no. DA06948 from the National Institute on Drug Abuse.

REFERENCES

Bratter, T. E., E. P. Bratter, and J. Heimberg. 1986. Uses and Abuses of Power and Authority Within the American Self-Help Residential Therapeutic Community: A Perversion or a Necessity? In *Therapeutic Communities for Addictions: Readings in Theory, Research and Practice*, edited by G. De Leon and J. T. Ziegenfuss, pp. 191–208. Springfield, IL: Charles C. Thomas.

Carroll, J.F.X., and B. S. Sobel. 1986. Integrating Mental Health Personnel and Practices into a Therapeutic Community. In *Therapeutic Communities for Addictions: Readings in Theory, Research and Practice*, edited by G. De Leon and J. T. Ziegenfuss, pp. 209–226. Springfield, IL: Charles C. Thomas.

De Leon, G. 1985. The Therapeutic Community: Status and Evolution. *International Journal of the Addictions*, 20(6, 7), 823–844.

De Leon, G. 1986. The Therapeutic Community for Substance Abuse: Perspective and Approach. In *Therapeutic Communities for Addictions: Readings in Theory, Research and Practice*, edited by G. De Leon and J. T. Ziegenfuss, pp. 5–18. Springfield, IL: Charles C. Thomas.

De Leon, G. 1988. Legal Pressures in Therapeutic Communities. *Journal of Drug Issues*, 18, 625–640.

De Leon, G. 1990–1991. Aftercare in Therapeutic Communities. *International Journal of the Addictions*, 25(9A, 10A), 1225–1237.

De Leon, G., and N. Jainchill. 1986. Circumstances, Motivation, Readiness and Suitability as Correlates of Treatment Tenure. *Journal of Psychoactive Drugs*, 18(3), 203–208.

Field, G. 1989. The Effects of Intensive Treatment on Reducing the Criminal Recidivism of Addicted Offenders. *Federal Probation* (December), 51–56.

Holland, S. 1978. Gateway Houses: Effectiveness of Treatment on Criminal Behavior. *International Journal of the Addictions*, 13(3), 369–381.

Hooper, R. M., and B. Wald. 1990. Drug Treatment Within a Correctional Facility. *American Jails* (September/October), 50–54.

Inciardi, J. A., S. S. Martin, D. Lockwood, R. M. Hooper, and B. M. Wald. 1992. Obstacles to the Implementation and Evaluation of Drug Treatment Programs in Correctional Settings: Reviewing the Delaware KEY Experience. In *Drug Abuse Treatment in Prisons and Jails*, edited by C. G. Leukefeld and F. M. Tims, pp. 176–191. NIDA Research Monograph No. 118, DHHS Publication No. (ADM) 92–1884. Rockville, MD: National Institute on Drug Abuse.

Inciardi, J. A., and F. R. Scarpitti. 1992. *Therapeutic Communities in Corrections: An Overview*. Paper presented at the Annual Meeting of the Academy of Criminal Justice Sciences (March 10–14, Pittsburgh).

Jones, M. 1980. Desirable Features of a Therapeutic Community in a Prison. In *Therapeutic Communities in Corrections*, edited by H. Toch, pp. 34–39. New York: Praeger.

Kerr, D. H. 1986. The Therapeutic Community: A Codified Concept for Training and Upgrading Staff Members Working in a Residential Setting. In *Therapeutic Communities for Addictions: Readings in Theory, Research and Practice*, edited by G. De Leon and J. T. Ziegenfuss, pp. 55–64. Springfield, IL: Charles C. Thomas.

Leukefeld, C. G., and F. M. Tims. 1988. *Compulsory Treatment of Drug Abuse: Research and Clinical Practice*. NIDA Research Monograph No. 86, DHHS Publication No. (ADM) 88–1578. Rockville, MD: National Institute on Drug Abuse.

Levinson, R. B. 1980. TC or Not TC? That Is the Question. In *Therapeutic Communities in Corrections*, edited by H. Toch, pp. 50–52. New York: Praeger.

Rouse, J. J. 1991. Evaluation Research on Prison-Based Drug Treatment Programs and Some Policy Implications. *International Journal of the Addictions*, 26(1), 29–44.

Sugarman, B. 1986. Structure, Variations, and Context: A Sociological View of the Therapeutic Community. In *Therapeutic Communities for Addictions: Readings in Theory, Research and Practice*, edited by G. De Leon and J. T. Ziegenfuss, pp. 65–82. Springfield, IL: Charles C. Thomas.

Weppner, R. S. 1983. *The Untherapeutic Community: Organizational Behavior in a Failed Addiction Treatment Program*. Lincoln: University of Nebraska Press.

Wexler, H. K., G. P. Falkin, and D. S. Lipton. 1990. Outcome Evaluation of a Prison Therapeutic Community for Substance Abuse Treatment. *Criminal Justice and Behavior*, 17(1), 71–92.

Wexler, H. K., G. P. Falkin, D. S. Lipton, A. B. Rosenblum, and L. P. Goodloe. 1988. *A Model Prison Rehabilitation Program: An Evaluation of the "Stay'n Out" Therapeutic Community*. New York: Narcotic and Drug Research, Inc.

Winick, C. 1990. Retention and Outcome at ACI, a Unique Therapeutic Community. *International Journal of the Addictions*, 25(1), 1–26.

Yablonsky, L. 1989. *The Therapeutic Community: A Successful Approach for Treating Substance Abusers*. New York: Gardner Press.

6

Dually Diagnosed Men in Different Community Treatment Programs: A Longitudinal Evaluation Study

Michael Rahav, Elena Guagenti-Tax, James Rivera, Richard Raskin, Benjamin Gross, Elizabeth L. Sturz, Elmer L. Struening, Bert Pepper, and Bruce G. Link

In recent years growing attention has been paid to the association between psychiatric disorders and substance abuse, often termed "dual diagnosis," "dual disorder," or "comorbidity." One recent investigation of the prevalence of dual disorders in the general population, the Epidemiological Catchment Area study, has shown that 30 percent of those who have ever had a psychiatric disorder have also had substance abuse problems. Also, 39 percent of those who have ever been alcohol abusers and 53 percent of those who have ever had drug abuse problems have had one or more psychiatric problems (Regier et al., 1990). The large degree of overlap between psychiatric disorder and substance abuse poses urgent questions to mental health and drug addiction therapists, researchers, and policy makers: Where and how should the dually diagnosed be treated? Should they be treated primarily as psychiatric patients or as drug and alcohol addicts? What treatment works best and for whom? What are the psychiatric diagnoses of the dually diagnosed independent of their substance abuse problems? How can their retention in and completion of treatment programs be secured? What characteristics of the dually diagnosed may suggest etiological clues to how comorbidity develops? How do the stigmas of mental illness and of drug and alcohol addiction affect the dually diagnosed? These questions have led to the research described in this chapter. Specifically, the aim of this chapter is to describe an evaluation research project that attempts to study dually diagnosed men in different community-based treatment modalities. After a brief introduction, five research goals and their corresponding methodology are explained. Since this research is in its initial stages, results are not available for presentation.

INTRODUCTION

In comparison with the deinstitutionalized mental patients of the 1960s and 1970s, the 1980s witnessed a new generation of patients, referred to as "un-institutionalized" (Pepper, Ryglewicz, and Kirshner 1982; Caton et al., 1989). Unlike their predecessors, this new generation has a high prevalence of alcohol and drug abuse (Minkoff, 1989), particularly among younger males (Drake and Wallach, 1989; Safer, 1987), and is at serious risk of being or becoming homeless.

Treating the dually diagnosed has been a challenge to all parties involved. The dually diagnosed have been shown to comply poorly with medication (Drake, Osher, and Wallach, 1989) and to respond poorly to traditional substance abuse treatment (McLellan, 1986). Nevertheless, the dually diagnosed are often excluded from treatment settings (Osher and Kofoed, 1989). Often they encounter disjointed treatment programs and are shuffled back and forth between psychiatric hospitals or clinics and drug and alcohol rehabilitation programs. In either treatment context, only one disorder is addressed as the primary problem, even though it is evident that both disorders should be treated concurrently and integrated into one treatment strategy (Lehman, Myers, and Corty, 1989; Ridgely, Osher, and Talbott, 1987; Kofoed et al., 1986; Hellerstein and Meehan, 1987). Treatment programs for mentally ill chemical abusers (MICA) have rarely been evaluated (Thacker and Tremaine, 1989). The treatment of MICAs has been described as being "in its infancy, characterized more by trial and error than by implementation of established treatment protocol" (Ridgely, Osher, and Talbott, 1987).

Outside psychiatric hospitals, treatment for the dually diagnosed is hardly ever available. Two main community-based treatment approaches, the therapeutic community (TC) and the community residence (CR), rarely admit MICA clients, as having both psychiatric and substance abuse problems disqualifies them from entering one program or the other. The two approaches are described and compared later as part of the discussion of research goal number 1.

Retention in treatment has been shown to be positively associated with successful outcome (Lewis and Ross, 1991), yet correlates of retention and dropout have rarely been investigated. One research goal of this study aims at identifying correlates of dropout.

Another important issue regarding the treatment of MICA clients pertains to their psychiatric diagnosis. It has been hypothesized that among MICA clients there are those with primary mental illness and substance abuse sequelae, those with primary substance abuse and psychiatric sequelae, and those who suffer from both disorders, which interact and exacerbate each other (Lehman, Myers, and Corty, 1989). Establishing a psychiatric diagnosis following prolonged abstinence from drugs and alcohol is one goal of this research.

One aspect of the treatment of MICA clients derives from the theory of stigma, stemming from work by Link and colleagues (Link, 1987; Link et al., 1989;

Link and Cullen, 1990; Link et al. 1991). Hypotheses derived from Link and colleagues' theory on stigma also constitute one of this study's research goals.

One of the most unknown questions about dual diagnosis is what exactly it is and how, why, and when it is likely to occur. Is it mental illness that increases the risk of becoming a substance abuser? Is it substance abuse that predisposes the abuser to higher risk of developing mental illness? Or is there a common etiological factor underlying both disorders? It may be just a statistical association confounded by variables such as help-seeking behavior (Berkson, 1946). Some of these etiological hypotheses are investigated in this chapter.

GOALS

This study attempts to cover five different areas of inquiry:

1. A comparison of the relative effectiveness of CR and TC treatment modalities on specific outcome criteria.
2. Identifying correlates and inferred causes of dropout.
3. Examining the psychiatric diagnoses of MICA patients following abstinence from drugs and alcohol.
4. Studying the effect of stigma on MICA patients.
5. Identifying etiological clues to the MICA syndrome.

These five research areas constitute, to a large extent, five different studies, discussed separately below. The sample and research design are discussed, however, only under research goal number 1.

RESEARCH GOAL NUMBER 1: EVALUATING THE OUTCOMES OF TWO COMMUNITY-BASED TREATMENT APPROACHES

The community residence (CR) and therapeutic community (TC) offer contrasting approaches to the treatment of MICA patients. The TC aims at a global change in lifestyle, including abstinence from illicit substances, elimination of antisocial activity, acquisition of work skills, and prosocial attitudes and values (De Leon, 1986), which may characterize the TC as a "high expectations environment." The daily schedule during the entire eighteen-month treatment regimen is rigidly and tightly structured, with movement through the TC stages and standards for graduation clearly defined. One key assumption of the TC model is that change in behavior will eventually bring about change in attitudes. The emphasis, therefore, is on compliance, conformity, and conscience. The TC model expects its members to adopt a clear, normative value system: "get up, go to work, live drug free, have a family, and so on." In exchange, the TC offers powerful bonding and the warm embrace of the staff and peers who become the client's extended family and community.

Historically, TCs were founded in the 1960s by recovering heroin addicts seeking to live in self-help/peer-support residences. Residents (or "family," as they called themselves) were self-funded and shared income and expenses. The program was holistic with housing and treatment combined in a highly structured and formalized manner designed to modify behavior. The atmosphere was one of "tough love," which, while constantly confronting antisocial behavior, also generated strong peer support for positive growth.

The CR, as opposed to the TC, may be referred to as a "low expectations environment," allowing a great deal of personal freedom and gentle counselling. CRs were started and privately funded in the 1960s by middle-class families who could not deal with their recently deinstitutionalized relatives at home. The CRs aimed at providing the least restrictive alternative to the psychiatric hospital, separating the housing and psychiatric functions from each other. CR staff provided licensed housing, assistance and training in the activities of daily living (ADL), the monitoring of medication compliance, and day program attendance. The CRs are prevented by law from providing certain services. Treatment services are provided outside the CRs, as arranged by the staff. Each client makes his or her own separate arrangements for psychiatric care and involvement in day programs, thus allowing different levels of compliance with the treatment program.

The CR represents a continuum of treatment approaches ranging from supervised congregate care with seven-day-a-week, twenty-four-hour-a-day staffing to supportive scattered site apartments with staff visits three to five times a week. As a client's ability to live independently improves, he or she moves to less supervised accommodations.

The question of which of the two approaches is more appropriate for MICA patients has never been investigated. A priori it is hard to predict which approach may be the right one in treating the dually diagnosed, who have been shown to be very heterogeneous in the nature and severity of their psychiatric and substance abuse disorders (Lehman, Myers, and Corty, 1989; Drake et al., 1991). From the comparison of CR and TC approaches, a hypothesis develops that one modality may be more appropriate for certain types of MICA clients, while the other modality may be preferable for others.

In this study, the CR and the TC are enhanced to allow them to treat people with both psychiatric and substance abuse problems. The TC is enhanced with psychiatric services, and the CR is enhanced with substance abuse rehabilitation services and vocational counselling.

The primary objective of comparing enhanced TC and CR is to identify the particular treatment program from which certain types of MICAs will benefit most. A client will benefit most by a program effective in preparing homeless, mentally ill substance abusers to live a constructive life in society. More specifically, the programs are assessed on their ability to move their clients along the following dimensions:

1. Reduction in psychiatric symptomatology and hospitalization.
2. Reduction in the use and abuse of drugs and alcohol.
3. Reduction in criminal activities and time spent in prisons.
4. Improvement of personal and social skills.
5. Improvement of vocational and educational development, work attitudes, and finding and holding a steady job.
6. Improvement in emotional maturity, ability to accept criticism, and self-control under stressful conditions.
7. Improvement in personal hygiene.
8. Establishing a stable housing situation.

Methods

The need to compare two long-term treatment approaches has determined the three main characteristics of this study design.

1. The study is longitudinal, to allow the measurement and evaluation of treatment outcomes along an extended duration of time (twenty-four months).
2. The study has a multiple time series experimental design where MICA clients are assigned randomly to either type of program, allowing the comparability of different interventions (i.e., treatment modalities).
3. The study is naturalistic, evaluating clients and treatment outcomes in the natural treatment environment.

The Treatment Environment

The enhanced TC in this study is Harbor House, a forty-five-bed, modified therapeutic community program that was developed by Argus Community, Inc., for the treatment of homeless, severely mentally ill, chemical-abusing men. Harbor House staff includes psychiatrists, psychologists, psychiatric social workers, and substance abuse counselors who together have developed an integrated model for the treatment of MICAs. In Harbor House, the rigorous TC structure is modified only enough to protect fragile residents. All treatment takes place under one roof, insuring that treatment is integrated and that residents do not manipulate it by pitting outside mental health professionals against TC professionals. Harbor House also offers its residents treatment through the New Identity Process (Casriel, 1972) and an extensive work program. Harbor House emphasizes similarity in background and culture between staff and residents. At least 30 percent of the direct care staff are recovering addicts. Harbor House emphasizes mutual self-help and a community theme. Residents are taught to bond with others, to trust others and themselves, and to live engaged with others in a community. Many activities are run by the residents themselves, and as they advance through the different treatment phases, responsibilities as well as privileges increase.

The enhanced CR is represented in this study by two organizations and a variety of programs they run in New York City. Services for the Underserved operates two of these programs: Montrose Community Residence and Patchen Avenue Community Residence. Montrose is a coed, forty-eight bed, supervised residence program in Brooklyn that provides group living arrangements with around-the-clock staff supervision. Patchen is a twenty-four-bed facility in Brooklyn for men who meet the homelessness criteria according to the New York City agreement (Dennis et al., 1991). The Bowery Residents Committee (BRC) operates the two other CR programs that participate in the study: Fulton House and the Metropolitan Apartment Program (MAP). Fulton House is a fully supervised residence program in the eastern section of Brooklyn. The MAP program is an intensive supportive community residence that operates apartments in various sites in Manhattan and provides daily staff supervision, counselling, and assistance in ADL.

The Sample

The sample of this study consists of homeless MICA clients who seek treatment in any of the community programs affiliated with the study. It is not a probability sample, nor is it a representative sample of the dually diagnosed population. Nevertheless, it probably mirrors accurately that population in New York City who seek community-based treatment for psychiatric and substance abuse disorders. The majority of cases in this sample are referred to treatment by psychiatric hospitals around New York City. The rest come from homeless shelters, psychiatric outpatient clinics, jails, and drug and alcohol treatment programs. By February 1992, this sample consisted of 230 MICA men. By the time this study is over, the sample size is expected to exceed 600 cases.

Beginning in February 1991, all inquiries about and requests for placement of MICA clients to the programs participating in the study were forwarded by these programs to the research department in Argus Community for prescreening and determination of suitability for placement in and random assignment to any of the participating programs. In addition to ''inheriting'' the MICA clientele and referral network from the participating programs, MICA clients were recruited to the study through ''direct marketing'' by correspondence and phone calls to hospitals, clinics, and homeless shelters in New York City. Table 6.1 below describes the 230 MICA men by their referral source.

Study Design

The goal of evaluating two different treatment programs requires that similar clients are assigned to the two programs. Such similarity allows the elimination of the rival hypothesis that differences found between programs are due to

Table 6.1
MICA Clients Referred to the Study, by Referral Source

Referral source	Frequency	Percentage
State Psychiatric Hospital	86	37.39
Psychiatric Ward in City General Hospitals	56	24.35
Psychiatric Ward in Private Hospitals	36	15.65
Homeless Shelters	21	9.13
Drug and Alcohol Clinics	8	3.48
Psychiatric Ward in VA Hospitals	6	2.61
MICA Programs	6	2.61
Court	6	2.61
Community Mental Health Centers	5	2.17
TOTAL	230	100%

different client populations, thus instead testing hypotheses about inherent differences in the programs themselves. The similarity of MICA clients in the different treatment programs is achieved by a two-step process (see Figure 6.1).

Step 1: Prescreening of all referrals by a Central Prescreening Unit (CPU) and selection of candidates who satisfy the criteria of suitability to enter any of the treatment programs involved in the study.

Step 2: Random assignment of those determined suitable into any of the programs involved in the study.

Suitability of referral to a treatment program is determined by integrating the minimal entry requirements of all the programs. By integrating these requirements, the study minimizes the possibility of a MICA client being found suitable for one treatment program but not for another. The determination of suitability attempts to balance two types of possible errors: excluding clients from treatment whom the programs themselves would have actually accepted (false negative error) and referring clients to treatment whom the programs themselves would not have taken (false positive error). Balancing these two types of error tends to lean toward the false positive error—that is, when there are doubts about a

Figure 6.1
Flow Chart Diagram of the Study Design

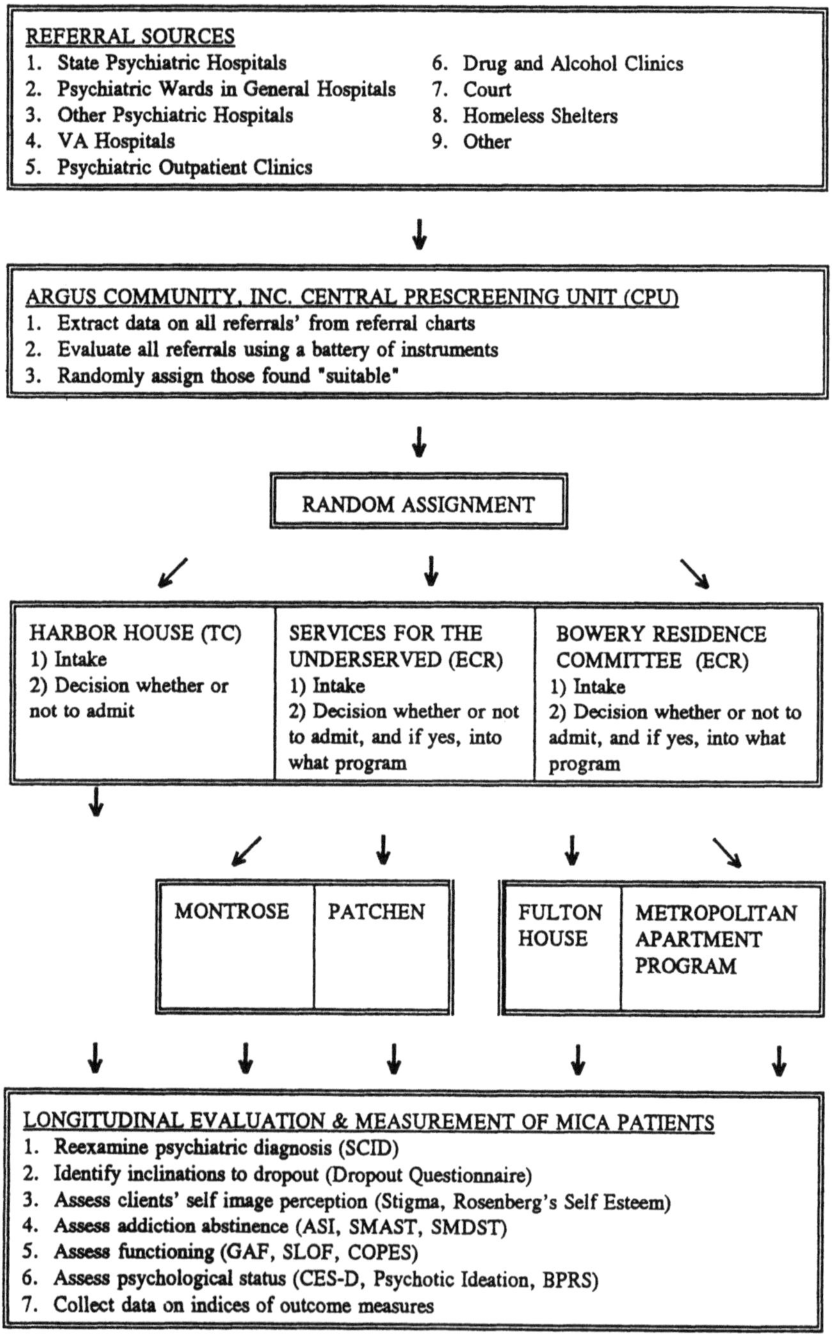

client's suitability, he is referred to treatment anyway so as to prevent depriving a suitable client from treatment by committing the false negative error. The programs themselves conduct thorough intakes for each of the study referrals and exercise the complete mandate as to whom to admit into treatment.

Criteria on suitability fall into three areas: demographic, diagnostic, and behavioral risk. Demographically, clients must be male, twenty-one years or older, and homeless or at risk for homelessness. Clients must have dual diagnoses of alcohol or drug dependence and a psychiatric disorder with at least two psychiatric hospitalizations. In addition, clients are assessed at the prescreening interview for severe psychopathology and impairment in cognition and judgment, grounds on which they may be excluded. Finally, recent history of assaultive behavior, arson, rape, or suicide attempts may deem a client unsuitable for referral to treatment.

RESEARCH GOAL NUMBER 2: CORRELATES OF DROPOUT

The second aim of this study is to identify client and program characteristics that may account for retention or dropout from programs. It has been shown that the longer the length of stay, the higher the posttreatment success rates (Simpson, 1979, 1981; Hubbard et al., 1989).

In searching for correlates of dropout, a number of hypotheses are being tested:

a. MICA clients' clinical characteristics, such as severity of psychiatric impairment, psychiatric diagnosis, severity of drug and alcohol addiction, type of drugs that have been abused, and so on, are associated with a client's tendency to drop out.
b. MICA clients' personal characteristics, such as family history, education, employment history, and so on, are associated with a client's tendency to drop out.
c. The various dimensions of the treatment environment—social, psychological, and physical—are associated with a client's tendency to drop out.
d. The outside environment, such as availability of housing, family support, friends, employment opportunities, and stressful events, are associated with a client's tendency to drop out.
e. The type of the treatment program, whether it is a TC or a CR, is associated with a client's tendency to drop out.

Method

Dropout is clearly measured by the actual act of clients "splitting" a program. Often, though, dropout occurs suddenly and impulsively. After the client has dropped out it is often difficult to locate him and obtain information about his reasons for leaving the program. It is for this reason that a questionnaire has been developed to elicit information from clients that might explain their tendencies to drop out and their motivation to stay. The questionnaire asks clients about their satisfaction with their treatment, the food, room, peers, and so forth. It tries to identify what clients are lacking, the pervasiveness of their thinking about splitting, and the reasons for staying in treatment. In addition, questions are asked about stressful life events that may have occurred while in treatment. The questionnaire is asked at repeated time intervals during the treatment course so that if and when certain clients drop out, information pertinent to their dropout has already been assembled.

In addition to eliciting information from clients, a questionnaire has been developed to obtain information about actual dropouts from the staff members who knew them best. This questionnaire identifies specific incidents, perceptions, and attitudes that might have contributed to dropout as well as examining various hypotheses about the exclient's standing and popularity among his peers, his motivation, his cooperation, and his desire to participate in the rehabilitative processes.

RESEARCH GOAL NUMBER 3: REEXAMINING THE PSYCHIATRIC DIAGNOSES OF MICA CLIENTS

When reaching the CPU, MICA clients already have significant histories of psychiatric treatment and psychiatric diagnoses. Although they may look similar, these MICA clients may actually represent different forms of the dual diagnosis syndrome. Some may suffer primarily from mental illness while their substance abuse is episodic, and others may have major substance abuse disorder with temporary psychiatric symptoms (Lehman, Myers, and Corty, 1989). Attempts to construct topologies for the dually diagnosed have floundered in part because the symptom picture changes during the acute, subacute, and maintenance phases of the treatment episode (Ries, 1991). This study provides a unique opportunity to evaluate MICA clients during a prolonged maintenance phase where they receive active substance abuse and psychiatric treatment and housing supports. The research goal is to compare the psychiatric diagnosis assigned to clients prior to their entering treatment with their diagnosis after prolonged stay in treatment.

Method

The data for research goal number 3 encompass the collection of diagnostic information from multiple sources. Used in conjunction with the Structured Clinical Interview for DSM-III-R (SCID), it allows for the determination of the current psychiatric diagnosis according to consistent criteria. The data are first collected after clients stay two months in treatment, when they have been abstinent from alcohol and illicit drugs for a minimum of two months. The second data set is collected after clients have lived in the residential setting for ten months. Alternative indicators of psychiatric and substance abuse problems are obtained through administration of the Addiction Severity Index (ASI), the Brief

Psychiatric Rating Scale (BPRS), the Center for Epidemiological Studies Depression Scale (CES-D), the Psychotic Ideation Scale, and other measures (see Figure 6.1). Occurrences of relapse are carefully monitored by residential treatment staff through observation and urine screenings.

RESEARCH GOAL NUMBER 4: THE EFFECTS OF STIGMA

Testing of hypotheses derived from Link and colleagues' theory of stigma (Link, 1987; Link et al., 1989; Link and Cullen, 1990; Link, Mirotznik, and Cullen, 1991) is the aim of research goal number 4. Their theory proposes that society determines people's perception of what it means to be a mental patient. These beliefs about how others treat patients become personally relevant to someone who is labeled a mental patient. The new patient may wonder, "Will others think less of me, reject me, because I am now a mental patient?" The label "mental patient" triggers a powerful expectation of rejection that disrupts social interaction and impairs performance. Thus, the more people so labeled expect themselves, as mental patients, to be devalued and discriminated against by others, the worse they do in terms of outcome variables such as self-esteem and work functioning. The theoretical reasoning of Link and his colleagues is extended in this study to MICA clients who have two potential sources of stigmatization: that of the mentally ill and that of the substance abusers. Research goal number 4 aims to investigate the extent and effect of these stigma on the clients' self-images, their interaction with their social surroundings, and their treatment and rehabilitation process. It also attempts to assess the effect of treatment on clients' perceived stigma and differences in perceived stigma between the different treatment modalities.

Method

Link and colleagues' measurement approach is augmented in this study to include questions about the stigma that a history of drug abuse imposes, questions on how MICA clients cope with stigma, and whether they have experienced rejection as a consequence of their mental illness or substance abuse history. The stigma questionnaire is asked repeatedly at different time intervals in order to detect change in clients' perceived stigma.

RESEARCH GOAL NUMBER 5: IDENTIFYING ETIOLOGICAL LEADS OF THE MICA SYNDROME

Research questions concerning etiological clues to the development and onset of the MICA syndrome were not part of the original study. They began to emerge as data on MICA clients seeking treatment started to accumulate. These data suggested the hypothesis that life history and family and psychosocial background may all play a role in the roots of the MICA syndrome. Many similarities in life histories and family background indicated that particular patterns of early childhood experiences and subsequent stages of educational and psychological development may be associated with the MICA syndrome.

Method

A great deal of the information needed for this investigation is serendipitous data obtained in the course of the referral process during which hospitals, other treatment facilities, and shelters send patients' charts, psychosocial and psychiatric evaluations, and other rich information hidden in the paperwork New York City requires. In order to identify and extract this information, a special form has been devised that allows systematic and reliable data extraction. In addition, a special personal history questionnaire has been developed by the research team for the testing of specific hypotheses about MICA clients' background and its possible etiological relation to the MICA syndrome. Thus, for example, elaborate questions are asked about existence and presence of parents; relationships with parents, including the love, affection, support, and encouragement shown to clients as children; the extent, if any, of abuse; and the care, guidance, and attention available to clients as children from parents and others.

CONCLUSION

In the first twelve months of this study (February 1991 to February 1992), 230 MICA clients passed through the doors of Argus Community Research Department and were screened, 90 percent of whom were randomly assigned to either enhanced TC or enhanced CR treatment. Data analysis has not yet begun. Nevertheless, the wealth and promise of this abundant data set are becoming more obvious and intriguing as every week sees another eight to ten new MICA clients referred to and prescreened by the research department. As these clients are to be recruited for two more years (and then followed up for another two years), it is estimated (by extrapolation) that the final sample size will be over 600 MICA clients. The size of this sample and the enormous volume and quality of data it will generate promise that research hypotheses set forth at the beginning of this study will be tested and the research goals will be achieved successfully.

ACKNOWLEDGMENT

This research was supported by grant number DA06968–02 from the National Institute on Drug Abuse.

REFERENCES

Berkson, J. 1946. Limitation of the Application of Four-Fold Tables to Hospital Data. *Biometric Bulletin*, 2, 47–53.

Casriel, D. 1972. *A Scream Away from Happiness*. New York: Grosset and Dunlap.
Caton, C.I.M., A. Gralnick, S. Bender, and R. Simon. 1989. Young Chronic Patients and Substance Abuse. *Hospital and Community Psychiatry*, 40(10), 1037–1040.
De Leon, G. 1986. The Therapeutic Community for Substance Abuse: Perspective and Approach. In *Therapeutic Communities for Addictions: Readings in Theory, Research and Practice*, edited by G. De Leon and J. T. Ziegenfuss, pp. 5–18. Springfield, IL: Charles C. Thomas.
Dennis, D. L., J. C. Buckner, F. R. Lipton, and I. S. Levine. 1991. A Decade of Research and Services for Homeless Mentally Ill Persons. *American Psychologist*, 46(11), 1129–1138.
Drake, R. E., F. C. Osher, and M. A. Wallach. 1989. Alcohol Use and Abuse in Schizophrenia: A Prospective Community Study. *Journal of Nervous and Mental Diseases*, 177, 408–414.
Drake, R. E., F. C. Osher, and M. A. Wallach. 1991. Homelessness and Dual Diagnosis. *American Psychologist*, 46(11), 1149–1158.
Drake, R. E., and M. A. Wallach. 1989. Dual Diagnosis Among the Chronically Mentally Ill. *Hospital and Community Psychiatry*, 40(10): 1041–1045.
Hellerstein, D. J., and B. Meehan. 1987. Outpatient Group Therapy for Schizophrenic Substance Abusers. *American Journal of Psychiatry*, 144, 1337–1339.
Hubbard, R. L., M. E. Marsden, J. V. Rachal, H. J. Harwood, E. R. Cavanaugh, and H. M. Ginzburg. 1989. *Drug Abuse Treatment: A National Study of Effectiveness*. Chapel Hill: University of North Carolina Press.
Kofoed, L. L., J. Kania, T. Walsh, and R. M. Atkinson. 1986. Outpatient Treatment of Patients with Substance Abuse and Coexisting Psychiatric Disorders. *American Journal of Psychiatry*, 143(7), 867–872.
Lehman, A., C. P., Myers, and E. Corty. 1989. Assessment and Classification of Patients with Psychiatric and Substance Abuse Syndromes. *Hospital and Community Psychiatry*, 40(10), 1019–1025.
Lewis, B. F., and R. Ross. 1991. *Retention in Therapeutic Communities: Challenges for the 90's*. Paper presented at the NIDA Technical Review of Research on Therapeutic Communities May 16–17, Bethesda, MD.
Link, B. G., 1987. Understanding Labeling Effects in the Area of Mental Disorder: An Assessment of the Effects of Expectations of Rejections. *American Sociological Review*, 52, 96–112.
Link, B. G., and F. T. Cullen. 1990. The Labeling Theory of Mental Disorder. A Review of the Evidence. In *Research in Community and Mental Health*, vol. 6, edited by James Greenley. Greenwich, CT: JAL Press.
Link, B. G., F. T. Cullen, E. L. Struening, P. Shrout, and B. P. Dohrenwend. 1989. A Modified Labeling Theory Approach to Mental Disorder: An Empirical Assessment. *American Sociological Review*, 54, 400–423.
Link, B. G., J. Mirotznik, and F. T. Cullen. 1991. The Effectiveness of Stigma Coping Orientations: Can Negative Consequences of Mental Illness Labeling Be Avoided? *Journal of Health and Social Behavior*, 32, 302–320.
McLellan, A. T., 1986. "Psychiatric Severity" as a Predictor of Outcome from Substance Abuse Treatment. In *Psychopathology and Addictive Disorders* edited by R. E. Meyer, pp. 95–135. New York: Guilford.
Minkoff, K. 1989. An Integrated Treatment Model for Dual Diagnosis of Psychosis and Addiction. *Hospital and Community Psychiatry*, 40(10), 1031–1036.

Osher, F. C., and L. L. Kofoed. 1989. Treatment of Patients with Psychiatric and Psychoactive Substance Abuse Disorders. *Hospital and Community Psychiatry*, 40(10), 1025–1030.

Pepper, B., H. Ryglewicz, and M. C. Kirshner. 1982. The Uninstitutionalized Generation: A New Breed of Psychiatric Patient. In *New Directions for Mental Health Services: The Young Adult Chronic Patient*, edited by B. Pepper and H. Ryglewicz, pp. 3–14. San Francisco: Jossey-Bass.

Regier, D. A., M. E. Farmer, D. S. Rae, B. Z. Locke, S. J. Kieth, L. L. Judd, and F. K. Goodwin. 1990. Comorbidity of Mental Disorders with Alcohol and Other Drug Abuse: Results from the Epidemiologic Catchment Area Study. *Journal of the American Medical Association*, 264(19), 2511–2518.

Ridgely, M. S., F. C. Osher, and J. A. Talbott. 1987. *Chronic Mentally Ill Young Adults with Substance Abuse Problems. Treatment and Training Issues*. Rockville, MD: Alcohol, Drug Abuse and Mental Health Administration.

Ries, R. K. 1991. *A Search for Typology in Dual Diagnosis*. Paper presented at the NIDA Conference on Drug Abuse Research and Practice (January 12–15, Washington, DC).

Safer, D. J., 1987. Substance Abuse by Young Adult Chronic Patients. *Hospital and Community Psychiatry*, 38, 511–514.

Simpson, D. D. 1979. The Relation of Time Spent in Drug Treatment to Posttreatment Outcome. *American Journal of Psychiatry*, 136(11), 1449–1453.

Simpson, D. D. 1981. Treatment for Drug Abuse: Follow-up Outcomes and Length of Time Spent. *Archives of General Psychiatry*, 38(8), 875–880.

III

CASE MANAGEMENT PROGRAMS

7

A Case Management Model for Intravenous Drug Users

Peter J. Bokos, Cheryl L. Mejta, Robert L. Monks, and Judith Mickenberg

In recent years, there has been a resurgence in the use of case management approaches in the human and social service fields. This resurgence seems to be a response to several factors. First, there has been a focus on improving service delivery and coordination for client populations with chronic and multiple problems. Second, there has been a focus on more effective utilization of the increasingly limited services available to these client populations. Case management approaches mostly have been utilized with chronically mentally ill patients. More recently, case management approaches have been used with chronically physically ill patients including persons with HIV (Human Immunodeficiency Virus). Although case management approaches have not been broadly adapted and applied to substance-abusing populations, this approach holds promise for improving the effectiveness of the current substance abuse treatment system.

Several characteristics of substance abuse, substance abusers, and the substance abuse treatment delivery system lend themselves to a case management approach. Substance abuse is considered to be a chronic illness characterized by repeated relapses. Substance abusers typically experience multiple problems associated with their substance use (e.g., medical, legal, social, financial, familial, and HIV-related problems). As a result of increased demand in conjunction with reduced federal and state funding, the substance abuse treatment delivery system has limited treatment slots available for substance abusers seeking treatment. Furthermore, the size of counselors' caseloads often prohibits coordination with other health and social service agencies in order to more comprehensively address clients' needs. Finally, substance abuse treatment programs generally lack resources to follow clients upon discharge from treatment in order to assess the client's ability to sustain changes he or she made during treatment and to intervene if problems surface. Case management, which emphasizes the integration and coordination of health and social systems to address the chronic, multiple, and individual needs of clients, may enhance the effectiveness of treatment for substance abusers.

This research study was designed to evaluate the effectiveness of a case management intervention compared to standard treatment in assisting intravenous drug users (IVDUs) in taking advantage of treatment opportunities in the Chicago area. Staff discussions at the time of the study design focused on four basic questions:

1. What exactly is case management?
2. Are there existing models of case management that could be utilized or adapted for utilization with IVDUs?
3. Are there special traits or characteristics of the IV drug user that would require unique definitions of the functions of the case manager?
4. How can interface between case management and drug treatment be effected?

WHAT IS CASE MANAGEMENT?

"Case management" is an ambiguous term that is applied to a number of activities and practices without specific definition. Usually case management is discussed in terms of functions rather than philosophical underpinnings or theoretical bases. Since the nineteenth century, these functions have been translated into a variety of models of case management that are highly similar. These models have many different constructs ranging from the case manager being a broker of services to the case manager, after client assessment, being a provider of services.

The contemporary concept of case management evolved in the 1960s according to Dybal (1980). He indicated that the proliferation of categorical social programs during this era resulted in a fragmented and inefficient service delivery system. Service integration was designated as a priority by then Secretary of the U.S. Department of Health, Education, and Welfare, Elliot Richardson. Thus, Dybal defined case management as a "system of locating, coordinating, and monitoring a defined group of services for a defined group of people" and as a "process whereby a fixed point of responsibility within a governmental agency, or its designee, is assigned to coordinate a comprehensive, community-oriented plan of services and informal supports for an individual or family" (p. 1).

Others have defined the case management function in slightly different words, but the definitions are variations on the same theme, as evidenced by O'Connor (1988): "David Austin and Penelope Caragonne (1988) define case management as a 'systematic problem solving process, consisting of a series of sequentially related tasks aimed at delivering a variety of services to a client' " (p. 97).

Sullivan (1981) suggested that "the dominant notion among theorists is that case management comprises five basic functions: assessment, planning, linking, monitoring, and advocacy" (p. 121). Johnson and Rubin (1983) summarized the ambiguity about case management when they wrote that confusion arises because of the imprecision with which these case management functions are translated into specific tasks and behaviors by the case manager.

EXISTING MODELS OF CASE MANAGEMENT

The seven most commonly referred to models of case management are traditional social work and mental health models (Weil et al., 1985: 407). Within the Generalist Service Broker Model, the case manager orchestrates the entire case management process and performs all case management functions. The case manager within the Primary Therapist Model serves as the client's primary therapist in addition to performing all case management functions. Case managers working within the Interdisciplinary Team Model form a team in which each case manager specializes in a case management function. The Comprehensive Service Center Model is similar to the notion of "one-stop shopping"; service centers provide clients with comprehensive services, which are coordinated by staff members. Within the Family as a Case Manager Model and the Volunteer as Case Manager Model, the family or volunteers respectively interface with professionals to obtain needed services for the client. Finally, the Supportive Care Model views communities as "case managers"—communities deliver some direct services to clients and link clients to other needed services.

Johnson and Rubin (1983) opined that these and other models that have been developed can be conceptualized on a continuum. At one end is the model in which the primary therapist functions as the case manager and is also responsible for treatment. At the other end is the case manager who has little contact with the client and is a broker of services, performing largely a clerical function.

The literature is replete with descriptions of case management models along this continuum. Examination of these models suggests that the five functions of case management as identified by Sullivan (1981) earlier are basic to most popular models of case management. Specific applications and implementation of the case management models and functions, however, seem to depend upon the case management program's underlying philosophy and goals and the characteristics of the relevant health and social service delivery systems.

INTERVENTIONS' CASE MANAGEMENT MODEL

Interventions is a substance abuse treatment, education, and research organization based in Chicago, Illinois, providing services in the states of Illinois, Indiana, Texas, and Wisconsin.

The case management model utilized by Interventions is an amalgamation of the several traditional social work and mental health models discussed earlier.

Figure 7.1
Case Management Problem-Solving Model

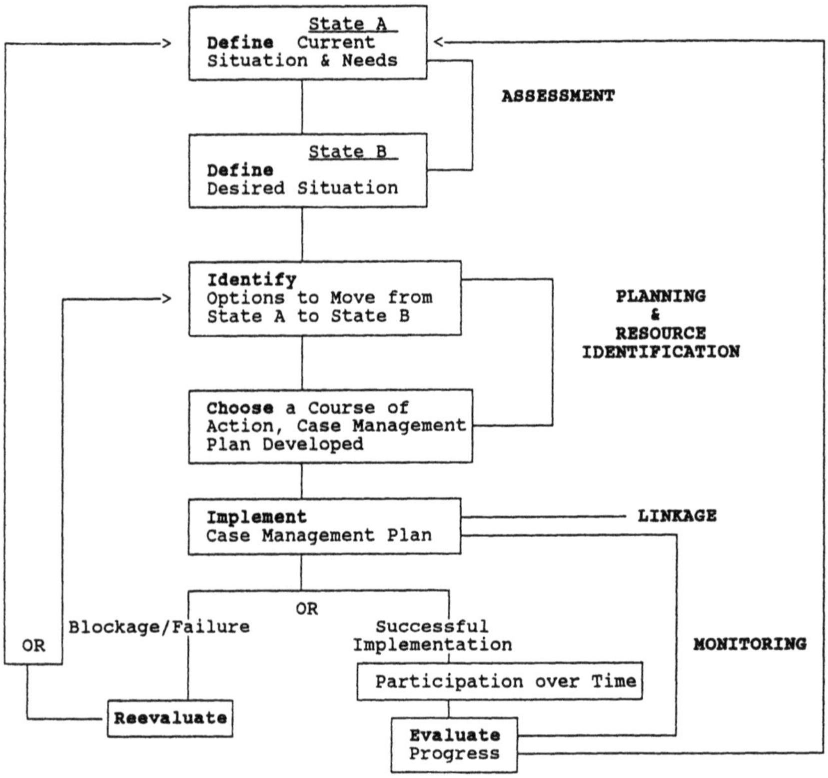

The Interventions model positions the case manager in the role of generalist. In this role, the case manager provides five basic functions: assessment, planning, linking, monitoring, and advocacy. More specifically, the case manager: (1) conducts a broad-based needs assessment with the client to identify presenting needs and problems; (2) develops an individualized case management plan that specifies the client's goals and a plan to attain those goals; (3) links the client with a variety of treatment providers and other services, which are selected to address the client's identified needs; (4) monitors the treatment process and progress; and (5) advocates on behalf of the client when needed.

Figure 7.1 depicts the case management process used by case managers throughout their involvement with clients. The case manager and client: (1) review the client's current situation and needs; (2) define the desired situation or goal; (3) identify options to move the client from his or her current situation to the desired situation; (4) select and implement from these options a course of action; (5) evaluate progress in attaining the desired situation or goal; and (6) review the client's situation for changes necessitating revised goals and additional case management activity.

Case management is a fluid process in which these functions are repeated as a client progresses through the stages of recovery, as new client goals are developed, as new needs or problems emerge, and/or as previously identified needs or problems remain unresolved.

The goal of case management with IVDUs is to effect resolution of the client's problems and changes in the client's psychological, social, physical, legal, and vocational status necessary for the client to become and remain abstinent from drugs. To accomplish this long-term goal, the case manager continually involves himself or herself in case management activities (assessment, planning, linking, monitoring, and advocacy). The specific nature of activities can best be understood by looking at three stages in the client's recovery process: treatment initiation and admission, treatment retention and completion, and posttreatment relapse avoidance and prevention.

Treatment Initiation and Admission

Usually, the first goal of the case manager is to get the client into an appropriate substance abuse treatment program. To accomplish this, the case manager must define the appropriate level of care needed, identify a substance abuse treatment program providing this level of care which has an available treatment slot, and identify and eliminate barriers to the client accessing treatment.

Assessment tools useful during this phase are the Addiction Severity Index (ASI) developed by McLellan and colleagues (1980) and the Substance Abuse Problem Checklist developed by Carroll (1984). Some barriers to treatment that the case manager might confront include unavailability of a treatment slot, lack of transportation, lack of child care, lack of financial resources to purchase care, missing prerequisite client documentation (e.g., ID, lab results, previous treatment records) to enter treatment, comorbidity (coexistence of alcoholism, medical problems, or psychiatric issues, which may preclude acceptance into a treatment program), poor reputation in the substance abuse treatment network, personal ambivalence about entering treatment, and treatment clinic hours inconsistent with client's availability. The case manager assists the client in eliminating barriers to treatment by: (1) providing temporary financial assistance to purchase treatment, transportation, or laboratory tests; (2) directing clients to treatment clinics compatible with the clients' needs and with available treatment slots; and (3) resolving other problems interfering with clients' admission into treatment. In addition to facilitating the treatment admission process, case managers in this phase often need to assist IVDUs in meeting their basic needs for food and housing.

Treatment Retention and Completion

After the client has been admitted into a substance abuse treatment program, the goal of case management is to facilitate treatment retention and completion. Once the client has been stabilized and he or she is attending substance abuse treatment regularly, other issues related to his or her recovery begin to emerge. Vocational or educational needs may surface. Relationship difficulties may occur. There may be pressure within the family system or peer group for a return to the previous drug-related level of functioning. Recreational issues may become important in that the client may not know how to spend his or her free time without using drugs. Basically, the case manager needs to assess what the client needs to live his or her life drug free. If a client leaves treatment or is terminated from treatment, the case manager needs to assess the source of the problem, help the client resolve the problem, and reengage the client in treatment.

Posttreatment Relapse

As previously noted, substance abusers are prone to repeated relapses. The primary goal of case management after the client completes treatment is to sustain changes the client made during treatment and to avert relapse. This is a particularly critical stage for case management since once the clients leave treatment, they often are on their own. To prevent relapse, an adequate after-care plan should be developed and implemented. With the client, the case manager should identify the client's high-risk relapse situations, assess the adequacy of the client's social support system, and identify residual problems or problems incompletely resolved. The after-care plan should include the identification of strategies to avoid high-risk situations and to avoid relapse if the client is in a high-risk situation. Identification of and linkage to appropriate support and self-help groups are particularly important in this stage. The first three to six months after treatment are a particularly critical relapse period. Maintaining contact with the client during this period to determine adherence to the after-care plan and to identify situations threatening the client's abstinence from drugs is an important case management function. Should the client relapse, the case manager can play an important role in interrupting the relapse, reengaging the client in an appropriate level of treatment, and/or establishing a new after-care plan based on an understanding of the client's relapse.

SPECIAL IV DRUG USER CHARACTERISTICS THAT AFFECT CASE MANAGEMENT FUNCTIONS

An effective case management model must consider the special traits, characteristics, and needs of the IVDU population. In large measure IVDUs have been abusing drugs for years and have become part of the drug culture. In this culture they perceive no way out, no other lifestyle. In Chicago, the IVDU population tends to be black, male, unemployed, single, impoverished, and has low self-esteem. Sometimes a person's low self-esteem is reinforced by relapsing after a number of treatment episodes. Failure breeds low self-esteem. Interventions' staff were convinced that their case management model would have to place a high degree of priority on relapse prevention, relapse identification, relapse interruption, and treatment reintegration planning. With this population, major service deficiencies related to basic needs (food, shelter, clothing, medical, and financial) are pervasive and require aggressive interventions.

In addition, the urban IVDUs are often discouraged from pursuing relationships with service systems outside of the drug treatment providers because they are frequently viewed as an undesirable if not undeserving potential client group. The case manager and case management system must at some stage negotiate and attempt to deal with these attitudes and concerns.

This population is oriented toward immediate gratification, which causes a problem when the case management services are utilized on a voluntary basis. Clients view themselves as consumers and must foresee an immediate benefit to justify continued participation. Their inherent frustrations must be offset by the anticipated gain.

This orientation toward immediate gratification and the case management process, which by nature is a long-term planning process, creates a dichotomy with which the case manager must deal. The case manager must understand that case management has been developed as a response to complex, multiproblem, chronic conditions. This understanding needs to be transmitted to the client so that the client can further understand that the case management process is a series of activities designed to stabilize the client, to support and maintain the client's abstinence, and to assist the client in developing an increased competency to function in relative autonomy within society. These activities and goals take time. The case manager must be prepared to explain these benefits to the clients and to assist them in coping with the frustrations associated with long-range goal planning and achievement.

A challenge for the case manager in working with this population is in developing and maintaining a viable working relationship with the clients and their natural value systems. Trust, openness, honesty, cooperation, and collaboration are concepts rarely practiced by the active and newly recovering drug addict. Furthermore, minorities and the historically poor usually hold suspect any representative of a formal organization, as well as the organizations themselves. These problems in providing direct service to the client and in matching the clients to other services pose problems for the case manager.

The typical adaptive behavior patterns of the drug addict cause stress in working effectively with the clients and others with whom they become involved. Another trait of IVDUs is their desire to maintain power and control over their situation. These clients protect this power and control by attempting to prevent key players involved in their treatment from communicating with one another. This behavior undermines the very core of case management, which is characterized as a unified, coordinated, cooperative system for sharing power and responsibility for negotiating and achieving desired goals.

The case manager must also engage these clients in HIV risk reduction behaviors if HIV transmission is to be prevented. The engagement is most difficult for reasons such as denial, apathy, grandiosity, self-destructiveness, lack of information, difficulty in obtaining materials needed to practice safer sex or safer drug use, and lack of cultural and social support. It takes a special case manager with special counseling skills to develop a relationship with these clients. The case manager does not act as a therapist but does participate in therapeutic activities that instigate client behavioral changes.

The IVDUs present, at one time, a multiplicity of problems, deficiencies, and disabilities. Their unconventional, sometimes unstable, and often rootless lifestyles require innovative, creative, and aggressive action by the case manager. Thus, this project, while based on a number of case management models and closely resembling the generalist model, is an adaptation that meets the unusual needs of an unusual group of people.

INTERFACE BETWEEN CASE MANAGEMENT AND DRUG TREATMENT

Case management should complement drug treatment. As pointed out in the preceding section, IVDUs are usually troubled with myriad needs. Most of these needs, outside of direct treatment services, are not being met by common treatment service modalities. If a person is to benefit from treatment, then treatment must be viewed as only one of the city's resources that must be tapped by or on behalf of the client. Obstacles that inhibit the person from benefiting from treatment must be removed. The case manager attempts to place himself or herself in the best position to be of help to the client in this respect.

The case manager, because he or she advocates for consumers of treatment services but is not a treatment provider, is in a position to stimulate the development of a delivery network for the desired services and to encourage the appropriate people to fill existing gaps in service. Often, services are fragmented, especially outpatient services, and do not provide the support, assistance, and opportunity patients need to succeed.

Dealing with gaps in the service delivery network is one of the most challenging aspects of the case management process. The development of new and creative linkages can be very rewarding for the client, the case manager, and the provider. The inability to adequately address the real human needs of clients who genuinely want assistance and who are actively working on their own behalf is one of the most significant and unfortunately common frustrations that all parties must address.

It is a well-established fact that patients willing to comply with the treatment program requirements consistently do better than those who are forced into treatment. The case manager at the assessment stage, utilizing motivational interviewing techniques (Miller, 1991), attempts to assist the client in developing a positive mindset that will allow him or her to participate in treatment with a positive attitude. The case manager helps to minimize the likelihood of participation by disengaged or unmotivated individuals.

The case manager can also be of great help to the treatment provider in several ways. One way is by assisting in after-care planning. After-care planning is essential if relapse is to be prevented or if it is going to be dealt with appropriately when it occurs. Since the major goal of treatment should be the reintegration of the client into the community as a productive, contributing member, the case manager can be of invaluable assistance to the primary counselor by locating and coordinating educational and job training opportunities for clients while in treatment. It is usually accepted that employment status correlates positively with less substance abuse. The case manager can help the client learn about how to access free leisure time and cultural activities.

It is also generally accepted that affiliation with drug-using subcultures can severely undermine any treatment benefit. The case manager by virtue of his or her monitoring function establishes regular contact with the client and helps the client establish new friendships and creates a new positive, wholesome lifestyle.

Finally, the case manager, unlike the counselors at the treatment facilities who usually have much larger caseloads, has time to create and maintain an extensive, varied list of community resources available to meet client needs. In a city the size of Chicago, the coordination of the various support systems and the awesome array of potential resources available is a gargantuan task—one that is undertaken by a case management system.

SUMMARY

The Interventions' Case Management Model, as a process, is an orderly, well-planned orchestration of individualized services needed to facilitate a patient's functioning as normally as possible. It is based on the principle that people who are successful in treatment and in after-care are those who know how to access community resources in developing and then using their own potential. It is our desire that the community be viewed as a reservoir of resources, not an enemy to be avoided, fought with, or destroyed.

The implementation and evaluation of this case management model currently are underway. Preliminary results suggest that case management, through its ability to identify available services, to purchase temporary services, and to reduce barriers, is highly effective in helping IVDUs access drug treatment.

ACKNOWLEDGMENT

This project was supported by Research Demonstration grant number DA06086 from the National Institute on Drug Abuse.

REFERENCES

Austin, D., and P. Caragonne. 1988. A Comparative Analysis of Twenty-Two Settings Using Case Management Components. *The Case Management Research Project.* Austin: School of Social Work, University of Texas.

Bargarozzi, D., and L. Pollane. 1984. Case Management in Mental Health. *Health and Social Work*, 9, 201–211.

Carroll, J. 1984. The Substance Abuse Problem Checklist: A New Clinical Aid for Drug and/or Alcohol Treatment Dependency. *Journal of Substance Abuse Treatment*, 1, 31–36.

Dybal, L. 1980. Human Services Development Series: Case Management in Selected Wisconsin Counties. *Wisconsin Department of Health and Social Services Report* (September), 1.

Johnson, P. J., and A. Rubin 1983. Case Management in Mental Health: A Social Work Domain? *Social Work*, 28 (January-February), 49–55.

McLellan, A. T., L. Luborsky, J. Cacciola, J. Griffith, P. McGahan, and C. O'Brien. 1988. *Guide to the Addiction Severity Index: Background, Administration, and Field Testing Results*. NIDA Treatment Research Report, DHHS No. (ADM) 88–1419. Rockville, MD: National Institute on Drug Abuse.

Miller, W. R., and S. Rollnick. 1991. *Motivational Interviewing: Preparing People to Change Addictive Behaviors*. New York: Guilford Press.

O'Connor, G. 1988. Case Management: System and Practice. *Journal of Contemporary Social Work* (February), 97–106.

Sullivan, J. P. 1981. Case Management. In *The Chronically Mentally Ill*, edited by J. A. Talbott, p. 121. New York: Human Sciences Press.

Weil, M., J. M. Karls, and Associates (eds.). 1985. *Case Management in Human Service Practice*. San Francisco: Jossey-Bass.

8

Assertive Community Treatment: Integrating Intensive Drug Treatment with Aggressive Case Management for Hard-to-Reach Populations

Steven S. Martin, Howard Isenberg, and James A. Inciardi

Community-based drug treatment can range from a few days of detoxification to a few months of drug-free outpatient counseling, to a year or more living in a therapeutic community, to a multi-year commitment to methadone maintenance (Anglin and Hser, 1990). In each of these modalities the focus is on providing medical, counseling, and psychological services to the client. Medical and psychological services are important, even primary, issues in treating drug abuse; however, case studies (Weppner, 1983; Wexler et al., 1988) have repeatedly highlighted the critical role of stressful life events (e.g., divorce, loss of job) in precipitating a relapse into drug use among recovering addicts. Integrating educational, vocational, and life skills management with more standard counseling treatment may more comprehensively address drug abuse symptomatology. Providing after-care resources to assist and buffer the client from life stressors may be a more effective means of preventing relapse.

Yet most treatment programs have no budget for educational or vocational development, and only a small minority report that their staff focuses on vocational counseling (Hubbard and Harwood, 1981). In fact, Anglin and Hser (1990: 404–405) report that relapse prevention training is not the norm in treatment, that educational and vocational services are rarely provided, and that provision of assistance in social and community support beyond referrals to self-help programs like Alcoholics Anonymous (AA) and Narcotics Anonymous (NA) is at very low levels.

Traditional outpatient drug-free treatment programs vary widely from dropin "rap" centers to highly structured programs providing mostly counseling or psychotherapy as the treatment mainstay (O'Brien, 1987). Simpson and Sells

(1982) report that, after outpatient treatment, opioid abusers decline in their daily drug use, arrest rates show a significant decline, and employment rates increase. While these results suggest some efficacy for traditional, counseling-focused outpatient treatment, other research suggests that treatment outcome is more likely to be successful when drug use is viewed as having a multitude of symptom patterns involving various dimensions of the individual's life (McLellan et al., 1981; Lipton, 1989). This perspective is remarkably akin to the rationale for the *biopsychosocial* approach, incorporated in the Assertive Community Treatment (ACT) model of rehabilitation used with the chronic mentally ill, and suggests the utility of its application for outpatient drug treatment with difficult populations who are not candidates for residential treatment.

An Assertive Community Treatment program has been instituted in Delaware under sponsorship of a grant from the National Institute on Drug Abuse (NIDA) to the University of Delaware. The program was developed by NorthEast Treatment Centers (NET) and the university and is run by NET.[1] The program design integrates an intensive outpatient biopsychosocial model of drug treatment with the community support system approach to assertive case management. This specific program is directed toward a particularly difficult subpopulation: parolees with an extensive drug abuse history. However, the general plan could be readily applied to other hard-to-reach groups, such as the dually diagnosed. In this chapter, we consider the theoretical bases and specific program aspects of the ACT model, using the Delaware program as an example.

ORIGINS OF ASSERTIVE COMMUNITY TREATMENT

The Assertive Community Treatment program is based on a continuity of care model for the community treatment of the chronic mentally ill that originated in Madison, Wisconsin, during the early 1970s (Test, Knoedler, and Allness, 1985). Often referred to as "assertive case management," the program's focus is proactive—to go out to help the client reenter the community by providing *in vivo* treatment in small client-to-staff ratios (Bond et al., 1991). Treatment goes beyond counseling to include material, interpersonal, and moral support in the areas of education, vocational training, use of leisure time, and self-care in dealing with the stresses and pressures of interpersonal living. The approach includes several components: (a) counselors actively keep track of their clients with numerous face-to-face contacts, rather than waiting for problems to arise; (b) staff are available to clients at all times; (c) staff treat clients normatively; (d) counselors have access to instrumental support for clients (e.g., job training, rent and food money, tools for work, transportation, child care); and (e) the more traditional forms of treatment, rehabilitation, and support group services are provided (Anthony and Margules, 1974; Cutler et al., 1984; Thompson, Griffith, and Leaf, 1990).

Although evaluations of the ACT approach with the mentally ill are limited, the results are generally positive. Studies demonstrate that, when compared with matched control patients who are discharged from inpatient psychiatric and other mental health settings *without* some form of case management program, those in the assertive treatment models tend to: (1) have better occupational functioning; (2) live in residential situations requiring some level of independence; (3) be less socially isolated; and (4) be rehospitalized less often and remain in the community longer before rehospitalization (Stein and Test, 1980; Test, 1981; Rapp and Chamberlain, 1985; Bond et al., 1988; Goering et al., 1988; Olfson, 1990).

APPLICATION OF ACT TO DRUG-INVOLVED TREATMENT CLIENTS

There are similarities between chronic mentally ill persons and drug users that would lead one to examine the potential for ACT in the drug abuse field. Both populations require treatment and a comprehensive network of continuing support in order to interrupt the relapse cycle and allow the client to remain stabilized in the community. The prevention of relapse has challenged the addiction treatment field despite several decades of research (Marlatt and Gordon, 1985; Vaillant, 1988), and, with the additional problems of criminal involvement, prison experience, injecting drug use, and HIV risk factors, the cycle of potential recidivism and relapse becomes even more complex, problematic, and costly to the individual and to society.

Mental health clients and substance abusers in treatment both may require a variety of rehabilitative services in order to "treat" the multiple areas of their lives affected by their disorders. It seems natural, therefore, to apply to both types of clients an approach that stresses multi-modal and holistic methods of assessment and treatment. While relapse prevention can also be addressed as a psychoeducational, skill development approach (Daley, 1986), other problem dimensions can also be treated effectively when properly integrated in a comprehensive rehabilitation program that provides reinforcement and support in the community (Brekke and Test, 1987).

There are also big differences between the ACT model in the mental health field and its application to drug treatment and to drug-involved parolees in particular. Most important is the expectation that the parolees' substance abuse and related problems can improve, and eventually they may cease to need the ACT assistance. As such, although it is not a short program, the ACT program for parolees has time limits and success goals, rather than the continuous availability of help envisioned for the mentally ill. Second, it is difficult to get treatment staff to leave their clinics and their passive role of waiting for clients to come to them and be assertive in going out to deliver treatment and support to clients in the community. This is a difficult barrier to overcome in the mental health field, and it is even more difficult in dealing with criminal justice clients as there is the perception of more physical risk and the underlying feeling that the clients are more responsible for their situation. Unfortunately, there is some evidence that substance abusers are less likely to receive the array of rehabilitative services available to the chronic mentally ill person (Solomon, 1986).

MODEL OF THE DELAWARE ACT INTERVENTION

In general outline, the provision of drug treatment and case management occurs in five stages, with transition into the fifth stage toward the end of six months:

1. intake evaluation and assessment;
2. intensive drug treatment, which includes group counseling, drug and AIDS education and discussion groups, individual counseling, and family assessment therapy;
3. moderate treatment, where education/vocation sessions come more to the forefront in group counseling and life skills planning, and treatment takes on a more supportive posture;
4. relapse prevention, where group sessions, education, vocational, and individual and family counseling all focus on support of relapse prevention; and
5. case management, where clients who have completed their active involvement in the treatment-oriented parts of ACT transfer into a case management phase, designed to support their transition into normal community life with instrumental support from case managers.

The program emphasizes the graduation process through these stages; however, this does not mean that the focus issues of each stage are exclusive. For example, vocational issues may be discussed in the intense treatment phase, and intensive drug counseling may occur when a case management client is brought back for treatment of a relapse incident.

After classification to parole status and selection for the program, each ACT client first receives an in-depth, comprehensive biopsychosocial intake evaluation. At intake, a trained intake coordinator conducts an admission interview, which includes questions on demographics, family background, residence and job history, drug use history and past treatment experience, psychiatric and physical evaluation, and an assessment of motivation for treatment. The coordinator also explains the program philosophy and rules and answers any questions. Clients sign a voluntary admission form.

Next, the client is assigned a primary counselor who develops a written, comprehensive, individualized treatment/service plan based on input from the client, results of intake evaluations,[2] and consultations with other members of the treatment team. The plan specifies identified problem areas, planned approaches for treatment, expected outcome, type and frequency of case management services needed, and criteria for goal completion. The treatment/service plan contains specific, measurable goals and objectives and a time frame for accomplishing them. The plan is reviewed every month thereafter by the treatment team in staff meetings to determine progress toward stated goals, overall progress, and newly identified problem areas.

The second stage is an intensive outpatient substance abuse treatment service. At the intensive treatment stage of the program, the group sessions, addiction and HIV prevention educational meetings, and other services are more frequent (most of the day for four to five days per week). The components of treatment during the intensive phase are designed to interrupt drug use behavior by providing individual, group, and family counseling aimed at breaking through denial and addressing issues that support the ongoing use of drugs. Drug education provides clients with information about the physical, emotional, behavioral, and spiritual effects of chemical use. AIDS education and support involving groups, discussion, and multi-media materials for clients and, if appropriate, their families lay the groundwork for further, individualized HIV prevention efforts. This component of the program is based, in part, on materials developed through a NIDA-funded outreach program in Miami (Chitwood et al., 1991), risk assessment and counseling protocols developed by the NIDA/National Institute of Alcohol Abuse and Alcoholism (NIAAA)-funded Center for AIDS and Substance Abuse Training (1989), and educational resources developed by NorthEast Treatment Center staff.

The ACT program is designed to be highly individualized because each person has a different addiction history and, therefore, experiences different needs. While the initial, intensive phase of treatment is the same for all participants, individual differences are taken into account during the third and later stages of the program. During stages three and four, the specific treatment components become less frequent, until finally a client is actively involved only once or twice a week until program completion. The program is designed as it is primarily to provide structure and intensive support for abstinence, which is crucial during the initial stages of recovery from substance abuse.

Stage three activities include individual, group, and family counseling; drug and AIDS education; and life skills development programs, all designed to provide clients with needed structure as well as meaningful activity. On-site AA/NA meetings help the newly recovering individuals adjust to the workings of the supportive fellowship in preparation for attending community-based twelve-step meetings.

The education and vocation programs are of particular importance. Remedial education in the areas of reading, math, and language arts is provided to appropriate clients based on evaluation results. The PACE Learning Systems (McKee, 1987), a self-paced program of special education, is used along with teacher assistance. GED preparation is available for those clients needing to complete their high-school-level education. Teacher assistance is available to facilitate the learning process.

Employability skills training, also utilizing the PACE Learning Systems, is effective in preparing clients for work. This program focuses on employability, job-retention skills, and valuable life or "survival" skills (e.g., how to live within a budget, buy a reliable used car). Employability skills training is used in conjunction with the Job Club (Azrin and Besalel, 1980). The Job Club involves a behavioral approach to assisting job seeking/job placement with consideration given to both immediate employment and long-term vocational needs. Group work in the Job Club includes a support group, career guidance, how to complete job applications and write resumés, finding employment sources, and practicing interviewing skills. Other vocational assistance comes from linking clients with existing community resources including rehabilitation agencies, the State Division of Vocational Rehabilitation, and other local, state, and federal vocational programs.

Clients may be involved in stages of the ACT program at various levels of frequency, based on client-specific needs. This may be particularly true during the relapse prevention stage. During this fourth stage of treatment, a client may continue to be involved in remedial education, vocational preparation, or actual employment. Relapse prevention skill training and support are based on a synthesis of available psychoeducational models (Zackon, McAuliffe, and Ch'ien, 1985; Daley, 1986). Skill development emphasizes the efficacy of lifestyle changes that produce increased self-esteem including, but not limited to, developing healthy, supportive friendships; coping with cravings and situations that are risks to relapse; effective use of leisure time; and stress management.

A major objective of the fourth stage is to routinize client participation in the supportive, self-help fellowship of Alcoholics Anonymous and Narcotics Anonymous. Moving from the on-site meetings, staff encourage clients to connect with a sponsor and regularly attend community-based meetings and twelve-step-sponsored social events. In addition, family consultation and crisis intervention services are geared toward maintaining the client in the community and preventing relapse. Involvement with collaterals also is an opportunity to further prevention efforts related to HIV issues, substance abuse, referral to Al-Anon, and other treatment or recommendations for maintaining the stability of the family unit.

Continued urinalysis monitoring seeks to confirm abstinence for documentation purposes and to determine substance use based on client behavioral indicators (suspicion of use). Urine tests and other indicators are used to identify clients experiencing difficulty meeting goals toward sustained abstinence. These clients are required to return to or increase their frequency of participation in the intensive treatment phase. The specific treatment strategy is based on the treatment team's decision and is documented in an update of the client's treatment plan.

The fifth and, as needed by the client, continuing stage of the ACT program is assertive case management. Case management provision is open-ended and emphasizes the relationship between client and counselor built in the earlier stages of treatment. Case management can include continued active participation in the supportive elements of the treatment program. The counselor, now case manager, is accessible to the client and prepared to provide individualized attention in the continuity of care (Bachrach, 1981). The overall goal for the integration of the assertive case management component with the clinical treatment program is to assist clients to become more active in their own treatment and eventually function as case managers for themselves. Giving clients a sense of instrumental empowerment permits them to transcend their typical role of dependency and prepares them to experience more participation in and responsibility for achieving their own stated goals.

Case managers act as advocates for the clients with other programs and other treatment and service providers within the local social service network. This includes linkage and networking toward maintaining an active resource pool that is used for obtaining needed services for clients. These services include: mental health treatment, medical and dental services, financial support, social services, and transportation.

Regularly scheduled case management contacts are initiated for each client to continually assess if the client: (1) has remained alcohol free and drug free; (2) has complied with vocational training and job placement plans; (3) is in a stable family and employment situation; and/or (4) is in need of further service or referral.

Effective case management during the followup period is expected to increase the likelihood of client involvement in recommended services, which is especially crucial in the first ninety days of recovery following release from treatment. In a study describing a population of recently discharged mentally ill patients, Tessler (1987: 40) reported that "evidence of gaps, interruptions, and other related signs of discontinuity during the first ninety days is important to the prediction of client outcome as indicated by measured variations in adjustment and complaints." Leukefeld and Tims (1988: 3) identified the first ninety days after drug treatment as posing the greatest risk of relapse, "when clients are exposed to drug-related stimuli, without the support of a structured program to help resolve their conflicts." Case management followup can provide the necessary structure and support to address these concerns, as well as prevent relapse through intensifying direct involvement with the client in the event of a crisis.

Discharge occurs in accordance with the client's progress, rather than being based on time spent in the program. Because treatment is individualized, time in treatment varies depending on the specific services required and the time necessary for the client to benefit from them within the existing structure of his or her life. The discharge and continuing care planning is the responsibility of the individual counselor, with input from the client and the treatment team.

SOME LOGISTICS OF THE DELAWARE ACT PROGRAM

The clinical staff of the Delaware ACT program includes a senior clinician, several licensed case managers/counselors, and an intake coordinator with addiction treatment experience and excellent diagnostic skills. The client-to-staff ratio is twelve to one. A case management utilization analysis by Harris and Bergman (1987) determined that the optimum staff-to-client ratio is about one to fifteen. Direct clinical staff are supported by administrative personnel, including a project director, a quality assurance director, and an administrative assistant. Staff take a team approach, and regularly scheduled team meetings are held during which staff can adjust client and program goals and objectives jointly, and each case manager can benefit from the input and support of other staff involvement with their clients.

The treatment team meets weekly to monitor client services, both inhouse and in the community, in order to ensure the stability and quality of the relationship between the client and treatment staff and with other service providers. During this team meeting the staff evaluates the progress of the clients in the planned services on an ongoing basis and adjusts services in response to each client's ability to benefit from them.

The full continuum of addiction treatment services of NorthEast Treatment Centers and the Recovery Center of Delaware includes a detoxification program, three inpatient programs with variable lengths of stay, and the outpatient after-care program of the NET Counseling Center, located in the same facility as the ACT program. All these resources, as well as other necessary services in the community, are available to ACT clients. The ACT effort also involves a well-developed working relationship with the Delaware Criminal Justice System for management of client progress through the treatment system (Treatment Alternatives to Street Crime [TASC] Program Brief, 1988).

CONCLUSION

The Delaware ACT project is expected to substantially reduce client drug use behavior and, thereby, the risk of rearrest, recidivism, and HIV infection among prison parolees. By borrowing from the mental health notion of aggressively providing services to clients in a community support framework and employing an integrated approach to substance abuse treatment, the model is an innovative approach being tested with a particularly difficult subpopulation. The community support system is "a network of caring and responsible people committed to assisting a vulnerable population to meet their needs and develop their potentials without being unnecessarily isolated or excluded from the community," as defined by the National Institute of Mental Health (1977: 1). Turner and Shifren (1979) suggest that this general concept could be adapted to other vulnerable populations. Certainly drug users (many of whom are injection drug users at risk of HIV infection) with past (and potentially current) involvement in criminal activity present a complex array of service needs when considered from a biopsychosocial perspective. Vulnerability to relapse, HIV infection, and return to illegal activity are all possible without a comprehensive approach to treatment.

A comprehensive, biopsychosocial approach to drug rehabilitation is expected to facilitate the necessary lifestyle changes supportive of a successful recovery program. Emphasis on treating the whole person—including socialization and relapse prevention skills as well as educational and employability skills training—can reduce the risk of relapse by developing adaptive behavior in areas deteriorated by previous drug use. In addition, the biopsychosocial model lends itself well to the creation of structure in the lives of a recovering person, an issue determined to be important by Vaillant (1988) in preventing relapse.

Besides the treatment components mentioned above, an assertive case management program that incorporates the features of the TASC model is expected to provide for the continuity of care and retention in services that are necessary to increase treatment completion rates for criminal justice clients. Collins and Allison (1983) found that the legal coercion or pressure necessary to ensure that a client enter and remain in treatment is most apparent in connection with TASC programs. Case management also serves the function of facilitating relationship building and trust, which is crucial to the task of assisting the client to develop the skills necessary to eventually assume his or her own case management duties and foster client empowerment (Rapp and Chamberlain, 1985).

ACKNOWLEDGMENT

This work was supported, in part, by grants number DA06124 and number DA06948 from the National Institute on Drug Abuse.

NOTES

1. NorthEast Treatment Centers is a nonprofit social service organization headquartered in Philadelphia, which operates over twenty-five programs in the Delaware Valley. NET provides a continuum of care for both substance abusers and troubled adolescents, including short- and long-term residential treatment, outpatient and intensive inpatient treatment, case management services, group homes, foster care, and inhome detention. NET also offers a variety of specialized programming for women, adult and juvenile criminal justice clients, and other high-risk populations.

2. Specific assessment tools are used at intake. For example, Biopsychosocial Assessment, developed by NorthEast Treatment Centers, asks about cultural and religious background, early childhood history, educational history, employment history, sexuality issues, family relationship dynamics, drug use and drinking history, and legal and emotional history; a baseline urine drug screen; and such standardized instruments as the Wide Range Achievement Test (WRAT), the Shipley-Hartford Institute of Living Intelligence Test (verbal intelligence), the Symptom Checklist (SCL–90) (to alert the clinician about immediate concerns of the client), the Minnesota Multiphasic Personality Inventory (MMPI–2), the Neurological Impairment Screen (NIS) developed by O'Donnell and Reynolds (1983) for neurological symptoms that may need medical attention, and the Beck Depression Inventory (depression and suicidal impulses). In addition to treatment assessment support, needs assessment includes the Progress Evaluation Scales (PES), a modification of a mental health level of functioning form developed by Ihilevich and Gleser (1988), and the Self-Directed Search (SDS), an occupational interest profile helpful in formulating educational and training plans.

REFERENCES

Anglin, M. D., and Y. Hser. 1990. Treatment of Drug Abuse. In *Drugs and Crime*, edited by M. Tonry and J. Q. Wilson, pp. 393–460. Chicago: University of Chicago Press.

Anthony, W., and A. Margules. 1974. Toward Improving the Efficacy of Psychiatric Rehabilitation: A Skills Training Approach. *Rehabilitation Psychology*, 21, 101–105.

Azrin, N. H., and V. A. Besalel. 1980. *Job Club Counselor's Manual: A Behavioral Approach to Vocational Counseling*. Austin, TX: Pro-Ed.

Bachrach, L. L. 1981. Continuity of Care for Chronic Mental Patients: A Conceptual Analysis. *American Journal of Psychiatry*, 138, 1449–1456.

Beck, A. T., A. Weissman, D. Lester, and L. Trexler. 1974. The Measurement of Pessimism: The Hopelessness Scale. *Journal of Consulting and Clinical Psychology*, 42, 861–865.

Bond, G. R., L. D. Miller, R. D. Krumwied, and R. S. Ward. 1988. Assertive Case Management in Three CMHCs: A Controlled Study. *Hospital and Community Psychiatry*, 39, 411–418.

Bond, G. R., T. F. Witheridge, J. Dincin, and D. Wasmer. 1991. Assertive Community Treatment: Correcting Some Misconceptions. *American Journal of Community Psychology*, 19, 41–51.

Brekke, J. S., and M. A. Test. 1987. An Empirical Analysis of Services Delivered in a Model Community Support Program. *Psychosocial Rehabilitation Journal*, 10(4), 51–61.

Center for AIDS and Substance Abuse Training. 1989. *Preventing HIV Disease among Substance Abusers: A Training Program*. Falls Church, VA: National Capital Systems, Inc.

Chitwood, D. D., J. A. Inciardi, D. C. McBride, C. B. McCoy, H. V. McCoy, and E. Trapido. 1991. *A Community Approach to AIDS Intervention*. Westport, CT: Greenwood Press.

Collins, J. J., and M. Allison. 1983. Legal Coercion and Retention in Drug Abuse Treatment. *Hospital and Community Psychiatry*, 34, 1145–1149.

Cutler, D. L., W. Terwillinger, L. Faulkner, G. Field, and D. Bray. 1984. Disseminating the Principles of a Community Support Program. *Hospital and Community Psychiatry*, 35, 51–55.

Daley, D. 1986. *Relapse Prevention Workbook*. New York: Learning Publications.

Goering, P. N., M. Farkas, D. A. Wasylenkl, W. J. Lancee, and P. Ballantyne. 1988. Improved Functioning for Case Management Clients. *Psychosocial Rehabilitation Journal*, 12(1), 3–17.

Harris, M., and H. C. Bergman. 1987. Case Management with the Chronically Mentally Ill. *American Journal of Orthopsychiatry*, 57, 296–302.

Hubbard, R. L., and H. J. Harwood. 1981. *Employment Related Series in Drug Treatment Programs*. Treatment Research Report. Rockville, MD: National Institute on Drug Abuse.

Ihilevich, D., and G. C. Gleser. 1988. *Evaluating Mental Health Programs: The Process Evaluation Series*. Lexington, MA: Lexington Books.

Leukefeld, C. G., and F. M. Tims. 1988. An Introduction to Compulsory Treatment for

Drug Abuse: Clinical Practice and Research. In *Compulsory Treatment of Drug Abuse: Research and Clinical Practice*, edited by C. G. Leukefeld and F. M. Tims, pp. 1–7. NIDA Research Monograph No. 86, DHHS Publication No. (ADM) 88–1578. Rockville, MD: National Institute on Drug Abuse.

Lipton, D. S. 1989. *The Theory of Rehabilitation as Applied to Addict Offenders*. Paper presented at the What Works Conference (October, New York City).

Marlatt, G. A., and J. R. Gordon (eds.). 1985. *Relapse Prevention: Maintenance Strategies in the Treatment of Addictive Behaviors*. New York: Guilford Press.

McKee, J. M. 1987. *A Training Program for Employability Skills*. Tuscaloosa, AL: PACE Learning Systems, Inc.

McLellan, A. T., L. Luborsky, G. E. Woody, C. P. O'Brien, and R. Kron. 1981. Are the "Addict-Related" Problems of Substance Abusers Really Related? *Journal of Nervous and Mental Disease*, 169, 232–239.

National Institute of Mental Health, Community Support Section. 1977. *Request for Proposals No. NIMH-MH–77–0080–0081*. Rockville, MD: National Institute of Mental Health.

O'Brien, C. P. 1987. Treatment Research. Drug Abuse and Drug Abuse Research. In *The Second Triennial Report to Congress from the Secretary, Department of Health and Human Services*. Rockville, MD: National Institute on Drug Abuse.

O'Donnell, W. E., and D. M. Reynolds. 1983. *Neurological Impairment Scale Manual*. Annapolis, MD: Annapolis Neuropsychological Services.

Olfson, M. 1990. Assertive Community Treatment: An Evaluation of the Experimental Evidence. *Hospital and Community Psychiatry*, 41, 634–641.

Rapp, C. A., and R. Chamberlain. 1985. Case Management Services for the Chronically Mentally Ill. *Social Work*, 30, 417–422.

Simpson, D. D., and S. B. Sells. 1982. Effectiveness of Treatment for Drug Abuse: An Overview of the DARP [Drug Abuse Reporting Program] Research Program. *Advances in Alcohol and Substance Abuse Treatment*, 2(1),729–742.

Solomon, P. 1986. Receipt of Aftercare Services by Problem Types: Psychiatric, Psychiatric/Substance Abuse and Substance Abuse. *Psychiatric Quarterly*, 58(3), 180–188.

Stein, L. I., and M. A. Test. 1980. Alternative to Mental Hospital Treatment. *Archives of General Psychiatry*, 37, 392–412.

TASC Program Brief. 1988. TASC Programs: Treatment Alternatives to Street Crime. *Bureau of Justice Assistance Program Brief*. Washington, DC: Bureau of Justice Assistance.

Tessler, F. C. 1987. Continuity of Care and Client Outcome. *Psychosocial Rehabilitation Journal*, 11(1), 39–53.

Test, M. A., 1981. Effective Community Treatment of the Chronically Mentally Ill: What Is Necessary? *Journal of Social Issues*, 37, 71–86.

Test, M. A., W. H. Knoedler, and D. J. Allness. 1985. The Long-Term Treatment of Young Schizophrenics in a Community Support Program. In *Training in Community Living—Ten Years Later*, edited by L. I. Stein and M. A. Test, pp. 17–27. San Francisco: Jossey-Bass.

Thompson, K. S., E. E. Griffith, and P. J. Leaf. 1990. A Historical Review of the Madison Model of Community Care. *Hospital and Community Psychiatry*, 41, 625–634.

Turner, J. E. C., and I. Shifren. 1979. Community Support Systems: How Comprehensive? *New Directions for Mental Health Services*, 2, 1–13.

Vaillant, G. E. 1988. What Can Long-Term Follow-up Teach Us about Relapse and Prevention of Relapse in Addiction? *British Journal of Addiction*, 83, 1147–1157.

Weppner, R. S. 1983. *The Untherapeutic Community: Organizational Behavior in a Failed Addiction Treatment Program*. Lincoln: University of Nebraska Press.

Wexler, H. K., G. P. Falkin, D. S. Lipton, A. B. Rosenblum, and L. P. Goodloe. 1988. *A Model Prison Rehabilitation Program: An Evaluation of the "Stay'n Out" Therapeutic Community*. New York: Narcotic and Drug Research, Inc.

Zackon, F., W. E. McAuliffe, and J.M.N. Ch'ien. 1985. *Addict Aftercare: Recovery Training and Self-Help*. Rockville, MD: National Institute on Drug Abuse.

9

Treatment Dropouts and Noncompliers: Two Persistent Problems and a Programmatic Remedy

Harvey A. Siegal, Richard C. Rapp, James Fisher, Phyllis Cole, and Joseph H. Wagner

While substance abuse treatment programs are currently treating record numbers of patients, noncompletion rates and the general problem of noncompliance with prescribed treatment regimens continue to negatively affect treatment efforts. The current generation of substance abusers is younger, more frequently involved with more than one drug, and often addicted to cocaine or its derivative "crack." Concurrently, these substance abusers present with more diverse and seemingly intractable problems than earlier drug-using populations. As a result this population seems to be harder to engage in treatment.

The Substance Abuse Intervention Programs (SAIP) at Wright State University School of Medicine and the Polysubstance Rehabilitation Program (PRP) at the Department of Veterans Affairs Medical Center (DVAMC), Dayton, Ohio, are involved jointly in a National Institute on Drug Abuse (NIDA)-funded demonstration research project. The Enhanced Treatment through Induction and Case Management Project has as its complementary goals improvement of treatment retention, compliance, and outcome by implementing (1) pretreatment induction procedures in the form of an innovative weekend intervention program and (2) intensive case management/advocacy strategies utilizing a strengths-based model. Initiated in 1990, the Enhanced Treatment Project examines the impact that the two interrelated treatment enhancements have on treatment retention and therapeutic compliance as well as both short- and long-term treatment outcomes.

BACKGROUND: DROPPING OUT OF AND NONCOMPLIANCE WITH DRUG TREATMENT

The problem of patients not completing a therapeutic regimen has been and continues to be vexing. This is particularly the case in virtually all of the social service or mental health disciplines, including substance abuse treatment. Baekeland and Lundwall (1975) published a comprehensive review of the literature that reported on prevalence of treatment dropouts in a variety of mental health programs. They found that in general psychiatric clinics 20 percent to 57 percent of patients fail to return after their first visit, and 31 percent to 56 percent attend four sessions or less. In group psychotherapy, 33 percent to 50 percent of patients drop out of treatment. From 32 percent to 79 percent of the psychiatric inpatients on ''open wards'' have been reported to sign out against medical advice (AMA) in the first few months of treatment.

The picture is not dissimilar in substance abuse treatment modalities. In outpatient alcoholism treatment programs, 52 percent to 75 percent of the clients drop out by the fourth session. Even in methadone maintenance treatment programs, where one might assume that client attrition would be diminished because of methadone's addicting nature, dropout rates vary significantly with 7 percent to 64 percent of the clients dropping out of treatment within six months. Clinics providing a higher dose of medication seem to have lower attrition rates than lower dose programs; this perhaps explains the large amount of variability in dropout rates in this modality. A range of 26 percent to 68.6 percent of patients fail to complete outpatient detoxification programs. Noncompletion rates for inpatient detoxification programs range from 23 percent to 39 percent. Finally, in drug-free therapeutic communities, where clients are expected to remain for a year or longer, 82 percent complete less than four months of residence (Baekeland and Lundwall, 1975).

More recent reports have remained consonant with Baekeland and Lundwall. In a DVAMC drug abuse detox/rehab unit with a two-week length of stay, the AMA rate was routinely about 50 percent per month and often went as high as 70 percent (Craig, 1985). In a study of 585 male veterans addicted to heroin, subjects were randomly assigned to either therapeutic community (TC) or methadone maintenance modalities. The TCs were able to retain 39 percent of those assigned; the methadone program retained 31 percent of those originally assigned to it (Bale et al., 1980). Joe and Simpson (1975), reviewing Drug Abuse Reporting Program (DARP) data, suggested that the percentage of clients still in treatment a year after admission was highest for methadone maintenance (46 percent). They also reported that the largest treatment disposition category in all other treatments was termination by ''quitting.'' Quitting accounts for 60 percent of TC patients leaving treatment, 64 percent of patients in drug-free treatment, and 67 percent in detoxification settings. In most of the modalities, it was found that, of those patients who dropped out, a large number left within a month after admission and over half were gone within three months (Joe and Simpson, 1975).

These high levels of early attrition are poor prognostic signs in light of the general finding linking time in treatment with a positive outcome (Stark and Campbell, 1988). In general, most studies report a positive correlation between outcome and treatment retention for alcoholics in all treatment conditions (Baekeland and Lundwall, 1975). The literature on drug abuse treatment is equally clear in associating a positive outcome with retention in treatment (Bale et al., 1980; McLellan et al., 1983; Simpson, 1979; Collins and Allison, 1983; Washton, 1986; Simpson, Savage, and Lloyd, 1979).

In addition to the difficulty substance abuse treatment programs have with nonretention of patients, these programs have also experienced limited success in assisting patients to comply with the overall process of treatment. If recidivism and improvement rates are at least an indirect measure of compliance, results have been less than satisfactory. One study documents an incidence of recidivism averaging around 50 percent or greater and overall poor improvement rates (McLellan et al., 1980). Somewhat more optimistically, it can be said that most studies of treatment outcome suggest that chemically dependent people receiving substance abuse treatment do better than those who do not receive treatment (Edwards et al., 1977; McLellan et al., 1982; Armor, Polich, and Stambul, 1978; Bale et al., 1980; Inciardi, 1975; Hubbard et al., 1984).

The problem of the apparent poor retention and compliance performance of drug treatment programs probably lies in both the nature of the programs and the nature of drug problems themselves. The addiction process is a complex one involving the interaction of multiple medical, social, psychological, legal, and family problems. This interaction may lead to continued substance abuse and thereby create particular treatment needs. Based on various therapeutic philosophies, treatment programs have tended to adequately address some client needs while ignoring others. It is not surprising, therefore, that while a program may be only 35 percent to 40 percent effective with its total patient population, a program may be much more effective in treating the particular sample of patients for which it is best suited (McLellan et al., 1980; Inciardi, 1975).

The problem of dropping out from substance abuse treatment and noncompliance with treatment regimens has been addressed in numerous ways. On one end of the continuum, some have suggested that a "cafeteria approach"—that is, allowing the patient to choose the kind of service and provider that seem to have greatest appeal—would both prevent early withdrawal and enhance the prospect for a successful outcome. Realistically, however, this approach has had its problems, and it appears that it has not achieved the desired therapeutic outcomes (Finney and Moos, 1986). On the other end of the continuum, several studies have found that court coercion is useful in holding clients in treatment and therefore has some clinical merit (Anglin, McGlothlin, and Speckart, 1981; Anglin, 1988; Inciardi, 1988; Leukefeld and Tims, 1988). However, others have concluded that the effect of court-mandated attendance on early withdrawal dissipates rather rapidly and does not predict retention at two months. This suggests that the potency of legal pressure fades quickly since the passage of time provides more occasion for relapse and lessens clients' fears about the consequences of noncompliance (Stark and Campbell, 1988).

For the purposes of this project two complementary techniques, treatment induction and case management/advocacy, are utilized to impact on the issues of treatment retention and compliance. Implemented in tandem, these two techniques hold the possibility of addressing both system-based and individual client issues that influence retention, compliance, and overall outcome.

INTRODUCING PATIENTS TO TREATMENT: THE WEEKEND INTERVENTION PROGRAM

Treatment induction attempts to motivate substance abuse patients to stay in treatment and to support the achievement of therapeutic goals. As we are using it here, "treatment induction" means a successful technique borrowed from the mental health disciplines. In the mental health setting, these "role induction procedures" are used to explain the process of psychotherapy to clients at treatment entry. By doing this, attendance is improved, attrition reduced, and favorable outcomes, especially with patients of lower socioeconomic status, are achieved (Stark and Kane, 1985; LaTorre, 1977; Orne and Wender, 1968).

Role induction has also been shown to have a positive impact on preventing attrition from outpatient drug treatment (Zweben, 1981; Stark and Kane, 1985; Fink et al., 1984). The process appears to work because it is able to reduce cognitive inaccuracies regarding the nature of treatment (Heitler, 1976), provide a more accurate reflection of the client's experience and current needs, and enhance the client's perceptions of the therapist's credibility, competence, and empathy (Stark and Kane, 1985).

A crucial task involves finding a way in which to induct or introduce patients into the process, content, and culture of treatment. A supportive environment is needed, even before treatment begins, in which patients can start the process of self-diagnosis, observe others engaging in their own self-diagnoses, and begin to consider a lifestyle that does not include the use of alcohol and other drugs. Such an environment exists in the form of the Weekend Intervention Program (WIP).

The WIP is a component of an interdisciplinary effort linking the area's courts and substance abuse treatment agencies. The WIP program was developed at Wright State University in 1978 and has been in continuous operation since that time. The program has been periodically updated to reflect changes in substance-abusing populations as well as changes in research and clinical development. The WIP is an intensive, three-day residential program to which persons involved in a drug or alcohol offense may be remanded by a court or other supervising agency. The majority of offenders attending the WIP have been involved in an impaired driving charge. Since 1978 the WIP has provided assessment and intervention to over 25,000 drug- and alcohol-impaired drivers.

This education/intervention program is based on marathon substance abuse counseling and a cognitive/behaviorally oriented health belief model. The WIP participants are encouraged, via small group counseling sessions, to explore their own relationships with alcohol and other psychoactive drugs while professional staff complete individual assessments for the referring courts and/or agencies.

The major programmatic goals of the WIP are: (1) to provide a comprehensive assessment of an individual's involvement with alcohol and other psychoactive drugs; (2) to confront participant denial and encourage self-evaluation; (3) to prepare participants for treatment when necessary; and (4) to increase their accessibility to treatment.

A particular strength of the WIP model is that the assessment/intervention is carried out in a supportive, gently confrontive atmosphere. Through the use of the marathon group approach the participant finds that it is more difficult to maintain defensive structures that impede involvement with the therapeutic process. This approach has a salutary effect on participants in several ways. It enlists their assistance by encouraging self-assessments of alcohol and drug abuse problems, and it provides group validation for the insights as they occur. The participant emerges from the WIP experience with a clearer understanding of why his or her alcohol and/or drug use might be a problem.

The counseling staff completes a comprehensive nine-page report on each participant. The diagnostic schema reflects the DSM-III-R categorization of alcohol abuse and dependency (American Psychiatric Association, 1987). Particular attention is paid to individual learning styles, cognitive functioning levels, and other ideographic factors that might have bearing on the choice of an outpatient or inpatient treatment program recommendation. The referring court or agency then receives an individualized report based on this information. Among the information provided to the referring court is an assessment of the most appropriate treatment program setting for each individual. For example, while some patients may achieve therapeutic goals in an outpatient program, others will need the highly structured, monitored environment provided by inpatient treatment.

Given the success of the Weekend Intervention Program with its population of substance-abuse offenders, it was believed that it would function in the same manner with those veterans selected as subjects in the Enhanced Treatment Project. Through their involvement in the intensive induction activities offered through the WIP, the likelihood of their completing the full treatment regimen increases.

Studies conducted at Wright State University School of Medicine have corroborated the effectiveness of this model for enhancing treatment compliance. A study conducted in 1986 on 754 WIP attendees indicated that over 85 percent of participants demonstrated significant changes in attitude and self-assessment scores over the course of the weekend program. WIP participants tended to rate their own problems with alcohol and drugs as more severe after their weekend experience, and they also demonstrated a greater appreciation of the benefits of drug treatment (Moore, 1989).

The participants in the 1986 study were divided into two groups depending on whether they had received a recommendation for followup drug or alcohol treatment. Treatment compliance was quantified for those persons in the followup group (235 WIP attendees were interviewed and compliance/noncompliance independently verified). Even when legal coercion into treatment was not a factor for a drunk-driving offender, fully 30 percent of those WIP participants who were recommended for followup alcohol and drug treatment voluntarily complied with the WIP recommendation (Moore, 1989).

Especially applicable to the proposed study was the finding that nearly all WIP participants who chose to attend treatment, either voluntarily or through coercion from a court, completed the full duration of treatment that was recommended for them (Moore, 1989). This illuminates the effectiveness of the WIP in accomplishing pretreatment sensitization.

Role induction by itself, however, seems to have a time-limited effect. In a study of an outpatient drug treatment center, Stark and Kane (1985) found that clients who received drug-treatment-specific role induction returned for followup visits at a significantly higher rate than control subjects. However, analysis of attendance rates after three months suggested that role induction had no continuing effect on treatment retention. It is for this reason that we elected to include a substance-abuse-specific case management/advocacy program component into this demonstration effort.

SUPPORT FOR TREATMENT PARTICIPATION: STRENGTHS PERSPECTIVE OF CASE MANAGEMENT/ ADVOCACY

While the Weekend Intervention Program may be an effective means of motivating patients for the early phases of treatment, additional techniques are needed to support longer term retention in treatment and adherence to other, perhaps more subtle compliance issues. Case management/advocacy (CM/A) was chosen as a complementary enhancement in this demonstration project for two related reasons. First, many findings document the utility of case management with other populations: persons who are experiencing chronic mental illness (Rapp, 1988; Kanter, 1989), homelessness (Rog, Andranovich, and Rosenblum, 1987), and advanced age (Goodman, 1987). Despite the long history of CM/A with these populations and some early evidence that case management and patient advocacy activities serve a powerful function in helping to encourage substance abusers to stay in treatment and to realize treatment goals (Kofoed et al., 1986), little systematic work to determine the connection has been undertaken. Second, it appears that CM/A activities can be used to address the causes related to patients quitting drug abuse treatment and/or not complying with treatment regimens. The causes of poor retention rates, noncompliance with treatment regimens, and overall poor treatment outcome are complex and include both patient and treatment system dimensions as well as the interface between those dimensions. It is the very nature of case management and advocacy to impact on these various dimensions.

Case management/advocacy in this chapter is defined as those activities oriented to assisting the client in reestablishing an awareness of internal resources such as intelligence, competence, and problem solving; establishing and negotiating lines of operation and communication between the client and external resources; and advocating with those external resources in order to enhance the continuity, accessibility, accountability, and efficiency of those resources. When substance abusers are already in treatment, the treatment system itself qualifies as a potential target of CM/A activities.

The conceptual stages of case management/advocacy that guide strengths-based interventions in the Enhanced Treatment Project are those described by Ballew and Mink in *Case Management in the Human Services* (1986). In addition to guiding the order of interventions, these stages—engagement, assessment, planning, accessing, advocacy, and coordinating—are used as the basis for documenting the activities of case manager/advocates.

Case management activities, generally categorized as engagement, assessment, and planning, address many of the patient and interface causes of treatment failure through negotiating expectations, interpreting the treatment process, clarifying roles, identifying patients' strengths in a meaningful way, anticipating barriers to treatment, and engaging in specific goal setting activities. The sum of these activities, coupled with the therapeutic interventions provided by substance abuse counselors, leads to a reduction in patient anxieties about issues raised in treatment and insecurities about the chances of succeeding in a straight world. Steer (1983) suggested that resolving these issues and thereby helping patients to develop a mastery over their abilities to successfully resist pressures to use drugs increase the likelihood of staying in treatment and participating in treatment activities.

Case management activities that impact on systems (both treatment and other social service) and the patient-system interface can lead to success in achieving access to needed resources and thereby influence treatment compliance and success. Techniques related to advocacy, negotiation, organization, and coordination can help patients see the value of the various treatment activities in which they are involved and provide a monitor to drug-free living (Fink et al., 1984; Craig, 1979). The advocacy function helps project participants thread their way through the complex maze of agency services to which they are entitled (Ogborne, Rush, and Dwyer, 1985).

Because many patients entering substance abuse treatment have other needs—such as housing, employment, and education—it is crucial that they receive assistance in accessing needed resources and in utilizing them effectively. Indeed, at least one comprehensive examination of treatment retention and compliance (Baekeland and Lundwall, 1975) identified patients who lacked basic resources such as housing and employment as most likely to drop out of treatment.

The CM/A strategies employed in the Enhanced Treatment Project are designed to serve as a quasi-therapeutic intervention, bridging the ground between "therapeutic" and "resource acquisition" interventions. This project also provides an excellent forum in which to begin a systematic exploration of the larger issues involved in CM/A work with substance abusers.

The model of case management/advocacy used in this demonstration project is based on a "strengths approach" developed by Rapp and Chamberlain (1985). In its original application, the strengths perspective of case management/advocacy was employed to assist a population of persons with mental illness in making the transition from institutionalized care to independent living. While the strengths perspective is predicated on five principles, two stand out. Its first principle demands that all case management/advocacy activities will be based on the strengths and assets of a client. By focusing on the strengths of an individual, CM/A empowers that person, thereby increasing the likelihood that he or she will complete goals such as finishing treatment and acquiring needed skills and services. Realizing this principle requires a radical departure in both the philosophy and techniques utilized in problem-based models, which focus on symptoms, weakness, and deficit.

A second primary principle places the client in charge of the direction of CM/A work. The client-driven nature of the model requires the worker (and client) to have a greater sensitivity toward client goals and available resources than in those models of CM/A that attempt to steer clients based on societal and/or institutional needs. The three remaining principles that guide the strengths perspective are the primacy of the client-worker relationship in seeking necessary resources, the field-based nature of CM/A activities, and the use of informal helping networks.

The adaptation of a mental health model to work with substance abusers was based on the similarities of the groups as a whole and early indications of the model's effectiveness. Persons with mental illness and those with substance abuse problems are generally disenfranchised. Both groups generally suffer from a lack of needed resources such as housing, jobs, basic living skills, and education. Both groups are stigmatized. Early research with the model was conducted with a small group of nineteen patients in a noncontrolled trial (Rapp and Chamberlain, 1985). In that initial evaluation more than 61 percent of resource-acquisition-oriented client goals were achieved, this with a client population generally seen as minimally capable of independent living.

As the foundation for engaging a veteran in the strengths perspective, case manager/advocates complete a strengths assessment. This assessment is completed not as a structured interview but in an open-ended discussion format. The exploration of past, often forgotten personal assets is guided generally by an examination of nine "life domains": life skills, finances, leisure activities, relationships, living arrangements, occupation/education, health, internal resources, and recovery. The exploration of strengths and assets is documented in narrative and scale form, the latter modeled on Progress Evaluation Scales derived from the work of Ihilevich and Gleser (1982).

Focus group techniques were used with both veterans and DVAMC staff to develop the scale items for the Enhanced Treatment Project Progress Evaluation Scales. Clients complete an initial rating of their own perceived functioning in each of the life domains. After completion of the strengths assessment, case manager/advocates rate the client on each life domain, and clients complete a subsequent rating based on their possibly changed perceptions of their own strengths. These ratings serve as the basis for a consensus rating between worker and client and the establishment of general goals in each life domain.

Work on specific goals follows from the general goals identified as part of the strengths assessment and are guided by a written plan. The case management plan is straightforward in intent, yet elaborate in the functions it can serve. The plan provides the veteran and case manager/advocate with a format for identifying *broad goals*, setting *measurable objectives*, and creating *strategies* that can be implemented to accomplish the objectives. Target and review dates are set for all objectives and strategies so as to prompt worker and veteran to review progress toward completion, revise plans, and/or drop unwanted or unsuccessful activities. All plan goals are categorized as fitting in one of the nine life domains. While the case management plan's primary function is as a goal setting tool, it also has utility as a research instrument and as an organizational and supervisory device.

A resource database and objectives/strategies database have also been created to assist case manager/advocates in their work with veterans. The resource database holds a comprehensive listing of both DVAMC and community resources that are cross-indexed along several parameters to allow for ease of use. The objectives/strategies database is a comprehensive listing of successful objectives and strategies that can be utilized in work toward completion of goals in any of the life domains.

All case manager/advocates in the Enhanced Treatment Project must have completed at least a bachelor's degree in a human services major such as social work, sociology, psychology, or rehabilitation counseling and at least five years of social service agency experience. Project case manager/advocates need not be extensively experienced in substance abuse treatment since they are not providing treatment per se.

After receiving a thorough overview of CM/A in general, case manager/advocates are exposed to the strengths perspective of case management/advocacy. Training manuals developed by Modrcin, Rapp, and Chamberlain (1985) are utilized, and works pertinent to the strengths perspective are reviewed (Kisthardt and Rapp, 1989; Rapp and Wintersteen, 1989). One of the originators of the model—Chamberlain—conducted on-site training in order to clarify practice issues. A great deal of training time is also spent on issues of confidentiality and how confidentiality could be maintained as part of a research project operating within a host institution. Case manager/advocates are also introduced to research concepts, methods, and instrumentation.

MONITORING AND EVALUATION

A total of 600 participants will be selected for this demonstration project for all veterans seeking drug treatment at PRP. Significant use of psychoactive drugs other than alcohol is a requirement for participation. Clients are randomly assigned to four groups receiving either no enhancement, treatment induction alone (WIP), CM/A alone, or both treatment induction and CM/A. Participants engage in a four-part, biannual series of research interviews spanning from intake to eighteen-month followup.

Baseline interviews, collected in the first few days of treatment, include the widely used Addiction Severity Index (ASI), the Symptom Check List–90 (SCL–90), a comprehensive intake form, and a readiness-for-treatment scale. The ASI has components on medical status, employment, drug and alcohol use, legal status, family and social relations, and psychiatric status. These components are important in identifying individual and environmental attributes that affect treatment effectiveness.

While the ASI is widely used in measuring substance abuse and need for treatment, it is not robust with respect to diagnosis of psychiatric problems, many of which are associated with substance abuse. The SCL–90 is included to generate additional information on symptoms of psychiatric problems that veterans are currently experiencing. In addition to these standardized interviews, a detailed intake schedule has been designed in order to investigate more deeply into the client's drug use, criminal history, and employment. All of these schedules are adapted for followup interviews, thus enabling before-and-after comparisons for participants in the four groups.

The treatment process is also monitored throughout the course of participation in the demonstration project. Participants in the WIP provide assessments at the end of the weekend. Participants in CM/A tracks work with case manager/advocates to specify goals, objectives, and strategies with target dates for completion in order to monitor outcome. For instance, weekly reports are generated which list objectives and strategies that have not been realized. This not only encourages case manager/advocates to keep up with their clients but also provides insight into potential trouble spots in planning recovery.

The breadth of data collected in this project permits a wide variety of analyses. Both outcome and process will be evaluated. Outcome refers to the impact of treatment enhancements on retention, compliance, and abstinence from drugs.

Process refers to the activities of treatment per se and the knowledge, attitudes, and practices of the staff and participants. Process evaluation very often produces useful management information, including the effects of pace-of-activity and the potential for bias in measuring outcome.

SUMMARY

The Enhanced Treatment Project holds the promise of addressing two persistent problems affecting substance abuse treatment: treatment retention and compliance. These are addressed through a dual-phase process consisting of an intensive treatment induction experience and subsequent, ongoing case management/advocacy service.

To address those issues affecting the early phase of treatment, patients complete an intensive treatment induction program. This allows them to begin their treatment highly motivated and better informed. Through the supportive but gently confrontive approach utilized in the Weekend Intervention Program, patients begin to resolve many of those defenses and issues that might otherwise jeopardize their treatment experience. Participants begin treatment with a much greater self-awareness of their substance abuse problem and a better understanding of the process, content, and culture of the therapeutic program in which they are about to engage.

While the treatment induction process may be effective in motivating patients in the early phases of treatment, case management/advocacy services—using the strengths perspective—are needed to support continued retention and the more pervasive compliance issues. The patient is simultaneously able to develop a mastery over his or her ability to make needed changes in alcohol/drug use and to function in the posttreatment world.

To date, each aspect of the program has been well received by both the DVAMC and the substance abusers presenting for treatment in its Polysubstance Rehabilitation Program.

ACKNOWLEDGMENTS

This research was supported by grant number 1R18DA06944–01 from the National Institute on Drug Abuse.

The authors wish to express their sincere gratitude to their coinvestigators at the Department of Veterans Affairs Medical Center, Dayton, Ohio: Judith Tangeman, M.D., acting associate chief of staff for extended care; Charles Lauricella, M.S.W., chief of social work service; Vicente Callejo, M.D., director of the Polysubstance Rehabilitation Program; and William O'Brien, Ph.D., chief of psychology service.

REFERENCES

American Psychiatric Association. 1987. *Diagnostic and Statistical Manual of Mental Disorders, Third Edition, Revised.* Washington, DC: American Psychiatric Association.

Anglin, M. D. 1988. The Efficacy of Civil Commitment in Treating Narcotics Addiction. *Journal of Drug Issues*, 18(Fall), 527–545.

Anglin, M. D., W. H. McGlothlin, and G. Speckart. 1981. Effect of Parole on Methadone Patient Behavior. *American Journal of Drug and Alcohol Abuse*, 8, 153–170.

Armor, D. J., J. M. Polich, and H. B. Stambul. 1978. *Alcoholism and Treatment.* Santa Monica: Rand Corporation.

Baekeland, F., and L. Lundwall. 1975. Dropping Out of Treatment: A Critical Review. *Psychological Bulletin*, 82(5), 738–783.

Bale, R., W. Van Stone, J. Kuldau, T. Engelsing, R. Elashoff, and V. Zarcone. 1980. Therapeutic Communities vs. Methadone Maintenance: A Prospective Controlled Study of Narcotic Addiction Treatment: Design and One-Year Follow-up. *Archives of General Psychiatry*, 37, 179–193.

Ballew, J. R., and G. Mink. 1986. *Case Management in the Human Services*. Springfield, IL: Charles C. Thomas.

Collins, J., and M. Allison. 1983. Legal Coercion and Retention in Drug Abuse Treatment. *Hospital and Community Psychiatry*, 34(12), 1145–1149.

Craig, R. 1979. Increasing Program Effectiveness Through Indigenous Program Evaluation. *Professional Psychology* (December), 808–819.

Craig, R. 1985. Reducing the Treatment Drop Out Rate in Drug Abuse Programs. *Journal of Substance Abuse Treatment*, 2, 209–219.

Edwards, G., J. Orford, S. Egert, S. Guthrie, A. Hawker, C. Hensman, M. Mitcheson, E. Oppenheimer, and C. Taylor. 1977. Alcoholism: A Controlled Trial of Treatment and Advice. *Journal of Studies on Alcoholism*, 38, 1004–1031.

Fink, E., S. Rudden, R. Longabaugh, B. McCrady, and R. Stout. 1984. Adherence in a Behavioral Alcohol Treatment Program. *The International Journal of the Addictions*, 19(7), 709–719.

Finney, J. W., and R. H. Moos. 1986. Matching Patients with Treatments: Conceptual and Methodological Issues. *Journal of Studies on Alcohol*, 47(2), 122–134.

Goodman. C. C. 1987. The Elderly Frail: Who Should Get Case Management? *Journal of Gerontology Social Work*, 11(3/4), 99–113.

Heitler, J. B. 1976. Preparatory Techniques in Initiating Express Psychotherapy with Lower Class, Unsophisticated Patients. *Psychological Bulletin*, 83, 339–352.

Hubbard, R. L., J. V. Rachal, S. G. Craddock, and E. R. Cavanaugh. 1984. Treatment Outcome Prospective Study (TOPS): Client Characteristics and Behaviors Before, During and After Treatment. In *Drug Abuse Treatment Evaluation: Strategies, Progress, and Prospects*, edited by F. M. Tims and J. P. Ludford, pp. 42–68. NIDA Research Monograph No. 51, DHHS Publication No. 84–1349. Rockville, MD: National Institute on Drug Abuse.

Ihilevich, D., and G. Gleser. 1982. *Evaluating Mental-Health Programs: The Progress Evaluation Scale*. Lexington, MA: Lexington Books.

Inciardi, J. A. 1975. The Evaluation of Addiction Treatment. *The Addiction Therapist*, 1(2), 2–5.

Inciardi, J. A. 1988. Some Considerations on the Clinical Efficacy of Compulsory Treatment; Reviewing the New York Experience. In *Compulsory Treatment of Drug Abuse: Research and Clinical Practice*, edited by C. G. Leukefeld and F. M. Tims, pp. 126–138. NIDA Research Monograph No. 86, DHHS Publication No. (ADM) 88–1578. Rockville, MD: National Institute on Drug Abuse.

Intagliata, J. 1982. Improving the Quality of Community Care for the Chronically Mentally Disabled: The Role of Case Management. *Schizophrenic Bulletin*, 8(4), 655–674.

Joe, G. W., and D. D. Simpson. 1975. Retention in Treatment of Drug Users: 1971–1972 DARP Admissions. *American Journal of Drug and Alcohol Abuse*, 2(1), 63–71.

Kanter, J. 1989. Clinical Case Management: Definition, Principles, Components. *Hospital Community Psychiatry*, 40(4), 361–368.

Kisthardt, W. E., and C. A. Rapp. 1989. *Bridging the Gap Between Principles and Practice: Implementing a Strengths Perspective in Case Management*. Lawrence: University of Kansas School of Social Welfare.

Kofoed, L., J. Kania, T. Walsh, and R. Atkinson. 1986. Outpatient Treatment of Patients with Substance Abuse and Coexisting Psychiatric Disorders. *American Journal of Psychiatry*, 143(7), 867–872.

LaTorre, R. A. 1977. Pretherapy Role Induction Procedures. *Canadian Psychological Review*, 18(4), 308–321.

Leukefeld, C., and F. Tims (eds.). 1988. *Compulsory Treatment of Drug Abuse: Research and Clinical Practice*. NIDA Research Monograph Number 86, DHHS Publication No. (ADM) 88–1578. Rockville, MD: National Institute on Drug Abuse.

McLellan, A. T., L. Luborsky, C. P. O'Brien, W. E. Woody, and K. A. Druley. 1982. Is Treatment for Substance Abuse Effective? *Journal of the American Medical Association*, 247(10), 1423–1428.

McLellan, A. T., L. Luborsky, G. E. Woody, C. P. O'Brien, and K. A. Druley. 1983. Predicting Response to Alcohol and Drug Abuse Treatments: Role of Psychiatric Severity. *Archives of General Psychiatry*, 40, 620–625.

McLellan, A. T., C. O'Brien, R. Kron, A. Alterman, and K. A. Druley. 1980. Matching Substance Abuse Patients to Appropriate Treatment: A Conceptual and Methodological Approach. *Drug and Alcohol Dependence*, 5, 189–195.

Modrcin, M., C. A. Rapp, and R. Chamberlain. 1985. *Case Management with Psychiatrically Disabled Individuals: Curriculum and Training Program*. Lawrence: University of Kansas School of Social Welfare.

Moore, D. 1989. *Factors Influencing Treatment Compliance Following Drunk Driver Intervention*. Proceedings of the 11th International Conference on Alcohol, Drugs and Traffic Safety (October 24–27, Chicago, IL).

Ogborne, A., B. Rush, and D. Dwyer. 1985. The Development of Community-based Treatment Systems: An Ontario Perspective. *British Journal of Addiction*, 80, 363–367.

Orne, M. T., and P. H. Wender. 1968. Anticipatory Socialization for Psychotherapy: Method and Rationale. *American Journal of Psychiatry*, 124(9), 88–98.

Rapp, C. A. 1988. *The Strengths Perspective of Case Management with Persons Suffering from Severe Mental Illness*. Lawrence: University of Kansas School of Social Welfare.

Rapp, C. A., and R. Chamberlain. 1985. Case Management Services for the Chronically Mentally Ill. *Social Work*, 30(5), 417–422.

Rapp, C. A., and R. Wintersteen. 1989. The Strengths Model of Case Management: Results from Twelve Demonstrations. *The Psychosocial Rehabilitation Journal*, 13(1), 23–32.

Rog, D., G. Andranovich, and S. Rosenblum. 1987. *Intensive Case Management for Persons Who Are Homeless and Mentally Ill*, vol. 1. Washington, DC: Cosmos Corporation.

Simpson, D. 1979. The Relation of Time Spent in Drug Abuse Treatment to Posttreatment Outcome. *American Journal of Psychiatry*, 136 (11), 1449–1453.

Simpson, D., L. Savage, and M. Lloyd. 1979. Follow-up Evaluation of Treatment of Drug Abuse During 1969–1972. *Archives of General Psychiatry*, 36, 772–780.

Stark, M. J., and B. K. Campbell. 1988. Personality, Drug Use, and Early Attrition from Substance Abuse Treatment. *American Journal of Drug and Alcohol Abuse*, 14(4), 475–485.

Stark, M. J., and B. J. Kane. 1985. General and Specific Psychotherapy Role Induction with Substance-Abusing Clients. *The International Journal of the Addictions*, 20(8), 1135–1141.

Steer, R. 1983. Retention in Drug-Free Counseling. *The International Journal of the Addictions*, 18(8), 1109–1114.

Washton, A. 1986. Nonpharmacologic Treatment of Cocaine Abuse. *Psychiatric Clinics of North America*, 9(3), 563–571.

Zweben, A. 1981. The Efficacy of Role Induction in Preventing Early Dropout from Outpatient Treatment of Drug Dependency. *American Journal of Drug and Alcohol Abuse*, 8(2), 171–183.

IV

MULTI-MODALITY AND OTHER ECLECTIC PROGRAMS

Passages: A Modified Therapeutic Community Day Treatment Model for Methadone Clients

George De Leon, Stanley Sacks, and Robert Hilton

METHADONE MAINTENANCE

Surveys of the literature on methadone maintenance document the effectiveness of methadone in reducing heroin use and criminal behavior and in improving health status among methadone clients (Hubbard et al., 1989; Lipton and Magura, 1991; Senay, 1985). As with other treatment modalities, methadone treatment outcome is positively related to retention in program; the longer one stays in treatment the better the outcome. However, continued use of other nonprescribed drugs among significant numbers of methadone-treated clients is amply documented.

The high rates of cocaine use/injection among methadone clients are of particular concern because of the relationship between intravenous drug use and AIDS. Preliminary data from several recent National Institute on Drug Abuse (NIDA) demonstration projects, designed to improve treatment and reduce the spread of AIDS, indicate considerable cocaine use/injection among methadone clients.[1]

Effective treatment of intravenous drug use among methadone clients constitutes a significant approach to the problem of AIDS. Enhanced treatment is an important strategy for those methadone clients who continue to engage in high-risk drug use and/or sexual behavior. One such approach to enhanced treatment is a day treatment model modified from therapeutic community (TC) residential treatment.

THERAPEUTIC COMMUNITIES

The perspective and approach of the traditional TC on drug abuse and recovery have been described in other writings (De Leon, 1986, 1989; De Leon and Rosenthal, 1989). Briefly, drug abuse is seen as a disorder of the whole person, reflecting problems in conduct, attitudes, moods, emotional management, and values. Many experience chronic deficits in social, educational, and marketable skills. The specific social goal of treatment is the development of a prosocial lifestyle marked by alcohol and drug abstinence and the elimination of antisocial behavior and attitudes. The psychological goal is to change the negative patterns of behavior, feeling, and thinking that predispose the individual to drug use.

A critical assumption of the TC is that stable recovery depends on an integration of the social and psychological goals. Rehabilitation, therefore, involves a multidimensional effort which requires an intensive mutual self-help process in a twenty-four-hour residential setting. The goals of the therapeutic community approach are to promote abstinence from drug use and antisocial behavior and to effect a global change in lifestyle, including attitudes and values.

The effectiveness of TCs in reducing drug use and criminality has been well documented in a number of program-based and multi-site evaluations. In general, positive outcomes are directly related to increased length of stay in treatment (De Leon, 1984; Hubbard et al., 1989; Simpson and Sells 1982). Studies show considerable reduction in all substance use including alcohol (De Leon, 1984, 1987), and improvement in psychological well-being following TC treatment (Brook and Whitehead, 1980, Biase, Sullivan, and Wheeler, 1986; De Leon, 1984, 1989; De Leon and Jainchill, 1981; Holland, 1986; Kennard and Wilson, 1979; Simpson and Sells, 1982).

A major strength of the TC approach for the reduction of AIDS-relevant risk behavior is that it views any drug abuse as an aspect of a disorder of the "whole person." The therapeutic community treatment focuses on those behavioral, attitudinal, emotional, and lifestyle factors that are likely to produce a stable and enduring change. In order to address the problem of cocaine injection/use (and other drug use and/or high-risk sexual behavior) among methadone clients, a day treatment model based on modified TC methods—Passages—was developed. Clients in the Passages program not only remain in their methadone regime but also attend Passages as an enhancement to their treatment.

THE PASSAGES MODEL

Table 10.1 provides an outline of the Passages program including the admission criteria, model, goal, structure, and process. This section describes the basic features of Passages and the fundamental assumptions of the recovery-oriented perspective to the goals of reduced drug use and reduced high-risk sexual behavior. The structure and process of the Passages model are then presented in some detail, highlighting modifications from standard TCs.

Basic Features

Although most of the key components of the standard TC are retained in the Passages model, they are modified for methadone clients in a day treatment setting. The modified TC approach includes greater emphasis on outreach and advocacy, increased flexibility in phase format, reduction in the intensity of personal and interpersonal interactions, graduated and guided implementation of all new expectations, and greater responsiveness to individual differences.

The day treatment, nonresidential nature of the program has given rise to the development of several innovations, including the Client Action Plan and the Passages Fellowship, designed to integrate individual and group goals and ensure sustained influence beyond the official hours of contact. Nevertheless, the central TC feature remains: Passages, like all TC programs, seeks to develop a culture where clients learn through a self-help process to foster change in themselves and others.

The Recovery-Oriented Perspective

The goal of Passages remains narrow: to reduce high-risk drug use and sexual behavior in methadone-maintained clients. However, the Passages approach to this goal is grounded in a recovery-oriented perspective described in other writings (De Leon, 1991a, 1992), which have evolved from the work in TCs and relate to other efforts (e.g., Nurco et al., 1983; Rawson et al., 1986; Zackon, McAuliffe, and Ch'ien, 1985; Zweben, 1989).

The recovery-oriented perspective is a process of change from a drug abuse lifestyle to a positive lifestyle characterized by abstinence from all nonmedically prescribed substances, the absence of all forms of antisocial and high-risk sexual behavior and attitudes, gainful employment (including both homemaker and student status), adherence to values of "right living" (self-reliance, honesty, a work ethic, and responsible concern for others), and commitment to sustain sobriety in a continuing recovering process. In this formulation the individual progresses through stages of recovery with characteristic indicators of change, such as early stage (denial, ambivalence) to later stage (sobriety, commitment).

Assumptions about Recovery for Methadone Clients in Passages. The implementation of a recovery-oriented model such as Passages for methadone clients, particularly those engaged in high-risk behavior, requires certain assumptions:

- Abstinence from all nonmedically prescribed substances is viewed as a prerequisite in the recovery process. Use of any nonprescribed substance impedes the recovery process, increasing the risk of reinforcing pharmacological abuse and other behaviors and attitudes related to the addict lifestyle or identity. However, abstinence is a stage in the recovery process which is achieved through trial and error. Thus, nonabstinence is accepted as an entry point for the change process, as long as clients are committed to the goals of abstinence, personal change, and the process of recovery.

Table 10.1
Overview of the Passages Day Treatment Model

MODEL	Community
GOAL	Recovery
ADMISSION CRITERIA	Cocaine injection/use, other drug use, and high-risk sexual behavior
STRUCTURE	
• Daily Regime	Morning Meeting Seminars Education Groups Communal Lunch Therapy Groups
• Role of Staff	Role Models and Guides
• Role of Peers	Self-help with supervision
• Work	Reduced scope/rotational Reduced stratification
• Privileges and Sanctions	By level Cardinal Rules Legislated by self-government
PROCESS	Phases and Stages Phase I Intensive Treatment (first 6 months) Stage 1 Engagement (months 1-2) Stage 2 Stabilization (months 2-4) Stage 3 Commitment (months 4-6) Phase II Transitional (next 6 months) Stage 4 Affiliation (months 7-9) Stage 5 Reentry (months 10-12)

SUMMARY: ***Create affiliation and self-help community to foster change***

- Methadone treatment provides a medicine that can be used to facilitate a recovery process insofar as it eliminates illicit opiate use and retains clients in a treatment setting. Passages provides the methadone client with the opportunity for entering the recovery process within the context of methadone treatment. Detoxification from prescribed methadone is *not* essential to recovery, although some clients may voluntarily choose detoxification at some point in the enhanced program. Such a decision is deferred to the end of the Passages program and is made in consultation with the clinic staff.
- Passages clients are generally in the early recovery stages, and the bounded time frame of the demonstration project limits the recovery goals of the project. Thus, the recovery stage and goals are assessed separately for each individual. Passages is geared to move the individual client on to the next stage in his or her recovery status.

Admission Criteria

The referral group for Passages consists of clients currently injecting/using cocaine and other substances and engaging in other high-risk sex or needle-use practices. In addition to substance use and other high-risk behavior, secondary criteria for inclusion in Passages include unemployment, dysfunction, and/or noncompliance with either the methadone regime or the overall procedures and rules of the primary methadone treatment program.

Structure

Passages is similar in all respects to traditional TCs, with variations suitable to the methadone population and setting. Some highlights of the treatment structure and key comparisons to standard TCs are described below.

The Daily Regime. The Passages program operates four days per week, from 9:00 A.M. to 2:00 P.M. In addition, Passages activities are held one evening per week and on one day of the weekend. Clients often arrive one hour before the official program begins and remain two hours after it ends to increase affiliation, socialization, and connection to the community. Many clients even attend during the one day per week in which there is no formal program.

The daily regime consists of a variety of structured group activities, including morning meeting, seminars, communal lunch, therapy, and other specialized groups that occur in a manner almost identical to any TC. For example, the morning meeting begins the day. It consists of a variety of energy-enhancing and community-building activities including: announcements, jokes, songs, horoscopes, personal stories, and concepts for the day. There are regular seminars held on topics of particular relevance to methadone clients, including entitlements, the world of work, and AIDS.

AIDS-Related Activities. Neither HIV-positive status nor an AIDS diagnosis precludes entry into Passages. The topic of AIDS is incorporated in the enhanced program because of its urgency and relevance for the methadone-using population. Passages offers AIDS seminars to clients and enrolls those interested in an affiliated TC-oriented AIDS group. Data collected from the Passages baseline instrument indicate a reasonably high level of AIDS-related knowledge but a low relationship between AIDS-related knowledge and risk behavior (Quintyne and Kang, 1992). Although each client's HIV/AIDS status is completely confidential, HIV-positive and AIDS clients who have become members of Passages have usually shared their problems with the group. More specific AIDS-related components are planned as the cohort group increases.

Role of Staff. Staff function in their traditional TC roles as role models and guides, but with an increased emphasis on providing instruction, practice, and assistance. Staff consist of TC-trained and TC-experienced workers recruited for this project because of their special interest in developing modified TC methods for new populations. In addition, staff recruitment is focused on those who have special skills in outreach, advocacy, and vocational development. The staff include a TC consultant, site director (part-time), assistant site director, and one or two counselors per site. The staff-to-client ratio (apart from the consultant) is approximately one to ten.

Role of Peers. Peer self-help remains a guiding principle. However, staff of the modified TC provide a greater degree of supervision and direct help to the clients compared to traditional TC staff. This is particularly true in the launch phase when differentiation in level of functioning among clients is reduced and work tasks are limited.

Peer Work Structure. A modified peer work structure exists, in which the hierarchy is flatter and task assignments more rotational than in traditional TCs. Peer work tasks include facility maintenance, food preparation and cleanup, facility traffic control, and orientation of new Passages clients.

Responsibilities. Clients' responsibilities are determined by their level, which is based on their performance and time in the program. The level system is less differentiated compared to standard TCs. All clients in the current treatment cohort entered Passages with the same status as "pioneers." At this time four levels are distinguished: level one, prospects; level two, new members; level three, pioneers; and level four, stipend trainees. Differences in levels are mainly described in terms of the client's degree of responsibility within the program, peer/work assignments, and autonomy of functioning on their individual objectives (Client Action Plan).

Sanctions. Passages clients are expected to follow all rules of the methadone site, as well as the rules of the Passages program. There are two cardinal rules for Passages: no drug use on the premises, and no violence or threat of violence. There is a "three strike" policy leading to discharge if cardinal rules are broken. Clients discharged from Passages are not necessarily discharged from their primary methadone program. However, those clients who are discharged from their methadone program cannot remain in Passages. All other sanctions are situation-specific and determined by the Passages client government group.

Process

The treatment process unfolds in the phase/stage format described by De Leon and Rosenthal (1989) with special modifications developed in the Passages project. Table 10.2 presents part of the phase/stage format and describes the objectives, methods, and outcomes of phase one, stage one. Each stage has an interrelated set of objectives, methods, and outcomes. All of the objectives of a particular stage are consistent with the general goal of that stage, and the methods and anticipated outcomes relate to the specific objective. For example, for Phase One (''Intensive Treatment'')/Stage One (''Engagement'') establishment of the client's needs is a major objective. The method for accomplishing this objective includes assessment, advocacy, and the development of an individualized plan of service (the Client Action Plan or CAP). The expected outcome is the identification of basic needs (housing, entitlements, child care, etc.). Similar sets of objectives, methods, and expected outcomes exist for the next stage—''stabilization'' (not shown in Table 10.1)—and for subsequent phases and stages in the modified TC process.

There are three key *process* differences between the standard TC and Passages: the planned duration of treatment phases and stages, emphasis on methods for retention, and individualization of movement through the program's phase/stage design. These differences are highlighted below.

Planned Duration of Treatment. The duration of treatment is shortened from an eighteen- to twenty-four-month stay in the standard residential TC to twelve months in Passages. Clients remain in the Passages Day Treatment program for the first six months, then progress to the evening and weekend Fellowship program for the next six months. All stages are condensed, and clients move through each stage of the entire program more quickly than in traditional TCs. The change in duration of treatment emanates not only from the time limits of the demonstration research project but also from emerging changes within the drug treatment field, which now emphasize providing shorter-term treatment models.

Retention Methods. A central issue addressed in Passages is retention in treatment. The client factors that contribute to retention difficulties include their relatively low level of functioning, their substantial service needs, and unstable living situations and status. In order to ensure client retention in the program, considerable effort and time are devoted to the engagement and stabilization process. The program's emphasis on advocacy, support, encouragement, and gradual assimilation are all designed to engage and stabilize methadone clients as they learn TC methods and begin the process of self-help.

Individual Rates of Change. Program movement in Passages is individualized. Almost all clients move through all of the stages of the Passages program. However, they move at different rates. Occasionally a client may even enter at a more advanced stage, or move quickly to an advanced stage either by rapidly going through or skipping a particular stage. Conversely, although basic time

Table 10.2
Phase One, Stage One of Passages

PHASE ONE - INTENSIVE TREATMENT: STAGE ONE ENGAGEMENT

I OBJECTIVES
- Orientation
    - Passages: purpose and history
    - Concepts of "right living" and recovery
    - TC principles and philosophy
- Assessment
    - Generate personal history of client
    - Establish baseline data for Client Action Plan (CAP)
- Immediate Needs
    - Special issues of housing, finance, health
    - Incorporation into CAP
- Forming Relationships
    - Staff to client
    - Client to client

II METHODS
- Seminars/Tutorials
    - Introduction to Passages' purpose and history
    - Basic concepts of "right-living" and recovery
    - Basic TC principles and philosophies
    - Physiological, psychological effects of drugs
    - HIV information
- Testing
    - Standardized instruments
    - Passages interview
- Advocacy
    - Individual staff intervention
    - Group and community
- Case Management/Individual Counseling
    - Staff/client collaboration on development of CAP
    - Individual counseling
- Community Groups
    - Forums for discussion and assistance with CAP
    - Sources of support and constructive criticism

III OUTCOMES
- Client Disclosure to Community
    - Drug use history
    - Criminal history
    - Lifestyle and personal situations
- Immediate Needs
    - Acquisition of housing
    - Investigate financial resources
- Vocational Issues
    - Formal evaluation
    - Articulation of limited goals in CAP
- Health
    - HIV risk reduction education
    - Assessment of status (testing) in appropriate cases
- General
    - Consistency in attendance, punctuality, and participation
    - Steps toward goal attainment (CAP)

frames are established for each stage (e.g., stage one "Engagement," one to two months), clients may progress more slowly if they need to further enhance their development at a particular phase or stage.

OTHER KEY MODIFICATIONS

Client Action Plan (CAP)

The purpose of the Client Action Plan (CAP) is to specify, monitor, and document client short-term goals, as established by the Passages clients and staff. The rationale for the development of the CAP tool includes the need to focus on specific matters, the necessity for integrating individual activities within a group dynamic, and the urgency for parallel client work on both immediate, practical matters and longstanding characteristic patterns of emotional and behavioral response.

An underlying assumption of the CAP approach is that the client is capable of substantial accomplishments. However, the path to these accomplishments involves attaining smaller objectives and building incrementally on the accumulated success. This approach is especially important to the methadone client because it sustains the hope for a successful future despite a long history of past failures and a present profile of considerable dysfunction. Moreover, the attainment of each objective reinforces the sense that the client is on the road to successful recovery.

The procedures for the CAP follow the format of *goal, objective, method,* and *outcome*. Within a general goal area (e.g., "improve personal responsibility"), the CAP focuses on specific objectives (e.g., "obtain elected office in the Passages government"), specifies methods for obtaining that objective (e.g., "keep notes on all government activities," "facilitate all needed government meetings"), and designates a specific time frame for the accomplishment of the objective, usually one week. Clients (and staff) learn to set objectives that are concrete, specific, attainable, measurable, and important.

The initial thirty-day CAP is often quite practical (e.g., locate housing, complete medical evaluation, obtain health information, make provisions for child care). Although clients focus on concrete matters in all CAPs, there is often a systematic progression in which the CAP increasingly highlights matters central to the client's personal development. There are two distinctive features to the CAP within the modified TC: the behavioral dynamic perspective and the unique role of the group.

The Behavioral Dynamic Perspective. Goal setting in the CAP has both behavioral change and emotional exploratory functions. Thus, while the Client Action Plan incorporates the behaviorally oriented elements of goal attainment methods, it underscores the psychological significance of the specific goal for the individual. Characteristic attitudinal and emotional obstacles to change often surface when the client is unable to accomplish specific tasks.

For instance, in the example cited above, the issue of "responsibility" was a core problem for that individual that impeded overall adult development. Chronic irresponsibility was evident in similar patterns of behavior in adolescence prior to and during regular drug abuse. In working on the specific objectives in the CAP, this individual simultaneously works on alteration of patterns of behavior while confronting some of the personal/emotional issues underlying those patterns. By placing immediate behavioral expectations in the foreground, both behavioral change and emotional change are facilitated.

The Role of the Group. The CAP is reviewed in individual meetings with Passages staff and in scheduled CAP group reviews. During the group session each client is expected to share the experience of attempting to attain difficult goals with the other program members, who provide feedback and support. Learning opportunities are maximized since each client has the opportunity to learn from his or her own efforts, the feedback of peers, and the activities of other community members in their own individualized CAPs.

Recruitment/Outreach

Recruitment efforts are designed to convey specialized information about the Passages program, such as the nature of the key modifications, that could be easily understood by clients and supported by staff. A recruitment protocol that provides information, encourages participation, and promotes affiliation has been established. The essential features of the recruitment protocol are: collaboration, multiple contacts, planned formal orientation, informal dropin for further orientation, individual bonding with others, and setting a positive tone.

Collaboration. Recruitment into Passages is a collaborative effort between Passages program staff and methadone clinic staff. The first step in this process is orientation of methadone staff to the enhanced program. The rationale, goals, and methods of the program are explained, understood, and accepted by methadone administrative and clinical staff so they can facilitate the recruitment effort. The support of site staff, especially the leverage provided by key management staff, is often critical to the recruitment process.

Multiple Contacts. The methadone clients require repetition of contact and content in order to comprehend and accept new information. Thus, recruitment efforts occur over time, with several repetitions, delivered in different styles and settings (but with the same information) and even by different staff.

Planned Formal and Informal Orientation. Formal orientation to the Passages program is conducted in a small group setting. It gives concrete information (where and when), describes the structure of the program primarily in terms of group activities, focuses on immediate needs (e.g., the attainment of housing), identifies the Passages staff (mainly as recovering addicts), and sets a positive tone for starting over in the process of personal change and recovery. The formal orientation is supplemented by informal contacts such as conversations after orientation, dropin sessions, and other discussions. In the informal contact, client concerns are addressed and the orientation material is reworked in personal terms. The main goal of the orientation is encouragement and letting clients know of the availability of a special program geared to their needs, even for those who are most discouraged.

Client-Staff Connection. Most important to the recruitment process is the forming of an individual connection or bond between the client and at least one staff member. A feasibility study completed by the Passages staff (De Leon, 1990) identified concrete service needs and individual counseling as two of the most important needs of the methadone client. For the methadone client, particularly the problematic methadone client that Passages seeks to serve, the program is explained in personal terms, and clients put their faith in person, not program.

Setting a Positive Tone. The tone of orientation is positive. All past efforts, even those from which the client is most discouraged, are viewed as a prelude to the current effort. The message of the Passages program may be summarized as follows: *Others have changed, I have changed, you can change; the process can begin today with the simple avowal of an effort to try by committing oneself to attending a Passages group and the recovery process.*

The Creation of a Positive Peer Culture

The earlier trials of the Passages program at the initial sites revealed that the creation of a positive peer culture where none existed can be overwhelmed by the weight of client problems. These include drug use, high-risk sexual behavior, poor psychological functioning, unstable family and living situations, and a variety of other practical issues. In particular, there were problems endemic to the clinic's negative peer subculture, such as underproductivity, gossiping, loitering, and, sometimes, mutual involvement in destructive activity.

The strategy pursued to create a positive peer culture was that of culture planning and development prior to the inclusion of clients with higher problem profiles. The key to this strategy was assembling an initial "seedling group" whose members were designated "pioneers" in a new endeavor. They were trained to function as facilitators in the transmission of the peer self-help culture to other methadone clients.

The seedling group consisted of the most highly motivated, higher functioning of the methadone clients (although most were still using drugs), as referred by the directors of the site and as further selected by the Passages staff. Over a six-month period, the selected clients were exposed to a rigorous and accelerated TC regime designed to strengthen them individually and collectively. This special regime consisted of all of the basic TC elements, but it especially highlighted their roles as "pioneers" in the establishment of a self-help culture in a methadone clinic and their training to provide leadership for other methadone clients to follow.

Several criteria had to be met by each client during this development: learning of TC concepts, significant progress on individual CAPs, and semiautonomous management of key program activities. Most important, each client was asked to contribute to the establishment of a self-help TC culture—that is, the identification of the Passages site as the home and the Passages membership as the family in which the development of the individual would proceed. When these individual and group criteria were met and the culture was judged sufficiently strong to absorb other, more problematic methadone clients, then the research phase of random assignment was initiated.

Advocacy (Case Assistance vs. Case Management)

One of the first modifications introduced into the Passages program was the focus on the immediate needs of the client. Many of the clients initially enrolling in Passages were homeless, in poor physical health, unaware of their eligibility for various entitlements, and had little sense of empowerment to effect their future. Furthermore, although appearing for treatment for continued drug abuse problems, they conveyed an urgency for basic services to meet primary needs. This initial clinical impression was later confirmed in a feasibility survey (De Leon, 1990) that established the prominence of these needs.

In order to accomplish the goal of meeting basic needs within the modified therapeutic community, Passages developed an advocacy approach based on "client assistance" as compared to the "case management" approach commonly employed in the human services field. The elements of the "client assistance" method include client-centered assessment, staff consultation, and integration of individualized treatment within the group context.

Client-Centered Assessment. Client needs are initially surveyed in the baseline research instrument and later clinically, in the initial CAP, which is designed to focus primarily on immediate needs, objectives, and methods to meet those needs.

Staff Consultation. Passages staff are assigned an individual client caseload to assist the client to accomplish objectives. They provide general information, resource information, suggestions on how to proceed, guidance, and feedback. Occasionally, staff may directly intervene in assisting clients. However, such instances are rare and are provided only when there is urgency and client-demonstrated powerlessness.

Individualized Client Goals and the Group Process. The group involvement so vital to the building of a peer community is accomplished by making the CAP a part of group discussion. Client goals are developed, discussed, and evaluated within the group context.

Overall, Passages focuses on advocacy issues in a client assistance model that places a premium on client self-reliance, peer input, and group disclosure. Staff in this process may help directly where indicated, but traditional case management approaches are modified to allow staff to assist the client in a manner consistent with their traditional TC roles as guides and role models.

Increased Emphasis on Instruction

In standard TCs, seminars and tutorials serve the dual function of enhancing cognitive learning and introducing new material and expectations. In Passages, seminars and tutorials receive an increased emphasis necessitated by such factors as the client's cognitive/learning impairment, reduced tolerance for emotional intensity, and lack of basic information and skills.

In Passages the time spent on instructive approaches is expanded in both frequency and duration. Instruction is provided until clients have a working knowledge of a particular area. Experiential learning is introduced only when there is considerable certainty that clients understand and that actual experience is necessary to complete the learning process. For example, before establishing the self-government process within Passages, a civics lesson module was introduced. Clients were taught about the structure and functioning of the U.S. government and the role of the branches of the government, using explicit examples. Finally, the application of the formal material to the Passages program was described and implemented.

Other examples of the instructive approach involve the teaching of self-disclosure through an extended period of formal tutorials and seminars, followed by modeling and guided implementation (e.g., staff personal self-disclosure, role playing) prior to the introduction of client self-disclosure groups. For some topics, such as AIDS awareness and risk reduction, education and discussion are used almost exclusively since client tolerance for this topic is limited.

Traineeships and Stipends

Staff in the TC are addicts with TC-recovery experience who role model the messages of recovery and "right-living." Prior to this first demonstration project, there existed no cadre of methadone clients with Passages-recovery experience. This consideration led to the development of a Passages trainee stipend program.

The goal of the trainee stipend program is to develop a new cadre of trained staff to work with methadone or other special substance-abusing populations in modified TCs or other programs. The trainee subgroup consists of clients currently in the Passages program selected to further strengthen the Passages/TC culture. These clients remain in Passages and also assist Passages staff in conducting the program while receiving special training and supervision in managing the daily regime of the program. In fact, their performance in their role as trainees is the subject of both professional supervision and the substance of personal development.

The entire trainee stipend selection and training program is designed to parallel the real world of work. Clients are selected on the basis of their progress in the launch phase of the TC (the CAP provides the performance measure); their formal application for candidacy, of which the most important feature is their personal statement; and personal interviews. The traineeship program consists of both didactic and experiential learning. Formal training consists of sessions in psychology, the mental health field, and a review of central TC concepts. Experiential learning consists of supervision in the conducting of TC groups and other activities.

Self-Government

The development of Passages within a methadone setting raised several issues unique to the site and program. These issues included standards of behavior, safety and security of the site, and the future direction of the program. In order to resolve these issues and further develop the group in a manner consistent with TC principles, a form of self-government was developed.

Passages' self-government began with instruction on participatory democracy. These seminars served the dual purpose of providing a civics review and of laying the foundation for the government system to be instituted in Passages. Following the instructive phase, clients and staff devised a system that included a legislative process to define rules and boundaries, a judicial system to enforce these rules, and an executive function to oversee the structure. Every client in the program participated in either the legislative or judicial process, whereas the executive office was elected. The selection of elected officials was based on nominations, brief campaigns, and majority vote.

The goal of self-government in Passages is to increase ownership of the program by increasing client responsibility for the standards of behavior, the safety and security of the membership, and the direction of the Passages program.

The Passages Fellowship

The Passages Fellowship extends Passages into evenings and weekends. The Fellowship includes standard TC-structured activities (seminars, tutorials, and groups), other self-help groups (twelve-step, Narcotics Anonymous/Alcoholics Anonymous groups, and a developing METH/ANON group), and more specialized recreational/leisure activities, such as socials and trips, both on and off the premises. The Fellowship provides some clients with extended hours, others with primary treatment hours, and many with opportunities for accelerated movement through the program phase/stage sequence. Housing the Fellowship meetings within the Passages program facility provides a physical space for socialization and recreation and a symbolic place to strengthen identification with the Passages community.[2]

Vocational Services

There are two Passages world-of-work vocational modules: training for human services (as described in the section on Passages trainee stipends) and training for other work, which involves vocational preparation in areas such as food, maintenance, and secretarial services.

Training for Other Work. Vocational planning is accomplished within the framework of the CAP, in which regular vocational goals are established, implemented, and monitored. Vocational assessment, still in development, will be undertaken using traditional vocational tests. In-depth interviews will be conducted by Passages staff to establish work skills, work experience, strengths, deficits, and reasons for past successes and failures. Clients will be tutored in job-finding skills, including resumé preparation, job search, and interviewing. A TC staff member with special skills in the vocational area will be hired to supervise and manage the work/vocational training component of the Passages program.

Unique Features. There are three unique features of Passages vocational training:

1. The program is integrated into the TC experience and is part of the TC culture. The client's individual vocational objectives and activities are developed, discussed, and monitored within the group context. Staff are TC trained with work/vocational training expertise.
2. An immediate apprenticeship experience is provided within Passages itself, as clients are assigned to job functions that include expediter, food service, maintenance, and scribe for record keeping. In these functions, their work performance is a part of their regular activities; it is monitored, discussed, evaluated, and modified on a regular basis. This aspect of the Passages vocational program provides clients with the opportunity for an intensive but sheltered work experience prior to beginning work in the outside world.
3. Once outside work begins, regular support groups are held in which clients review and discuss their work experience and receive support and guidance as they negotiate and integrate the new work experience into their overall recovery and personal development plans.

Vocational Issues. The goals of the vocational module reflect the resources and work experience of the client. Specifically, there are three main vocational goals:

1. *Trainability*: preparation for additional vocational training programs for those with no work experience.
2. *Employability*: preparation for entry-level jobs for those with minimal skills and little work experience.
3. *Marketability*: preparation for return to the work force for clients with marketable skills and a documented work history.

The Passages program views work as essential to the recovery process, reflecting the psychological facts of self-efficacy and self-esteem, as well as the values of earning, self-reliance, and responsibility. The focus in Passages is to foster the socialization and personal growth changes that are the foundation for *sustaining* the work role. Thus, the Passages vocational preparation module is phased in *after* the client has stabilized in a recovery orientation. Therefore, work and recovery are viewed as interactive. Initially, the stability of recovery is a prerequisite for sustaining work, which then becomes a prerequisite for sustaining recovery.

Child Care Services

Many Passages clients have the concrete need for child care services during the day treatment hours of Passages. In addition, many have never developed proper child care skills and responsible attitudes toward child rearing. In order to facilitate registration and retention in the Passages program, child care services are planned at one of the sites for clients in need during the day treatment program. Child care staff and services in the child care setting will be integrated into the regular treatment program. Regular joint activities will be held, and observations from the child care setting will be discussed with Passages clients and staff. Clients' CAPs will directly address the issues of increasing child care responsibilities and enhancing child care skills.

SPECIAL ISSUES

The feasibility of implementing the Passages model in a freestanding methadone clinic setting has been demonstrated, and clinical changes in the initial cohort of clients at the present site are encouraging. However, there are issues that bear on application of the model to other methadone centers.

Recruitment and Retention

The issues of recruitment and retention must be solved for the success of any program, especially a program such as Passages, which seeks to provide enhanced treatment for some of the more hard-to-treat methadone clients. Overall recruitment and retention rates for the Passages program at the first two sites were low. Enrollment rates averaged approximately only one in every ten clients from the clinic roster (De Leon, 1990). Attendance was low and steadily decreased during treatment at both site one and site two.

These recruitment and retention rates were confounded by a number of site-specific and startup issues such as space availability, collaboration, and program design. At the present site (site three), most administrative and programming issues have been more adequately resolved. The clinic provides considerable administrative leverage, encouraging client participation in Passages by direct counseling and by mandating attendance at the formal orientation session for all clinic services including Passages. Attendance at the enhanced program remains voluntary, although if irregular it is addressed by both the Passages and clinic staff. Recruitment and attendance have been more successful, but sample size remains a potential problem.

Recruitment Strategies: Mandating Enhanced Treatment

The project experience at the three sites underscores the need for effective strategies to increase recruitment and retention in enhanced methadone treatment. There were three types of factors that influenced the recruitment and retention of clients in a variety of ways, particularly during the initial stages of program launch: clinic factors, client factors, and program factors. In brief, successful recruitment and retention involve collaboration and influence from the clinic (or site), providing clients with outreach and advocacy services as well as an extended opportunity for stability, and the creation of a positive, home- and family-like environment and TC culture.

Recruitment strategies also depended on the nature of the project. In a time-limited demonstration project such as Passages, there is pressure to rapidly develop a treatment sample that is statistically robust for research purposes. Thus, a variety of tactics were considered, including financial incentives and mandating clients to enhanced treatment. However, from the longer range perspective of integrating a program such as Passages into general clinic services, a voluntary approach is more desirable. At the present site, for example, Passages is gradually becoming more attractive to clients and clinic staff based on the clinic's actual experience with Passages program members. Recruitment is facilitated by the positive image of Passages members, who also engage in direct outreach to others, and the accessibility of the program in the form of seminars and an open-house policy. With ample time these factors will most likely establish normative influences on enrollment and be preferable to mandatory pressures.

Nevertheless, mandating the enhanced treatment must be considered if recruitment rates remain below the level necessary for adequate evaluation of the demonstration model. The issue of mandating has been previously addressed in the drug treatment field, particularly in TC programs where external pressure, either by court order or family, resulted in successful outcomes for some clients (e.g., De Leon, 1988; Hubbard et al., 1988).

The incorporation of mandated enhanced treatment into a regular methadone program raises concern about primary treatment obligations to the client. Methadone treatment has often been provided as a "treatment-on-demand," with few constraints placed on eligibility unless noncompliance with the methadone regime is demonstrated over a period of time. Mandating an enhanced treatment would require that continuance in a methadone regime be made contingent on attendance in a enhanced treatment, a policy which is counter to much current practice.

Staff Training

Implementing a modified TC model in methadone settings underscores the need for appropriate staff. The development of this work force involves reorienting experienced TC workers, training current methadone workers in modified TC approaches, and developing a new work force consisting of current methadone clients who have recovery experiences in the modified TC model.

Reorienting staff with TC experience is focused on increasing their understanding of methadone clients, modified TC counseling methods, and the policies and procedures of the methadone field. Retraining of TC workers involves increasing their understanding of the careers and lifestyles of methadone clients, particularly those who are lower functioning, incorporating all of the modifications necessary in the adapted model such as outreach, advocacy, CAPs, and working in a recovery-oriented as opposed to a drug-free model. TC staff need to understand and accept the differences between the methadone client and other former TC clients (including themselves) in motivational level, degree of participation, speed of change, and so on and to incorporate these differences into modified TC treatment strategies.

Two other alternatives exist with regard to the training of a new work force. First is the training of current methadone workers in TC and in modified TC approaches. This strategy has the advantage of building upon the workers' understanding of methadone clients and the methadone treatment system's policies and procedures. The second alternative, training of the existing work force in modified TC approaches, is currently underway in the Stipend Trainee Program presented above.

THE EVALUATION PLAN FOR PASSAGES

The project's evaluation plan involves several comparisons to assess the effectiveness of Passages treatment: (a) profile descriptions of the study sample; (b) before and after changes in treated clients who serve as their own control; (c) changes in the enhanced treated clients vs. a standard treated (methadone only) comparison group; and (d) replication of the model at a different site.

Study Sample. The study sample consists of methadone clients who are eligible and volunteer for Passages and are assigned either to the Passages program or to a delayed treatment comparison group. Eligible clients are those who reflect risk behavior in terms of drug use or sexual practices and who are also free to attend the Passages day program. The specific criteria are: (a) use of cocaine or other substances in the previous thirty days, evident by self-report and/or urine toxicology (of these, the highest priority subjects are needle users); and (b) self-reported high-risk sex practices within the last six months. Clients in all groups are stabilized on methadone for at least thirty days, then followed for at least another thirty days to be considered for eligibility.

Most of the study sample are drawn from recent (i.e., within six months of clinic entry) admissions to the methadone clinic to limit the confounding effects of duration of methadone treatment and the enhanced Passages treatment. However, among eligible clients with longer stays in the clinic, a small number are assigned to one of the groups and followed. This addresses a clinic need to help with difficult clients but also provides some comparison among Passages clients with varying time in methadone treatment.

The two Passages-eligible groups (treated and delayed) provide critical comparisons for the purposes of research. However, other comparison groups are followed. One consists of Passages-eligible clients who refuse or cannot participate in the enhanced treatment but consent to remain in the project. Another group contains clients who are eligible based on the drug-use criteria and do not consent to be interviewed but whose status can be assessed through clinic records.

Assessment. The experimental and comparison cohorts are assessed at three points: baseline, six months, and twelve months. Measures are drawn from the Addiction Severity Index (McLellan et al., 1980), the AIDS Initial Assessment Inventory (National Institute on Drug Abuse, 1988), and the Drug Abuse Treatment for AIDS-Risk Reduction (DATAR) (Simpson, 1991). A psychological test battery is also used, including the Beck Depression Inventory (Beck, 1961), the SCL–90-R-Index Client (Derogatis, Rickels, and Rock, 1975), the Manifest Anxiety Scale (Bendig, 1956), the Diagnostic Interview Schedule (DIS) (Robins et al., 1989), and scales measuring motivation and readiness for treatment, (i.e., the CMRS) (De Leon and Jainchill, 1986).

Random Assignment. Standard random assignment of clients is not used, mainly because of its potentially disruptive effects within the clinic. Instead, a minimal bias assignment procedure, which has been successfully implemented in previous studies of retention (De Leon, 1991c), is used. In this "on/off" procedure, sequential cohorts of eligible admissions during a certain period (e.g., January through March) are enrolled in Passages, and eligible admissions in the following period (e.g., April through June) are assigned to a waiting list. The sequential periods of open-and-closed enrollment continue until the minimal sample size for the research is accomplished (e.g., N <> 90) in each group.

The sample size for Passages is limited by program capacity, time frame, and followup design of the project. Passages day treatment serves a maximum of twenty-five clients. There is a planned treatment duration of six months, with a six-month phase-down period of nighttime after-care groups. Despite these restrictive parameters, the study sample and analytic design provide a valid test of the effectiveness of the Passages program.

SOME PRELIMINARY FINDINGS

The evaluation effort of the Passages program is currently under way at the main experimental site; outcome and progress results are not yet available. However, considerable data of relevance to the initial research aim of the project have been collected at the two earlier sites at which the program was terminated because of poor recruitment. A full exposition of these findings is contained in several reports of the project (De Leon, 1990, 1991a). This section briefly summarizes the findings from these reports based on initial interview assessments and attendance data.

Figure 10.1
Comparison of Average Weekly Attendance at Three Sites

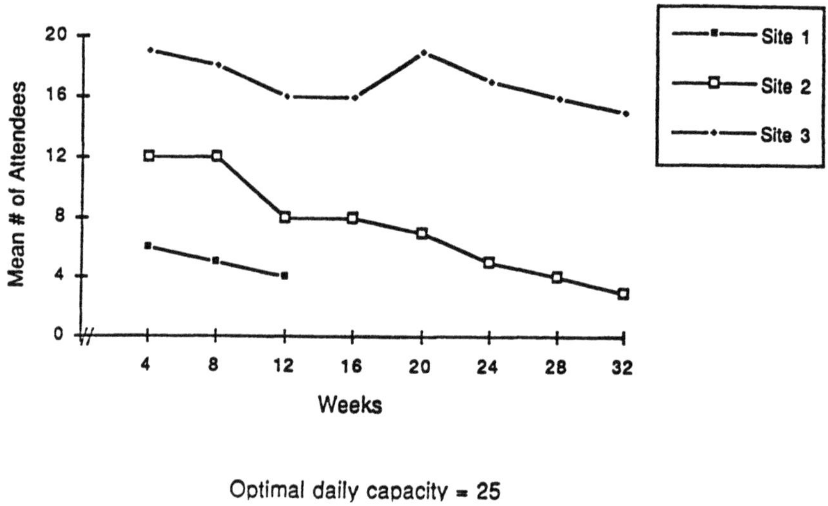

Profiles. Overall, the social and psychological profiles of several hundred clients assessed at both sites reveal considerable dysfunctionality reflected in their nonprescribed drug use, high-risk sexual behavior, poor employment, psychological symptoms, and arrest history. Despite some differences in the severity of dysfunction at site two as compared to site one, client profiles at the different methadone clinics were striking in their similarity. This conclusion is supported in preliminary analysis of profile data collected at the third, current site.

Passages Enrollees. Compared with non-Passages interviewees, the Passages group is clearly more dysfunctional as reflected in their social deficits, poorer psychological scores, and higher current cocaine/crack use. Thus, even among clinic clients who are eligible for Passages (i.e., use of drugs and/or high-risk sexual behavior), those who actually enroll in the enhanced treatment are clearly more socially and psychologically dysfunctional. The implications of this finding for the relevance and effectiveness of the model for particular subgroups of methadone clients remain to clarified in the research at the current site.

Recruitment and Attendance Rates at Three Sites. Overall, there was low recruitment and attendance in the first two sites. The Passages program at the present site three is stable and appears to be developing a sufficient sample size to test the validity of the model. Figure 10.1 shows that weekly attendance at site three is clearly higher and more regular than at sites one and two, which confirms the impression that Passages at site three is functioning more successfully than in the previous trials. Clinical assessments of client status at site three are positive, but firm conclusions on drug use and other variables await quantification.

SUMMARY

Passages is a day treatment program based on TC methods adapted for methadone clients. The goal of the program is to reduce cocaine use/injection and other drug use and high-risk sexual behavior. The Passages approach is grounded in a recovery-oriented perspective, which involves a process of change from a drug-abuse lifestyle to a positive one that is drug-free and prosocial. Methadone is a prescribed medicine that can facilitate the recovery process insofar as clients are committed to the goals of abstinence from all nonprescribed substances and to personal and lifestyle change.

The enhanced program retains what is central to TC methods, that is the peer community with modifications for the methadone client in a day treatment modality. These methods include greater emphasis on outreach and advocacy, increased flexibility in phase format, reduction in the intensity of interpersonal interactions, guided implementation of all new behavioral expectations, and greater responsiveness to individual differences. Key innovations include the integration of an individual Client Action Plan within the group context and the creation of an extended program or Fellowship. It also includes the trainee stipend group, designed to increase the substance abuse work force by providing current methadone clients with training in modified TC methods.

Preliminary findings indicate that there are similarities in client profiles at two sites, with some differences in level of functioning, considerable self-reported drug use at baseline, and greater dysfunction at baseline among Passages clients. At a third site, where the model has been successfully launched, attendance is higher and more regular than at the first two sites. Decreases in drug use and improvement in level of functioning have been clinically observed during the first six months of Passages treatment. A fourth site will be included in the project. Replication of effects at this site will provide an additional test of the model.

The effectiveness of the Passages program remains to be rigorously assessed in subsequent phases of this project. Thus far, however, the feasibility of implementing the model in a freestanding methadone clinic setting has been demonstrated, and clinical changes in the initial cohort of clients at the present site are encouraging. The prospect for generalizing the model to other clinics is optimistic.

ACKNOWLEDGMENTS

The authors acknowledge the contribution of Allen J. Bernhardt, M.S.W., to the conception and launch of the Passages program and Reuben Jimenez, site director, and Michael Guiro, assistant site director, for their dedicated and effective management of the program. The authors also acknowledge the contribution of Ronald Brady, M.D., medical director of the Bridge Plaza Treatment and Rehabilitation Services, Professional Corporation (PC), for his collaboration and support of the project, and Joyce Edwards, treatment administrator, for her assistance and coordination at the Bridge Plaza site.

NOTES

1. Although data are imprecise and still being developed, preliminary findings are: recent cocaine use, 55 percent to 79 percent, and recent cocaine injection, 10 percent to 45 percent (Compton, 1992).

2. Some of the affiliation issues for recovering addicts in TCs are reviewed in De Leon (1991b), and a discussion of fellowship groups in after-care for methadone-maintained clients is presented in Zackon, McAuliffe, and Ch'ien (1985) and Nurco et al. (1983).

REFERENCES

Beck, A. T., C. H. Ward, M. Mendelson, J. Mock, and J. Erbaugh. 1961. An Inventory for Measuring Depression. *Archives of General Psychiatry*, 4, 561–571.

Bendig, A. T. 1956. The Development of a Short Form of the Manifest Anxiety Scale. *Journal of Consulting Psychology*, 20, 384.

Biase, D. V., A. P. Sullivan, and B. Wheeler. 1986. Daytop Miniversity—Phase 2—College Training in a Therapeutic Community—Development of Self-Concept among Drug Free Addict/Abusers. In *Therapeutic Communities for Addictions: Readings in Theory, Research and Practice*, edited by G. De Leon and J. T. Ziegenfuss, pp. 121–130. Springfield, IL: Charles C. Thomas.

Brook, R. C., and I. C. Whitehead. 1980. *Drug Free Therapeutic Community*. New York: Human Science Press.

Cacciola, J., J. Griffith, and A. McLellan. *Addiction Severity Index*: Instruction Manual, 1–33. Unpublished.

Cocaine Abusers in Family and Individual Therapy. 1985. Grant No. RO 1 DA 03916–01 A2. Drug Use History Instrument. New York: Narcotic and Drug Research Inc.

Compton, W. M. 1992. Personal Communication.

De Leon, G. 1984. *The Therapeutic Community: Study of Effectiveness*. NIDA Treatment Research Monograph Series, DHHS Publication No. (ADM) 85–1286. Rockville, MD: National Institute on Drug Abuse.

De Leon, G. 1986. The Therapeutic Community for Substance Abuse: Perspective and Approach. In *Therapeutic Communities for Addictions: Readings in Theory, Research and Practice*, edited by G. De Leon and J. T. Ziegenfuss, pp. 5–18. Springfield, IL: Charles C. Thomas.

De Leon, G. 1987. Alcohol Use Among Drug Abusers: Treatment Outcome in a Therapeutic Community. *Alcoholism: Clinical and Experimental Research*, 2(5), 430–436.

De Leon, G. 1988. Legal Pressure in Therapeutic Communities. In *Compulsory Treatment of Drug Abuse: Research and Clinical Practice*, edited by C. G. Leukefeld and F. M. Tims, pp. 160–175. NIDA Research Monograph 86, DHHS Publication No. 88–1578. Rockville, MD: National Institute on Drug Abuse.

De Leon, G. 1989. *Therapeutic Communities Methods in Methadone Maintenance (Pas-*

sages). Grant application No. R18 DA 06131–01. Rockville, MD: National Institute on Drug Abuse.

De Leon, G. 1990. *Therapeutic Communities Methods in Methadone Maintenance (Passages), Year One Report of Project Activities*. Grant No. R18 DA 06131–02. Rockville, MD: National Institute on Drug Abuse.

De Leon, G. 1991a. *Therapeutic Communities Methods in Methadone Maintenance (Passages), Year Two Report of Project Activities*. Grant No. R18 DA 06131–03. Rockville, MD: National Institute on Drug Abuse.

De Leon, G. 1991b. Aftercare in Therapeutic Communities. *International Journal of the Addictions*, 25(9A, 10A), 1225–1237.

De Leon, G. 1991c. Retention in Drug Free Therapeutic Communities. In *Improving Drug Abuse Treatment*, edited by R. W. Pickens, C. G. Leukefeld, and C. R. Schuster. NIDA Research Monograph No. 106, DHHS Publication No. (ADM) 91–1754.

De Leon, G. 1992. *The Therapeutic Community: Brief Guide to Perspective and Method*. Unpublished manuscript.

De Leon, G., and N. Jainchill. 1981. Male and Female Drug Abusers: Social and Psychological Status Two Years After Treatment in a Therapeutic Community. *American Journal of Drug and Alcohol Abuse*, 8(4), 465–496.

De Leon, G., and N. Jainchill. 1986. Circumstance, Motivation, Readiness and Suitability (CMRS) Scales as Correlates of Treatment Tenure. *Journal of Psychoactive Drugs*, 8(3), 203–208.

De Leon, G., and M. D. Rosenthal. 1989. Treatment in Residential Therapeutic Communities. In *Treatments of Psychiatric Disorders*, edited by T. B. Karasu, pp. 1379–1396. Washington, DC: American Psychiatric Press.

Derogatis, L. R. 1983. *SCL–90-R: Administration, Scoring and Procedures Manual II*. Towson, MD: Clinical Psychometrics Research.

Holland, S. 1986. Psychiatric Severity and Response to Treatment in a Therapeutic Community. In *Bridging Services—Proceedings of the 9th World Conference of Therapeutic Communities*, edited by A. Acampora and E. Nebelkopf, pp. 122–131.

Hubbard, R. L., J. J. Collins, J. V. Rachal, and E. R. Cavanaugh. 1988. The Criminal Justice Client in Drug Abuse Treatment. In *Compulsory Treatment of Drug Abuse: Research and Clinical Practice*, edited by C. G. Leukefeld and F. M. Tims, pp. 57–79. NIDA Research Monograph No. 86, DHHS Publication No. (ADM) 88–1578. Rockville, MD: National Institute on Drug Abuse.

Hubbard, R. L., M. E. Marsden, J. V. Rachal, H. J. Harwood, E. R. Cavanaugh, and H. M. Ginzburg. 1989. *Drug Abuse Treatment: A National Study of Effectiveness*. Chapel Hill: University of North Carolina.

Kennard, D., and S. Wilson. 1979. The Modification of Personality Disorders in a Therapeutic Community for Drug Abusers. *British Medical Journal of Psychiatry*, 52, 215–221.

Lipton, D. S., and S. Magura. 1991. Methadone Maintenance: A Policy Paper. A report for *Criminal Justice Policy Review* for New York State Division of Substance Abuse.

McGahan, P., J. Griffith, R. Parente, et al. Composite Scores from the Addiction Severity Index, 1–14. Unpublished.

McLellan, A. T., G. E. Luborsky, C. P. O'Brien, and G. E. Woody. 1980. An Improved

Diagnostic Evaluation Instrument for Substance Abuse Patients: The Addiction Severity Index. *Journal of Nervous and Mental Disease*, 168(1), 26–33.

Moos, R. 1974. *Ward Atmosphere Scale*. Palo Alto, CA; Consulting Psychologists Press, Inc.

National Institute on Drug Abuse, Treatment Research Branch. 1988. *AIDS Initial Assessment Questionnaire*. Funded by NIDA Treatment Branch, Rockville, MD.

Nurco, D. M., N. Wegner, P. Stephenson, A. Makofsky, and J. W. Shaffer. 1983. *Ex-Addicts Self-Help Groups*. New York: Praeger.

Quintyne, R., and S. Y. Kang. 1992. *Reported AIDS Related Practices of Addicts in a Methadone Maintenance Program*. Proceedings of the Thirteenth Annual Scientific Session, The Society of Behavioral Medicine (March 25–28, New York City).

Rawson, R. A., J. L. Obert, M. J. McCann, and A. J. Mann. 1986. *Cocaine Treatment Outcome: Cocaine Use Following Inpatient, Outpatient, and No Treatment*. NIDA Research Monograph No. 67, DHHS No. (ADM) 86–1448. Rockville, MD: National Institute on Drug Abuse.

Robins, L., J. Helzer, L. Cottler, and E. Goldring. 1989. *NIMH Diagnostic Interview Schedule (DIS), Version III Revised.*

Rounsaville, B., T. Koste, M. Weissman, and H. Keber. 1985. *Evaluating and Treating Depressive Disorders in Opiate Addicts*. Rockville, MD: National Institute on Drug Abuse.

Senay, E. C. 1985. Methadone Maintenance Treatment. *International Journal of the Addictions*, 20(6/7), 803–821.

Simpson, D. D. 1990. *Drug Abuse Treatment for AIDS-Risk Reduction (DATAR) Project*. Fort Worth: Institute of Behavioral Research, Texas Christian University.

Simpson, D. D., and S. Sells. 1982. Effectiveness of Treatment for Drug Abuse: An Overview of the DARP Research Program. *Advances in Alcohol and Substance Abuse Treatment*, 2(1), 7–29.

Sorenson, J. 1985. *Client Attitudes Toward Tapering Interview*. San Francisco: University of California.

Zackon, F., E. E. McAuliffe, and J. Ch'ien. 1985. *Addict Aftercare: Recovery Training and Self-Help*. NIDA Research Monograph Series, DHHS Publication No. (ADM) 85–1341. Rockville, MD: National Institute on Drug Abuse.

Zweben, J. E. 1989. Recovery-Oriented Psychotherapy: Patient Resistances and Therapist Dilemmas. *Journal of Substance Abuse Treatment* 6, 123–132.

11

A Behavioral Model for the Treatment of Cocaine Addiction

R. J. Lamb, Martin Y. Iguchi, Stephen D. Husband, and Jerome J. Platt

Like drug addiction in general, cocaine addiction has two defining characteristics, cocaine-produced reinforcement and cocaine-produced adverse effects. Cocaine functions as a reinforcer in the cocaine addict, as it maintains behavior that leads to its ingestion. Cocaine use produces adverse effects for both the addict and society, and addiction occurs when cocaine use continues despite these adverse consequences. It is important to realize that these adverse consequences include the drug-maintained behavior itself, as this behavior begins to dominate the addict's repertoire to the exclusion of other behaviors and promotes chains of behaviors that include criminal and other antisocial activities related to obtaining drugs. Therefore, the first goal in addiction treatment is the elimination of drug-maintained behavior.

Our understanding of how and why drugs such as cocaine maintain behavior has undergone considerable revision over the last thirty years. A major factor in this revision was the discovery that cocaine and other drugs of abuse were reinforcers not only in the deviant group that the public characterized as drug addicts but in laboratory animals as well (Goldberg, 1976). The study of drugs as reinforcers in laboratory animals (Young and Herling, 1986) produced data incompatible with earlier conceptualizations of drug addiction. Specifically, the conceptualizations that drug addiction is *caused* by certain personality traits, social conditions, or genetic factors have been challenged; instead, these factors are viewed as potential determinants of an individual's vulnerability or susceptibility to drug-produced reinforcement. From this perspective, cocaine-maintained behavior is an example of operant behavior controlled by the same or similar factors and principles as other types of operant behavior (Schuster and

Johanson, 1981; Goldberg and Kelleher, 1977). Unfortunately, cocaine is a very effective and easily established reinforcer, and once established as a reinforcer it can maintain a larger amount of behavior (Griffiths, Bradford, and Brady, 1979) and is frequently chosen over other reinforcers (Aigner and Balster, 1978).

This view of cocaine addiction, as drug-reinforced behavior governed by the same principles as other types of operant behavior, led to a strategy for eliminating cocaine-maintained behavior. This strategy consists of five overlapping and interrelated treatment elements: (1) establishing abstinence; (2) reducing the impact of environmental stimuli that act as discriminative, reinforcing, and eliciting stimuli associated with cocaine use; (3) developing new repertoires of behavior that effectively compete with drug use; (4) eliminating deficits in social and problem-solving skills that increase the probability of relapse; and (5) incorporating technologies for the maintenance of appropriate behaviors.

ESTABLISHING ABSTINENCE

To increase the probability and duration of abstinence we advocate the use of several strategies. These strategies include: (1) the explicit reinforcement of abstinence (i.e., contingency management), (2) instructing the patient how to organize time so that events that initiate behavioral chains leading to drug use are avoided, and (3) the development of skills necessary to respond appropriately to unavoidable high-risk situations.

For most patients, there will be occasions when they are faced with circumstances under which drug use is highly probable. Patients need to be taught to (1) recognize such situations, (2) identify that they represent a high risk, (3) use strategies to escape from or change their situations, and (4) learn from these situations how to avoid similar problems in the future. In order to deal successfully with these high-risk situations, the patient needs to be provided with and rehearse self-instructions (cognitions) and behavioral strategies so that they are readily available when needed.

Instructional control in the form of explicitly scheduling a patient's time outside of the treatment setting is used early in treatment in order to minimize opportunities for drug use and to decrease exposure to stimuli occasioning drug use. In explicitly scheduling a patient's time there are several goals. The first is avoiding early links in the behavioral chain that lead to drug use. These early elements are often easier for the patient to avoid, and, by avoiding them, drug use itself becomes easier to avoid. In developing a plan to avoid these early elements, the therapist must discover what they are for each patient and then assist the patient in understanding the reason for avoiding them. The second goal is scheduling of the patient's time such that early links in the chain leading to drug use are replaced with other behaviors. It is important that these and other protherapeutic behaviors are then followed by events that function as reinforcers of the patient's behavior. Finally, this scheduling of a patient's time is intended to create a structure by which the patient's life becomes more structured.

By helping the patient learn to plan activities so that high-risk situations are avoided, or are effectively dealt with when they are not avoided, abstinence is more likely to occur, be reinforced, and come under contingency control. To assure that abstinence is reinforced early in treatment, a contingency management program is used.

Contingency management has been shown to be effective in changing target behaviors in drug addicts. For instance, Stitzer and her coworkers (1977) showed that, with methadone maintenance clients, making take-home doses of methadone contingent on counseling attendance increases counseling attendance. Also, making take-homes contingent upon the regular payment of clinic fees increases timely fee paying (Stitzer and Bigelow, 1984).

Further, contingency management is effective in reducing drug use in addicts. For instance, Miller (1972) demonstrated that contingency contracting can be used to reduce alcohol intake in alcoholics. Stitzer, Bigelow, and Liebson (1979) demonstrated that, in methadone maintenance clients, reinforcing opiate-free urines with take-home medication privileges or money reduces heroin use, while reinforcing benzodiazepine-free urines with money or take-home privileges reduces benzodiazepine use (Stitizer et al., 1982). Similarly, reinforcing clients for urine free of any illicit substance results in a general decrease in illicit substance abuse (Iguchi et al., 1988).

More relevant, contingency management techniques alone and in combination with other behavioral techniques are effective in reducing cocaine use in cocaine abusers (Crowley, 1986; Higgins et al., 1991). For instance, in the study by Higgins and coworkers (1991), the effects of a behavioral treatment package containing contingency management as one element of the package were compared to a traditional twelve-step program. Patients enrolled in the behavioral treatment package were both more likely to remain in treatment and to achieve significant abstinence than patients assigned to the twelve-step program. It is likely that the changes produced by this contingency management program were enhanced because it was one element in a community reinforcement approach to drug treatment that emphasized the development of alternative repertoires of behavior that compete with drug use (Hunt and Azrin, 1973).

DRUG-RELATED STIMULI

In 1927, Kolb discussed the role played by environmental stimuli in relapse to drug use. Since that time, evidence for the powerful role of environmental determinants in drug-seeking behavior has been empirically derived from laboratory studies of animal and human drug self-administration. These studies have shown that stimuli paired with drug injections can increase behavioral output, retard the extinction of drug-seeking behavior, and reinstate previously extinguished drug-seeking behavior (Goldberg, Schindler, and Lamb, 1990). Another set of laboratory data also supports the role of environmental stimuli in relapse to drug use. In these studies, abstinent cocaine and opioid abusers' conditioned responses to stimuli previously associated with drug use were measured (Childress et al. 1988). These studies demonstrated that conditioned responses occur in response to environmental stimuli, that such responses are associated with self-reports of drug craving, and that such responses and reports of craving can be extinguished by repeated exposure to the eliciting stimuli in the absence of drug administration. Childress and her colleagues (1988) also noted that emotional incidents can reinstate previously extinguished conditioned responses. This emphasizes the importance of the finding that many relapse incidents are associated with negative emotional states such as anger or depression (Brownell et al., 1986).

The importance of the role of environmental stimuli in relapse is further underscored by careful retrospective studies such as those of Vaillant (1969); these studies provide numerous reports consistent with the role of environmental stimuli as major determinants of relapse to drug use. For example, studies of Vietnam veterans addicted to heroin in Vietnam found that, upon return to the United States, most of these individuals ceased heroin use despite having access to heroin (Robins, Davis, and Goodwin, 1974). Veterans most likely to have continued heavy use of heroin were those who had used drugs prior to their service in Vietnam.

Establishing abstinence reduces the effectiveness of environmental and internal stimuli as discriminative, eliciting, and conditioned reinforcing stimuli because they are no longer reliably related to drug use. Thus, they become less effective in occasioning and maintaining drug use and drug-seeking behavior. Therefore, the second treatment goal of reducing the effectiveness of drug-related stimuli is dependent upon achieving the first goal.

COMPETING BEHAVIOR

Increasing the probability and duration of abstinence is made easier when behaviors incompatible with drug use are explicitly arranged to take the place of drug use. Developing such alternative behaviors not only aids in the elimination of drug use but also expedites changes in the discriminative, eliciting, or reinforcing properties of stimuli that previously occasioned or helped maintain drug use and drug-seeking behavior by pairing them with new behaviors and outcomes.

Our efforts concentrate on developing repertoires of behavior that compete with drug use in three different areas: (a) enhancing employment or educational opportunities, (b) improving family and marital relationships, and (c) establishing appropriate leisure activities and social interactions.

One problem patients often face early on in abstinence is the lack of non-drug-related activities. Several strategies are available to address this problem. The first involves identifying both productive and leisure activities for each patient and then scheduling these activities so that they are mutually supporting and reinforcing. In doing this, the therapist models and shapes the personal and interpersonal problem-solving skills the patient needs to acquire. Another strategy is to link the development of protherapeutic leisure activities to the contingency management system. For instance, Higgins and coworkers (1991) reinforced abstinence from cocaine with "points" that patients could use to purchase sporting equipment, health club memberships, and similar things that facilitate alternative behaviors to drug use.

One major determinant of an individual's behavior is the immediate social network of significant others, spouse, or family. Such individuals can provide powerful contingencies and stimuli for either drug use or abstinence. Clearly, when these contingencies and stimuli promote abstinence the patient's likelihood of success is greater. In order to make effective use of these available contingencies, behavioral couples therapy is utilized.

Behavioral couples therapy differs from other marital and family therapies in that it proceeds from a molecular analysis of the family system, which suggests interventions matched to specific target behaviors (Bednar, Burlingame, and Masters, 1988). Based on social learning and operant exchange theories, behavioral couples therapy employs two major operational components. The first involves a clear description of the family system, identifying the target behaviors to be modified. The second involves identification of the stimuli and contingencies regulating these behaviors. Behavioral couples therapy focuses primarily on individual behaviors and the manner in which family members control the contingencies governing these behaviors. Techniques employed in treatment typically are cognitive-behavioral in nature and include prompting, modeling, skill training, behavior rehearsal, and the like (Beck, 1975; Meichenbaum, 1977).

Behavioral couples therapy provides several important benefits to the patient. It helps to eliminate or minimize reinforcement following undesirable behavior in a relationship—for example, enabling. Behavioral couples therapy also helps to create an environment in which appropriate behavior is reinforced and thus "trapped" by its consequences. By removing or diminishing sources of discord and fostering improved communication in significant relationships, this therapy is designed to minimize a set of drug-use-trigger stimuli while creating and reinforcing a set of competing behaviors to drug use.

Obtaining employment can also have a number of important benefits. Employment occupies a large portion of an individual's time, often is incompatible with drug use, and hopefully introduces the patient to non-drug-using acquaintances with whom leisure time many be spent. Further, employment can be maintained by a powerful generalized reinforcer—money—increasing its likelihood of being sustained. Because jobs may come and go due to events over which the patient may have little control, a generalizable set of job-finding and job-keeping skills needs to be taught.

Several areas that need to be addressed in improving a patient's employment situation are: (1) expectations and motivations related to changing the employment situation; (2) job-finding skills; (3) general social and vocational skills; and (4) specific vocational skills. Each of these factors plays an interrelated role in a patient's employment situation.

Programs for developing specific job-finding skills in drug abusers and alcoholics are relatively well documented, such as the Job Finders Club (Azrin, Flores, and Kaplan, 1975) and the Job Seekers Workshop (Hall et al., 1977; Hall et al., 1981a; Hall et al., 1981b). Such programs typically consist of explicating, modeling, practicing, and then implementing the steps necessary in finding and obtaining a job from within an environment that supports the acquisition of these skills in stages.

Identifying appropriate potential jobs for the patient is an important first step, and the expectations and motivations of the patient as well as any specific vocational skills must be taken into account. One cannot expect to acquire and succeed at a job for which one does not have the requisite skills, and if a patient expects that he or she deserves a job for which he or she does not have the required skills, the therapist needs to assist the patient in realistically assessing expectations, skills, and the available alternatives. Otherwise, it is likely that the patient will fail, which may produce negative affective states and unstructured time, which can set the occasion for relapse. A related problem occurs when the patient expects that a job cannot be found no matter how much effort is expended; in this case, the patient often does not see the use of trying and is not motivated to change the situation. In order to overcome this the therapist can utilize several strategies. These include exploring past successes with the patient to show that this expectation is not necessarily true; breaking the process down into small steps that the patient feels he or she is able to accomplish; and helping the patient appreciate the benefits that might accrue with successful employment. This can be done by exploring the benefits of past employment, speculating on the benefits of future employment, and possibly sampling these benefits through the contingency management program.

SKILLS FOR CONTINUED ABSTINENCE

Drug abusers are frequently described as lacking the cognitive and behavioral skills necessary for coping effectively with the social situations and problems that arise in daily living. Maintaining a schedule, showing up on time, using appropriate social skills, and knowing how to solve interpersonal problems in an appropriate manner are all necessary for adequate adjustment and creating the behavioral flexibility necessary for continued abstinence. The absence of such skills can create traps that doom the patient to failure in one area after another, often leading to an undermining of treatment success and setting the occasion for return to drug use.

In the areas of interpersonal cognitive problem solving (Platt and Husband, 1991; Platt and Metzger, 1987; Appel and Kaestner, 1979; Platt, Scura, and Hannon, 1973) and general social skills (Marlatt and Gordon, 1985; Platt and Hermalin, 1989), many substance abusers have clear deficits that can undermine initial success and ultimately lead to failure. This is especially true in situations related to drug refusal (Monti et al., 1988). Substance abusers often tend not to plan ahead or to consider all of the potential consequences of their behavior. Many substance abusers also frequently have difficulty generating viable options and alternatives if their initial, often impulsive, strategy is frustrated. The lack of these basic skills can affect their quality of adjustment and create an increased risk for relapse. Therefore, training in problem-solving and social skills is viewed as essential for patient success.

While not all substance abusers lack appropriate social skills, those who do would appear to be at greater risk for return to drug use. Deficient social skills can undermine successful treatment in several ways. First, a lack of social skills makes the development of successful and maintainable social behaviors that compete with drug use more difficult. Further, such deficiencies frequently result in adverse outcomes from social interactions that can lead to conflict and negative affective states that have, in the past, served as discriminative and eliciting stimuli for drug use. Finally, a history of ongoing failure makes the development of appropriate self-instructional sets, based upon the expectancy and belief of possible success, substantially more difficult. For this reason, it is important to assess the patient's social skills and remedy the observed deficits. Because of the heterogeneity of social skills among cocaine abusers, these skills may be most efficiently developed at an individual level, adapting from one of the well-documented programs in existence for the treatment of groups (Monti et al., 1989). Social skills training should include an explanation of the behaviors to be learned, the reasons for learning these skills, and common mistaken beliefs that people have about these skills. Social skills training includes modeling, rehearsal, feedback, and assignment of specific practice tasks to accomplish in the community. While drug addicts and alcoholics may or may not lack general social skills, they do lack specific skills related to drug refusal and responding appropriately to situations that place them at high risk for drug use. As discussed earlier, these skills need to be developed to facilitate abstinence.

While development of appropriate social skills may reduce the number of interpersonal problems a patient encounters, such problems are an unavoidable part of everyday life. The ability to consistently achieve satisfactory resolution of these problems is important for both adequate social adjustment and for successful recovery. The lack of interpersonal problem-solving skills can undermine recovery in much the same way as the lack of specific social skills: the lack of such skills may hinder the development of behaviors competing with drug use, lead to negative affective states, and result in a continuing history of social failure. Because many drug addicts are deficient in interpersonal problem-solving skills (Appel and Kaestner, 1979; Platt, Scura, and Hannon, 1973), a psychoeducational group approach can be both behaviorally and cost effective: Training in Interpersonal Problem Solving (TIPS) is one such approach (Platt et al., 1988; Platt and Husband, 1991). Like specific social skills training, TIPS includes modeling, rehearsal, feedback, and assignment of specific practice tasks to accomplish in the community. TIPS covers a number of skills prerequisite to effective interpersonal problem solving and fosters the development of skills necessary for interpersonal problem solving such as the generation of alternatives, anticipating the consequences of one's actions, articulating the steps needed to accomplish a particular solution, taking the perspective of others, and understanding how the past affects the present and future. Such training can be effective in increasing interpersonal problem-solving skills among drug addicts.

MAINTENANCE OF BEHAVIOR

Once learned, improved problem-solving and social skills should be maintained because these behaviors are generally and contingently reinforced by the positive outcomes they bring about. In addition to developing these skills and other behaviors that are naturally reinforced in the community, several other technologies to increase the maintenance of therapeutic effects are incorporated into treatment. One such technology is the development of self-instructional sets to avoid lapses and to prevent lapses from becoming relapses. These self-instructional sets may be developed through a procedure known as cognitive restructuring (Marlatt and Gordon, 1985). Further, patients are assigned tasks to accomplish outside of the treatment setting. This is expected to support clients in behaving responsibly when not under the direct supervision of clinic staff, and should increase the generalization of skills they have learned. Also important, this treatment orientation makes clear to patients that they are expected to take an active part in their rehabilitation. Finally, the stimulus control provided by the program for appropriate behavior is faded out over time and replaced by sources of stimulus control within the patient's environment.

Because treatment is delivered in the patient's daily environment, the patient's ongoing success or failure can be monitored. This monitoring allows the therapist to examine which treatment goals are being met and which are not. It also allows the therapist to reinforce and encourage (prompt) appropriate behaviors and to help the patient to problem-solve failures. Further, the patient is taught to be an active participant in treatment in order to experience being an effective mediator of the environment. In developing new behaviors to compete with drug use, care is taken to choose behaviors that will be naturally reinforced and maintained in the patient's daily environment. For this reason, we concentrate on developing behaviors such as employment and appropriate family and social interactions that typically are contingently reinforced in the community. By examining patient success and failure in various areas, the therapist can gain an understanding of how likely these new behaviors are to be self-maintaining and to make adjustments as needed. Ideally, by developing productive behaviors through their own actions, patients begin to describe their role in the world differently—that is, beliefs about self and the world begin to change.

Self-descriptions and self-instructions, also known as beliefs and cognitions, can play an important role in the maintenance of behavioral change. Because of changes in the stimulus properties of environment events and the self-task these events occasion, protherapeutic behaviors are more likely to occur and detrimental behaviors are less likely. For instance, drug use after a period of abstinence can either set the occasion for behaviors such as problem solving, which may help the patient avoid further drug use, or it can set the occasion for complete relapse. Marlatt and Gordon (1985) termed this latter process the abstinence violation effect. In high-risk situations, patients who have been reinforced for effecting positive environmental change and for implementing appropriate sets of self-instructions are more likely to emit such behaviors than those without such a history. Thus, effective therapy aims to build both an appropriate set of cognitions and a history of effectively reinforced appropriate behavior.

One problem associated with intensive treatment programs such as this is that the treatment program itself can become a discriminative stimulus for appropriate behavior. Thus, stimulus control for appropriate behavior may fade with temporal distance from the program, making drug use more likely. Care should be taken to establish natural environmental controls and reinforcement of appropriate behavior while slowly decreasing the explicit role of the treatment environment. This fading of contact builds on the framework of the individual counseling provided earlier but moves from the behaviorally oriented treatment, designed to establish abstinence, to a more cognitively oriented treatment designed to prevent lapses and relapse. The goal of this program is for the patient to move from external to internal sources of behavioral control. Thus, the explicit instructional control of behavior, the explicit external contingencies for abstinence, and the counseling sessions themselves are all diminished over time. Internal sources of control are built upon the foundations of generic problem solving and relapse prevention begun earlier in the treatment program.

SUMMARY

Effective treatment of cocaine addiction, of necessity, utilizes a number of complementary treatment elements to initiate and maintain abstinence. In implementing these treatment elements a variety of behaviorally oriented approaches may need to be used. For instance, a contingency management program primarily may be implemented through individual counseling, while other elements of the behavioral treatment package are implemented through couples therapy. Training in job-finding skills may take place in social work sessions, and interpersonal problem-solving training may take place in groups. By bringing a variety of different treatment approaches to bear in a coordinated manner, the stimuli promoting abstinence are enhanced and the likelihood of success increased. As with any therapeutic approach, however, much of the effectiveness of the program is dependent upon implementation by counselors who are willing and able to utilize appropriate and theoretically sound techniques.

ACKNOWLEDGMENTS

We would like to acknowledge the thoughtful readings and helpful comments on earlier versions of this chapter by Mark Belding and Kimberly Kirby. This work was supported by grant number R18 DA06986 and grant number R18 DA06096 from the National Institution on Drug Abuse.

REFERENCES

Aigner, T. G., and R. L. Balster. 1978. Choice Behavior in Rhesus Monkeys: Cocaine versus Food. *Science*, 201, 534–535.

Appel, P, and E. Kaestner. 1979. Interpersonal and Emotional Problem-Solving among Narcotic Drug Abusers. *Journal of Consulting and Clinical Psychology*, 47, 1125–1127.

Azrin, N. H., T. Flores and S. J. Kaplan. 1975. Job-Finding Club: A Group-Assisted Program for Obtaining Employment. *Behavior Research and Therapy*, 13, 17–27.

Beck, D. F. 1975. Research Findings on the Outcomes of Marital Counseling. *Social Casework*, 56, 153–181.

Bednar, R. L., G. M. Burlingame, and K. S. Masters. 1988. Systems of Family Therapy: Substance or Semantics? *Annual Review of Psychology*, 39, 401–434.

Brownell, K. D., G. A. Marlatt, E. Lichtenstein, and G. T. Wilson. 1986. Understanding and Preventing Relapse. *American Psychologist*, 41(7), 765–782.

Childress, A. R., A. T. McLellan, R. Ehrman, and C. P. O'Brien. 1988. Classically Conditioned Responses in Opioid and Cocaine Dependence: A Role in Relapse? In *Learning Factors in Substance Abuse*, edited by B. A. Ray, pp. 25–43. NIDA Research Monograph No. 84, DHHS No. (ADM), 88–1576. Washington, D.C.: U.S. Government Printing Office.

Crowley, T. J. 1986. Doctors' Drug Use Reduced During Contingency Contracting Treatment. *Alcohol and Drug Research*, 6, 299–307.

Goldberg, S. R. 1976. The Behavioral Analysis of Drug Addiction. In *Behavioral Pharmacology*, edited by S. D. Glick and J. Goldfarb, pp. 283–316. St. Louis: C. V. Mosby Co.

Goldberg, S. R., and R. T. Kelleher. 1977. Reinforcement of Behavior by Cocaine Injections. In *Cocaine and Other Stimulants*, edited by E. H. Ellinwood, Jr., and M. M. Kilbey, pp. 523–544. New York: Plenum Press.

Goldberg, S. R., C. W. Schindler, and R. J. Lamb. 1990. Second-Order Schedules and the Analysis of Human Drug-Seeking Behavior. *Drug Development Research*, 20, 217–229.

Griffiths, R. R., L. D. Bradford, and J. V. Brady. 1979. Progressive Ratio and Fixed Ratio Schedules of Cocaine-Maintained Responding in Baboons. *Psychopharmacology*, 65, 125–136.

Hall, S. M., P. Loeb, K. Coyne, and J. Cooper. 1981a. Increasing Employment in Ex-Heroin Addicts I: Criminal Justice Sample. *Behavior Therapy*, 12, 443–452.

Hall, S. M., P. Loeb, M. LeVois, and J. Cooper. 1981b. Increasing Employment in Ex-Heroin Addicts II: Methadone Maintenance Sample. *Behavior Therapy*, 12, 453–460.

Hall, S. M., P. Loeb, J. Norton, and R. Yang. 1977. Improving Vocational Placement in Drug Treatment Clients: A Pilot Study. *Addictive Behaviors*, 2, 227–234.

Higgins, S. T., D. D. Delaney, A. J. Budney, W. K. Bickel, J. R. Hughes, F. Foerg, and J. W. Fenwick. 1991. A Behavioral Approach to Achieving Initial Cocaine Abstinence. *American Journal of Psychiatry*, 148, 1218–1224.

Hunt, G. M., and N. H. Azrin. 1973. A Community Reinforcement Approach to Alcoholism. *Behavioral Research and Therapy*, 11, 91–104.

Iguchi, M. Y., M. L. Stitzer, G. E. Bigelow, and I. A. Liebson. 1988. Contingency Management in Methadone Maintenance: Effects of Reinforcing and Aversive Consequences on Illicit Polydrug Use. *Drug and Alcohol Dependence*, 22, 1–7.

Kolb, L. E. 1927. Clinical Contribution to Drug Addiction: The Struggle for Cure and the Conscious Reasons for Relapse. *Journal of Nervous and Mental Disorders*, 66, 32–43.

Marlatt, G. A., and J. R. Gordon 1985. *Relapse Prevention: Maintenance Strategies in the Treatment of Addictive Behaviors*. New York: Guilford Press.

Meichenbaum, D. H. 1977. *Cognitive Behavior Modification*. New York: Plenum.

Miller, P. M. 1972. The Use of Behavioral Contracting in the Treatment of Alcoholism: A Case Report. *Behavior Therapy*, 3, 593–596.

Monti, P. M., D. B. Abrams, R. M. Kadden, and N. L. Cooney. 1989. *Treating Alcohol Dependence: A Coping Skills Training Guide*. New York: Guilford Press.

Monti, P. M., D. J. Rohsenow, D. B. Abrams, and J. A. Binkoff. 1988. Social Learning Approaches to Alcohol Relapse: Selected Illustrations and Implications. In *Learning Factors in Substance Abuse*, edited by B. A Ray, pp. 141–160. NIDA Research Monograph No. 84. DHHS No. (ADM) 88–1576. Washington, DC: U.S. Government Printing Office.

Platt, J., and J. Hermalin. 1989. Social Skill Deficit Interventions for Substance Abusers. *Psychology of Addictive Behaviors*, 3, 114–133.

Platt, J. J., and S. D. Husband. 1991. Interpersonal Cognitive Problem-Solving Interventions with Addicts. In *Community-based AIDS Prevention: Studies of Intravenous Drug Users and Their Sexual Partners*, pp. 316–323. Proceedings of the First Annual NADR Meeting. DHHS Publication No. (ADM) 91–1752. Rockville, MD: National Institute on Drug Abuse.

Platt, J. J., and D. S. Metzger. 1987. Cognitive Interpersonal Problem-Solving Skills and the Maintenance of Treatment Success in Heroin Addicts. *Psychology of Addictive Behaviors*, 1(1), 5–13.

Platt, J., W. Scura, and J. Hannon. 1973. Problem-Solving Thinking of Youthful Incarcerated Heroin Addicts. *Journal of Community Psychology*, 1, 278–281.

Robins, L. N., D. H. Davis, and D. W. Goodwin. 1974. Drug Use by U.S. Army Enlisted Men in Vietnam: A Follow-up on Their Return Home. *American Journal of Epidemiology*, 99, 235–249.

Schuster, C. R., and C. E. Johanson. 1981. An Analysis of Drug-Seeking Behavior in Animals. *Neuroscience Biobehavioral Reviews*. 5, 315–323.

Stitzer, M. L., and G. E. Bigelow. 1984. Contingent Methadone Take-Home Privileges: Effects on Compliance with Fee Payment Schedules. *Drug and Alcohol Dependence*, 13, 395–399.

Stitzer, M. L., G. E. Bigelow, C. Lawrence, J. Cohen, B. D'Lugoff, and J. W. Hawthorne. 1977. Medication Take-Home as a Reinforcer in a Methadone Maintenance Program. *Addictive Behaviors*, 2, 9–14.

Stitzer, M. L., G. E. Bigelow, and I. Liebson. 1979. Reinforcement of Drug Abstinence: A Behavioral Approach to Drug Abuse Treatment. In *Behavioral Analysis and Treatment of Substance Abuse*, edited by N. A. Krasnegor, pp. 68–90. NIDA

Research Monograph No. 25, DHEW Publication No. (ADM) 79–839. Washington, DC: U.S. Government Printing Office.

Stitzer, M. L., G. E. Bigelow, I. A. Liebson, and J. W. Liebson, and J. W. Hawthorne. 1982. Contingent Reinforcement for Benzodiazepine-Free Urines: Evaluation of a Drug-Abuse Treatment Intervention. *Journal of Applied Behavioral Analysis*, 15, 493–503.

Vaillant, G. E. 1969. The Natural History of Urban Narcotic Drug Addiction—Some Determinants. In *Scientific Basis of Drug Dependence*, edited by H. Steinberg, pp. 311–361. London: J.& A. Churchill.

Young, A. M., and S. Herling. 1986. Drugs as Reinforcers: Studies in Laboratory Animals. In *Behavioral Analysis of Drug Dependence*, edited by I. Stollerman and S. R. Goldberg, pp. 9–67. New York: Academic Press.

12

Cognitive Enhancements to Treatment in DATAR: Drug Abuse Treatment for AIDS Risks Reduction

D. Dwayne Simpson, Lois R. Chatham, and George W. Joe

It is widely agreed that drug abuse treatment can be effective for many drug users (see Anglin and Hser, 1990; Ball and Ross, 1991; De Leon, 1989; Gerstein and Harwood, 1990; Hubbard et al., 1989; Pickens, Leukefeld, and Schuster, 1991; Platt, Husband, and Taube, 1990–1991; Simpson and Sells, 1982, 1990; Tims and Ludford, 1984). As noted by Rawson (1990–91), however, sociopolitical factors and the increasing spread of AIDS among intravenous drug users (IVDUs) during the 1980s have had a major impact on the substance abuse treatment system in the United States. Economic inflation in the last decade resulted in declining financial support for drug abuse services, which were already underfunded. At the same time, efforts to respond to the AIDS epidemic among IVDUs have created pressures to spread scarce treatment services even further. As a result, in order to enlarge service delivery capacity, major attempts have been made to reduce or remove important aspects of therapeutic regimens such as methadone maintenance regulations and counseling intensity. Such changes in clinical practice, many believe, may erode the integrity of the national treatment system.

After years of neglect, the AIDS crisis had the effect of sharply increasing federal research funds during the late 1980s, including grants allocated to develop and evaluate psychosocial intervention programs for drug users. The projects described in this book were funded by the National Institute on Drug Abuse for the purpose of exploring enhancements to treatment effectiveness, thereby reducing the spread of HIV and the AIDS virus, associated with sharing injection equipment as well as drug-related sexual activities.

The Drug Abuse Treatment for AIDS Risks Reduction (DATAR) project described in this chapter shares the general goals stated above. It is a direct outgrowth of the Institute of Behavioral Research (IBR) treatment evaluation research program conducted since 1970, especially studies carried out as part of the Drug Abuse Reporting Program (DARP, see Simpson and Sells, 1982, 1990). In particular, the DARP studies helped establish that "treatment works" and that posttreatment outcomes improve in direct relation to the length of time clients stay in treatment (Simpson, 1979, 1981). The most effective intervention strategies and the essential elements involved in the therapeutic process, however, are yet to be identified. For that reason, it is important to conduct research that places special emphasis on measuring and assessing treatment process—loosely defined as the interactions involving client and counselor attributes, service delivery, and program structure.

The purpose of the DATAR project is to improve treatment retention, reduce drug abuse relapse rates, and improve psychosocial adjustment of IVDUs through enhanced intervention strategies. Simultaneously, innovative approaches are used for identifying some of the crucial therapeutic elements that contribute to greater treatment efficacy. Implementation of the project has taken place in four general stages. First, a multi-site study design has been selected in which funds have been provided to three multi-modality community-based drug abuse treatment agencies for the delivery of DATAR services. Second, enhancements to the therapeutic process have been conceptualized in terms of a comprehensive intervention sequence based on some of the most promising strategies available and incorporating "cognitive learning" principles. Third, an integrated data collection system has been developed that provides extensive behavioral and psychosocial assessments of clients, counselors, and the treatment process over time. Finally, a project management system has been created that provides clinical training resources as well as the monitoring of counseling services, data collection, and DATAR-related agency performance. The latter activity has required the establishment of a management information system, which serves both IBR and the agencies with easily understood information about performance. Each of these stages is described below in more detail.

DESCRIPTION OF TREATMENT AGENCY SELECTIONS

In order to expand treatment opportunities for IVDUs considered at highest risk of HIV exposure, state-licensed public nonprofit agencies located in Corpus Christi, Dallas, and Houston, Texas, were selected as collaborators in the DATAR project. Each is a large, multi-modality community-based treatment agency providing methadone maintenance (MM) and outpatient drug-free services. However, only MM clients are included in this project. DATAR funds are used to provide nonfee services to an average of 120 MM clients at each site. This number represents less than half of the total MM treatment capacity of these agencies. Overall, comparable numbers of African-American, Anglo, and Mexican-American clients are expected to be served. The average age at admission is 35, and about one-third of the admissions are females. In addition to heroin, cocaine use is a highly prominent drug abuse problem.

Each counselor carries an average client caseload of twenty and also is responsible for maintaining DATAR records. Each agency operates its own inhouse urine-testing laboratory (using the Cyva Emit System) for monitoring program compliance as well as compliance with Food and Drug Administration (FDA) regulations.

MAPPING AS A COGNITIVE ENHANCEMENT TO COUNSELING

Several of the most promising intervention strategies were selected for use in the DATAR project, similar to ones identified in recent treatment review articles by Brown (1990–1991) and Condelli and colleagues (1991). They include a range of psychoeducational, cognitive, behavioral, and skills-training approaches to be used in an integrated intervention sequence. It is hypothesized that these strategies and the therapeutic context for their delivery can be *enhanced* by the use of "mapping"—a cognitive learning strategy designed to improve the fundamental step of information input and cognitive integration (see Dansereau, 1985; Lambiotte et al., 1989; Evans and Dansereau, 1991). The incorporation of mapping as part of the counseling process is the most unique aspect of treatment enhancements in the DATAR project.

The rationale for considering a cognitive enhancement approach in the therapeutic process is based on the assumption that an accurate understanding of one's behavioral problems and related risk information is needed to facilitate rational and long-range decision making. The impulsive and hedonistic coping style characteristic of many drug abusers is antagonistic to this goal. As a result, "lectures" with low cognitive involvement are ineffective. Platt and his colleagues (Platt and Metzger, 1987; Platt et al., 1988) explored similar issues and found that addicts have conceptual difficulties in means-end thinking, involving step-by-step problem solving. They identified five major skills needed: (1) alternative thinking, (2) consequential thinking, (3) means-end thinking, (4) perspective taking, and (5) social-casual thinking. A broad-based program called Training in Interpersonal Problem Solving (TIPS) has been used by Platt to address these skills deficits.

The research program of Dansereau and his associates at Texas Christian University since the late 1970s has yielded a large body of evidence showing the effectiveness of mapping as a "thinking" tool. With only minor modifications, it also appears to be applicable to drug abuse treatment objectives. Much of Dansereau's earlier work involved the use of knowledge applications among college students, but the techniques have also been used with grade-school students and appear to be effective across a wide range of ages and levels of education. These methods are currently being applied to the field of drug abuse education and prevention at the high school and college levels (see Dees et al.,

1991; Dees, Dansereau, Peel, Knight, and Loftis, forthcoming; Dees et al., 1992). Dansereau currently is collaborating with IBR staff to adapt mapping to the drug abuse counseling process.

Mapping represents a blend of various attitudinal, memory processing, and skills learning models proposed to account for the flow from externally presented information to behavior change (see Boatler et al., 1992). In essence, it is believed that mapping serves as a communication tool to improve information storage and retrieval, which in turn facilitates cognitive integration of knowledge with resulting behavioral implications. Three forms of mapping—information, process, and reference—are used in the DATAR project. *Information mapping* stresses efficient transfer of knowledge; *process mapping* addresses time-related and conceptual processes involved in sequential transactions and the identification of factors influencing individual decisions and actions; and *reference mapping* provides graphic illustrations of a large, complex body of information useful in educational training sessions. Mapping is performed in a manner similar to that used in the construction of organizational flow charts, but with rules involving links and nodes for defining and labeling relationships between connecting ideas.

Procedurally, DATAR counselors are formally trained to use mapping techniques (especially process mapping) as part of individual and group counseling. Information and reference mapping are incorporated as part of several psychoeducational and intervention training modules.

COMPONENTS OF THE INTERVENTION PROCESS

The intervention process used in the DATAR project is conceptualized in five major (and sometimes overlapping) phases: (1) background and psychosocial assessments, (2) AIDS psychoeducation, (3) cognitive assessments and goal setting, (4) behavioral intervention, and (5) life skills and maintenance training. In general, each phase involves manual-driven data collection procedures and intervention training modules. These manuals are available on request.

Phase 1: Background and Psychosocial Assessments

The social history interview conducted at intake by many treatment agencies is open-ended and narrative in format, making electronic data storage, retrieval, and analysis difficult. Such narrative interviews frequently are augmented by the Addiction Severity Index (ASI, see McLellan et al., 1980) as a brief behavioral and psychosocial assessment. Routine professional testing and psychological services seldom are available or affordable at community-based drug treatment agencies, and some important client characteristics (such as antisocial tendencies and motivation levels) have been difficult to assess even within formal psychological test protocols. Another consideration for outpatient programs is that the amount of time allocated for client assessments is often limited by the length of scheduled appointments and client attention span.

Client assessments are conducted at the time of admission to DATAR using the *intake form*. This is a comprehensive interview schedule with precoded behaviorally based responses, developed on the basis of past treatment evaluation research experiences, advice from other researchers in the field, and formal reviews and input by the counseling staff. It includes sociodemographic background, family background, peer relations, criminal history, health and psychological status, drug history, and AIDS risk assessment. In addition, counselor comments and ratings of client problem severity using expanded ASI-type problem domains (which also are used in staff reviews to discuss new intakes) are included at the end of the structured interview.

A brief *self-rating form* is used to assess the client's self-perceived psychosocial functioning and motivation. It contains seven- to ten-item scales representing psychological functioning (self-esteem, depression, anxiety, decision making), social functioning (childhood problems, hostility, risk taking, socialization), and motivation for treatment (self-assessment of drug use, desire for help, and treatment readiness). The form is prepared specifically for drug treatment clients, and the scales have favorable psychometric properties. This form meets the objective of providing client information for several domains believed to be important for predicting treatment outcomes. For example, motivational assessments may be especially important for the prediction of short-term dropouts (see De Leon and Jainchill, 1986). With further study, the self-rating form response format will be amenable to conversion to a computer-administered instrument. A Spanish version of the form also is available.

Phase 2: AIDS Psychoeducation

Public health, drug abuse treatment agencies, and community-outreach programs for IVDUs (see Brown, 1991) have developed AIDS-relevant information and education programs, but these have not been adequately evaluated because of the short amount of time they have been in effect. Therefore, one of the major DATAR intervention modules focuses on providing information about AIDS-risky behaviors. As summarized in a recent review by the Office of Technology Assessment (1988), however, it is clear that knowledge by itself does not sufficiently motivate IVDUs to change risky needle use or sexual behaviors. Modifications of voluntary health behaviors appear to require several elements, as noted in previous research based on the Health Belief Model (Janz and Becker, 1984). These include individual perceptions concerning personal susceptibility, barriers to change, benefits expected to occur, and severity of the consequences of high-risk behaviors.

The *AIDS/HIV Module* (Boatler, 1991) describes a sequence of four group sessions and two individual sessions designed to deliver knowledge about HIV and AIDS-risky activities and to explore behavioral alternatives. Information and reference maps are used to present target information, ranging from common myths about AIDS to technical medical information concerning transmission of the virus and treatment. This strategy is expected to result in improved understanding and recall of information about AIDS-risky behaviors and to link this information to perceived behavioral consequences. In addition, it should make clients more aware of their personal susceptibility, the benefits of behavior changes, and the severity of the consequences of AIDS—three of the four elements important for change according to the Health Belief Model. Preliminary evidence supports the efficacy of this training module for increasing knowledge and reducing risky, behaviors, especially during the first few months of treatment (Boatler, Knight, and Simpson, 1991).

Phase 3: Cognitive Assessments and Goal Setting

In addition to the need to understand AIDS-risk factors within an appropriate cognitive framework, it is necessary for the counselor and client to have clear communication about other problems and solutions surrounding drug-related behaviors. Early treatment is a critical period of time for client dropouts, and improvements in communication are expected to contribute to better retention. The process of cognitive appraisal (e.g., Annis and Davis, 1988) is central to this phase and is at the basis of understanding behavioral consequences, setting new goals, forming expectations, and considering coping strategies. To accomplish this, the mapping approach described earlier is extended directly into the general counseling sessions of the intervention process. By using "bottom-up" mapping information and process to retrace current problem behaviors that brought the client into treatment, the counselor can recreate and elaborate on sequential events involved in critical decisions and behavioral outcomes. Part of the purpose of the counselor at this stage is to raise enough "cognitive dissonance" within the client to cause the client to consider making significant behavioral changes (Donovan, 1988).

This learning strategy process is practiced with the client to explore goal-setting options in a step-by-step sequence. The goal of this process is to enable the client to see that good decision making examines behavioral alternatives while recognizing or anticipating behavioral consequences. Examples of applications include drug using and sexual situations as well as routine daily activities such as financial budgeting, completing household chores, and so on. Both information and process maps are used by counselors as the basis of the cognitive appraisal process, as a means of facilitating communication, and as an aid in the organization of the therapeutic process over time. For example, counselors are asked to produce a map during or at the end of each session to summarize issues addressed and to use these maps to provide continuity in focus from one session to the next. It is believed that even clients at low literacy levels can learn to map their knowledge, attitudes, and beliefs about their problems and relevant coping strategies. Copies of the maps created during counseling sessions are tabulated and filed for review by clinical supervisory staff and are expected to be useful in evaluating counseling process and recurrent client problems.

Phase 4: Behavioral Intervention Techniques

As discussed by Grabowski, Stitzer, and Henningfield (1984), behavioral intervention techniques include a wide assortment of strategies (e.g., behavior modification, behavior therapy, contingency contracting and management, and token economy), all based on operant principles, to guide and reinforce goal-directed changes. Although their formal transition from the laboratory to general clinical settings has been limited in the drug abuse field, Bigelow, Stitzer, and Liebson (1984) reported some promising results with contingency management (CM) procedures that seem highly applicable to MM treatment settings. This strategy also is conceptually and procedurally well-integrated with the cognitive assessment and goal-setting phase already discussed.

Reinforcement parameters suggested by the work of Stitzer and Bigelow for contingency manipulation in MM programs include methadone take-home privileges, medication schedules, clinic attendance and urinalysis schedules, counseling requirements, and treatment fees. Important elements in its implementation involve selection of appropriate (and available) positive reinforcers within the context of a packaged contingency plan well-tailored to the goals for each individual client. Behavioral criteria must be explicit and readily measured, including on-site urinalysis, to maximize immediacy of the contingencies.

An early application of CM in the DATAR project (Rowan-Szal, Simpson, and Holcom, 1992) addressed the need to improve attendance at scheduled group and individual counseling sessions and to submit "clean" urines. Procedurally, each counselor made a posterboard in his or her office with clients identified only by coded client ID numbers, on which records of individual performance were recorded. Adhesive stars were attached to the board to represent each session attended on time and each occasion urinalysis results tested negative. Reinforcements included a small "acknowledgment" gift (e.g., candy bar, gum, soda, or chips), which the client was allowed to select from a basket on the counselor's desk for each star earned, and a larger gift (e.g., food or gas coupons, bus tokens, sunglasses, and t-shirts), which was earned only after accruals of several stars. Preliminary evidence suggests these efforts can be used effectively to improve targeted behaviors, and that even using stars on a community bulletin board to provide simple acknowledgments of behavioral progress and encourage social comparisons may have a positive impact.

In the long run, however, CM reinforcement parameters should become generalized as Donovan (1988) suggested and gradually be transferred from the treatment agent to other authorities in the environment of the client (and internalized) in order for the effects to endure over time. That is, the interactive role of family, friends, and employers as behavioral reinforcers must be strengthened.

Procedurally, this could include the involvement of a spouse or "significant other" in a positive support role in the treatment process, as suggested by the work of Sorensen and Bernal (1987). Success in recruiting and involving such support as well as its behavioral impact on client outcomes needs further attention, especially with regard to Mexican-American cultural traditions and women.

Phase 5: Life Skills and Maintenance Training

Adoption of, and adjustment to, a drug-free lifestyle requires many personal and socioenvironmental changes. The CM intervention strategy is designed to reinforce appropriate behavioral changes, but it does not necessarily cause appropriate behaviors to be elicited or to be maintained indefinitely. Continued counselor guidance and special-needs training are the sources for many initial client changes, which may then be reinforced and later sustained through social support networks. As noted by Platt and Metzger (1987), these changes may require development of some new personal skills in interpersonal problem solving and improved self-esteem that contribute to self-efficacy. Also required are learning how to assess and deal with temporary setbacks or failures in short-term goals, such as relapses, and how to recognize and avoid environmental situations (or cues) that threaten targeted behavior changes.

Several specific training modules that appear applicable to these needs are scheduled to be developed and tested over the course of the DATAR project, but not all clients will receive every type of module. Most modules will be planned to last no more than four to eight weeks, scheduled in conjunction with local needs and circumstances at each individual agency. Particular attention is given to assertiveness training, relapse prevention training, and support training.

Assertive Training (AT). Based on her review of research on drug-dependent women, Doyle (1982) concluded that "dependency, low self-esteem, high levels of anxiety, limited interpersonal and resource networks, and difficulty in negotiating with others are consistently reported to be more common in drug dependent women than they are in men with similar drug problems" (p. 214). These problems seem to be even more accentuated among Mexican-American women because of their adult male-dominated society and the practice of "machismo," which are characteristic of Hispanic cultures. These problems are consistent with reported treatment experiences in Texas.

The Corpus Christi and Dallas agencies each operate specialized women's treatment components in their programs, focusing primarily on health promotion and education strategies. Because women clients are faced with increased threats of exposure to HIV through needle sharing and sex with IVDU husbands and boyfriends, it is important to address the potential need for these women to develop assertiveness, communication, and health-care skills. Doyle (1982) discusses AT and explains assertiveness as involving the ability to recognize one's rights and responsibilities in a situation and to be able to respond in a manner that preserves them.

In response to the needs of women in drug treatment for interventions that address self-esteem, communication skills, and preventive health information involving safer sex strategies, DATAR staff developed a six-session module entitled "Time Out! For Me." Each two-hour group meeting is designed to be facilitated by women counselors at the DATAR sites who are given special training on implementing the module. Right or wrong, the term "assertiveness" is often viewed negatively among women, especially women from ethnic cultures that stress passivity as a virtue. Therefore, within the context of the Time Out! module, the terms "communicating effectively" or "getting through to people about your needs, thoughts, and feelings"—rather than "assertiveness"—are used. Much of the content, however, is based on classic assertiveness training.

The Time Out! module focuses on communication skills within the situational context of women's intimate sexual relationships, with the goal of increasing self-esteem, enhancing communication effectiveness, and improving knowledge and attitudes about sexual and reproductive health—including the adoption of preventive health measures such as breast self-examination and routine Pap tests and pelvic exams. Safer sex strategies for avoiding HIV infection and other sexually transmitted infections are also stressed.

The importance of I-statements, listening skills, nonverbal communication, and effective refusal are discussed in a small group format with opportunity to practice these skills through role play and the creation by participants of situational scripts that incorporate effective communication styles. Videos, overhead transparencies, instructional flip charts, anatomical teaching models, and handouts are used to enhance knowledge and maintain interest. The Time Out! manual uses a step-by-step format to guide facilitators. Materials for producing handouts and transparencies are included in the manual, along with activity sheets, session evaluation forms, and a pretest/posttest instrument.

Relapse Prevention Training (RPT). The benefits associated with training clients to recognize and accept the possibility of having a temporary relapse and teaching them how to develop response alternatives have been demonstrated in work by Marlatt and associates (Marlatt and Gordon, 1980; Marlatt and George, 1984). Education about early warning signs as well as psychological and environmental circumstances that tend to trigger relapse is therefore expected to be useful in helping some clients avoid high-risk situations. As reviewed by Tims and Leukefeld (1986) studies have shown that relapse rates are very high, especially in the first few months after treatment. The psychological impact of a lapse can be cushioned by proper education, which includes training the client to recognize that a lapse, if handled correctly, need not progress to full-blown relapse.

The RPT module used in the DATAR project is based on six lessons selected from a manual entitled *Addict Aftercare: Recovery Training and Self-Help* (RTSH) (Zakon, McAuliffe, and Ch'ien, 1985). A form of psychosocial treatment for drug addiction, RTSH was originally developed as an outpatient group after-care modality. RPT is an abbreviated version of RTSH and has been adapted to meet the particular needs of DATAR clients (Knight and Simpson, 1992). It consists of lessons ranging in focus from identifying the various stages of recovery to identifying and learning how to handle high-risk situations. In addition to the educational component, the client's own experiences along with the experiences of others are an integral part of RPT. For example, information maps, worksheets, and role playing are utilized to assist in the integration of acquired lesson information with relevant personal experience.

Support Training (ST). One of the most common self-help support group concepts today in the alcohol and drug abuse field involves Alcoholics Anonymous (AA), Narcotics Anonymous (NA), and Cocaine Anonymous (CA), as well as Al Anon, Co-Dependency Anonymous (CODA), and Families Anonymous (FA) for the families of addicts. Unfortunately, these and other after-care approaches designed to assist with community reintegration of addicts are often poorly attended by many community treatment agency referrals, and they have not been adequately evaluated because of problems in program implementation (Hawkins and Catalano, 1985).

Although comprehensive and well-designed after-care evaluations are very difficult, after-care efforts should be tried and assessed as part of ST during treatment. Educating both the client and the treatment staff about the after-care alternatives that are available in the community, the basic philosophies represented (e.g., twelve-step and self-help), the operating structures, and the benefits and challenges to be expected may help improve client referral and participation success. This process may also help identify strengths and weaknesses of existing programs and lead to the creation of new self-help groups supervised, or sponsored by, the treatment agency itself.

Another important after-care resource is a "significant other" (SO) support person, or network of friends and family members. Within the AIDS risk reduction objectives of this project, the involvement of SOs becomes even more significant if they represent sexual partners or drug use partners. Work by Sorensen and Bernal (1987) on drawing family members or SOs into treatment participation with MM clients suggests the value of such efforts. Thus, a separate adjunct to the ST training is needed to examine the role of SOs in intervention—that is, their recruitment into the treatment setting for periodic sessions and the impact of this on client outcomes. SO recruitment strategies need to be developed and evaluated (especially for Mexican-American IVDUs), based on low-intervention efforts (e.g., informal client invitations to SOs) versus high-intervention efforts (e.g., formal agency written requests conveyed through clients, or personal requests by counselors to participate with clients in designated group sessions). Part of the SO intervention strategy focuses on AIDS-risk education as well as appropriate family/support group behaviors.

INTEGRATED DATA COLLECTION SYSTEM

Treatment evaluation studies in the past have usually examined each modality as a "black box" without penetrating its exterior. Further advancements require that the intervention process be fractioned into separate components and examined in more detail. As suggested by Finney and Moos (1986), this first requires attention to the development of therapeutic components that address client needs and to the proper delivery of intended services. Second and equally important is the simultaneous assessment of client deficits (such as psychopathology-related limitations, see McLellan, 1986) and resources (such as social and coping skills), along with psychological abilities (including information processing, reasoning, and problem-solving skills, see Platt et al., 1988). Especially critical to the entire intervention process is an effective communication and education model that enhances information storage and decision making of clients in the therapeutic exchange.

Particular emphasis is therefore placed on examining "treatment process," including what takes place in counseling sessions and the interactions between counselor and client. These data are gathered through an integrated set of DATAR data collection instruments administered at intake and periodically throughout treatment. With collaborative inputs from other treatment evaluation researchers as well as DATAR treatment program staff, they have undergone numerous cycles of review, revision, and retesting. These forms are currently in use at the treatment agencies participating in the DATAR project. Data are sent to the central research staff at the IBR each week, where they are edited, keyed, and "cleaned." Based on the continuous monitoring and analysis of field information, these instruments are revised periodically to improve psychometric properties and measurement efficiency.

The forms are completed by counselors, clients, and a data coordinator at each DATAR site. Following intake, a battery of forms dealing with client behavioral and psychological status, as well as the therapeutic process, is repeated at the end of treatment months one, two, three, six, nine, and twelve. This schedule provides for quarterly assessments during treatment in the first year (or until termination), with more intensive monthly data collection during the first quarter. In addition, separate forms are completed for each client counseling session—including individual, group, family, and other—and an overall tracking record is maintained for monitoring client services throughout the course of treatment. Posttreatment followup forms for conducting face-to-face interviews one year after termination include most of the same information collected at intake. To insure uniformity in data collection, all new staff at the treatment sites are trained by the DATAR research staff on the administration of forms.

The *intake form* includes sections on sociodemographic background, family and peer relations, health and psychological status, criminal involvement, and drug history. Average administration time is sixty minutes. The *self-rating form* is completed (in ten minutes) by the client immediately prior to the intake interview, often while waiting for the session to begin. It includes short scales for psychosocial functioning and motivational assessments, as described earlier. These scales, however, are not used as clinical diagnostic instruments. This form also is administered as part of the monthly battery given at the end of each successive month in treatment.

After each therapeutic contact, a *counseling session report* is completed by the counselor (in five minutes), which describes the length and type of session as well as the issues addressed. At the end of the first month and at successive time intervals, a battery of other during-treatment forms is completed. The *monthly status report* is completed during an individual counseling session (ten to fifteen minutes) and reassesses major behavioral criteria—such as employment, criminal involvement, AIDS-risky behavior, and drug use—during the past month; these questions represent a subset of the intake form. The *client evaluation of treatment*, completed by the client in five minutes, obtains client ratings of the counselor and the program in general. This form is not made available to the counselor for review but is sent directly to the IBR research staff after being completed in a private setting apart from the counselor's office. The *counselor evaluation of client* is completed by the counselor (five minutes) for the purpose of describing client functioning and therapeutic strategies used during the past month.

The *client tracking form* serves as the overall monitoring record of client services and transactions and is updated monthly by data coordinators at each site. The report contains information on counseling session attendance (including missed appointments), methadone dosage and other medications prescribed, urinalyses results, ancillary services provided, and treatment termination.

The *counselor background record* is completed by each counselor and includes information about formal education, training certifications, and personality characteristics.

Posttreatment followups are scheduled for all clients one year after termination from DATAR, conducted according to a procedures manual detailing sequential steps for relocating and interviewing former clients (a subsample will be selected for two-year followup interviews as well). Materials used as part of the *followup interview* include an information sheet, consent forms, interview form, client rating form, urinalysis form, and fieldwork followup activities record. These data are collected by a member of the research staff (not a program counselor); the interview requires sixty minutes.

MANAGEMENT SYSTEM

Without an effective plan for project implementation and management, even the best intervention strategies may never find empirical support. As discussed by McAuliffe and Ashery (1992), intervention evaluation projects that rely on collaborative relationships with treatment agencies to follow research protocols and deliver enhanced services, such as in DATAR, are challenging. Under conditions of cooperation and mutual trust, however, such projects also can be very effective treatment demonstration models. To be successful, such efforts require that decisions be balanced in terms of the clinical services and research needs of the project, and that both the treatment and research leaders be willing to accept negotiated settlements of procedural issues.

There are several additional critical elements comprising the overall management system. First, enrichment of treatment services—such as using mapping techniques and special intervention modules in the DATAR project—requires careful counselor training and monitoring. Centralized and field-based training contacts with program staff have been frequent and have increased rapport and trust, which in turn has contributed to an overall improvement in the therapeutic skills and self-confidence of the counselors. Through mutual sharing of new skills and the attention resulting from being part of a "special study," these improvements appear to have generalized throughout the agency and occasionally have led to conflicts or jealousy among counselors and clients who receive different roles and assignments. However, the general effect of enhanced counseling and data collection training in the project has been to raise the general quality of services at each agency. This effect also has led to concern among research staff that it will reduce the chances of demonstrating enhanced treatment outcome differences in the evaluations being conducted.

Another important element in the management plan is the careful tracking of client services and compliance with targeted contact levels. Ideally, the DATAR project requests that four group and two individual counseling sessions be attended each month by clients in the outpatient MM programs. Compliance levels usually average less than half of this, but by developing key agency performance indicators and focusing attention on them—such as session attendance, as well as rates of "clean" urines and retention of clients—agency performance has improved over time. This process occurs through a systematic flow of communications using simple visual displays and brief narrative reports. For instance, charts on client caseloads and a one-page summary table of monthly data submitted are faxed to each site during the first week of each month. In addition, a newsletter has been developed to inform agency personnel about general project findings.

Finally, a sophisticated quality-control process has been developed to insure that high data standards are established and maintained. The system includes a computerized tracking system for all DATAR forms due and received. To insure the quality of the data, all forms are carefully edited and corrected, using agency inquiries when needed. This review and feedback process insures accuracy of records, field staff accountability for data completeness, and internal consistency of treatment records. A tracking system for identifying missing forms has been developed that provides easy-to-read computer printouts of missing client records for each agency as well as for each field staff member. Such information helps identify field staff who fall below performance standards in their record-keeping and conveys compliance expectations for each field worker. Recognition of favorable performance and of performance improvement is given frequently. This system has been crucial in helping field and central research staff maintain the large and complex DATAR database.

CONCLUSIONS

The DATAR project has faced significant substantive and methodological challenges, but few deviations from the original plan for the project have been necessary. Identifying and assessing relevant treatment process variables involved in recovery continue to represent extremely important methodological challenges for the drug abuse field. Progress to date suggests that most of the research objectives for evaluating enhancements for improving treatment outcomes in DATAR will be accomplished, and preliminary data are encouraging regarding the choice of strategies selected.

REFERENCES

Anglin, M. D., and Y. I. Hser. 1990. Treatment of Drug Abuse. In *Drugs and Crime*, edited by M. Tonry and J. Q. Wilson, pp. 393–460. Chicago: University of Chicago Press.

Annis, H. M., and C. S. Davis. 1988. Assessment of Expectancies. In *Assessment of Addictive Behaviors*, edited by D. Donovan and G. A. Marlatt. New York: Guilford Press.

Ball, J. C., and A. Ross. 1991. *The Effectiveness of Methadone Maintenance Treatment: Patients, Programs, Services, and Outcome*. New York: Springer-Verlag.

Bigelow, G. E., M. L. Stitzer, and I. A. Liebson. 1984. The Role of Behavioral Contingency Management in Drug Abuse Treatment. In *Behavioral Intervention Techniques in Drug Abuse Treatment*, edited by J. Grabowski, M. L. Stitzer, and J. E. Henningfield, pp. 36–52. NIDA Research Monograph No. 46, DHHS Publication No. (ADM) 84–1282. Washington, DC: U.S. Government Printing Office.

Boatler, J. F. 1991. *TCU/DATAR Project: AIDS/HIV Module*. Fort Worth: Texas Christian University, Institute of Behavioral Research.

Boatler, J. F., D. F. Dansereau, L. R. Chatham, and D. D. Simpson. 1992. *Mapping: Charting New Roads to Recovery*. Fort Worth: Texas Christian University, Institute of Behavioral Research.

Boatler, J. F., K. Knight, and D. D. Simpson. 1991. Assessment of an AIDS Intervention Program During Drug Abuse Treatment. Submitted for publication. Fort Worth: Texas Christian University, Institute of Behavioral Research.

Brown, B. S. 1990–1991. AIDS and the Provision of Drug User Treatment. *International Journal of the Addictions*, 25(12A), 1503–1514.

Brown, B. S. 1991. Introduction: A Report on the National AIDS Demonstration Research Project. In *Community-Based AIDS Prevention: Studies of Intravenous Drug Users and Their Sexual Partners*, Proceedings of the First Annual NADR National Meeting, October 15–18, 1989, pp. 1–8. DHHS Publication No. ADM 91–1752. Washington, DC: U.S. Government Printing Office.

Condelli, W. S., J. A. Fairbank, M. L. Dennis, and J. V. Rachal. 1991. Cocaine Use by Clients in Methadone Programs: Significance, Scope, and Behavioral Interventions. *Journal of Substance Abuse Treatment*, 8, 203–212.

Dansereau, D. F. 1985. Learning Strategy Research. In *Thinking and Learning Skills: Relating Instruction to Research*, vol. 1, edited by J. W. Segal, S. F. Chipman, and R. Glaser, pp. 209–239. Hillsdale, NJ: Erlbaum.

Dees, S. M., D. F. Dansereau, J. L. Peel, J. F. Boatler, and K. Knight. 1991. Using Conceptual Matrices, Knowledge Maps, and Scripted Cooperation to Improve Personal Management Strategies. *Journal of Drug Education*, 21, 211–228.

Dees, S. M., D. F. Dansereau, J. L. Peel, and K. Knight. 1993. Using Scripted Cooperation to Communicate Information about the Consequences of Alcohol and Cocaine Use. *International Journal of the Addictions*, 28(2), 153–166.

Dees, S. M., D. F. Dansereau, J. L. Peel, K. Knight, J. F. Boatler, and M. Loftis. 1992. Using Knowledge Maps and Scripted Cooperation to Inform Students about Patterns of Behavior Related to Recurring Abuse of Alcohol. *Journal of Addictive Behaviors*, 17, 307–318.

De Leon, G. 1989. Psychopathology and Substance Abuse: What Is Being Learned from Research in Therapeutic Communities. *Journal of Psychoactive Drugs*, 21(2), 177–188.

De Leon, G., and N. Jainchill. 1986. Circumstances, Motivation, Readiness and Suitability as Correlates of Treatment Tenure. *Journal of Psychoactive Drugs*, 18(3), 203–208.

Donovan, D. M. 1988. Assessment of Addictive Behaviors: Implications of an Emerging Biopsychosocial Model. In *Assessment of Addictive Behaviors*, edited by D. Donovan and G. A. Marlatt, pp. 3–48. New York: Guilford Press.

Doyle, K. M. 1982. Assertiveness Training for the Drug Dependent Woman. In *Treatment Services for Drug Dependent Women*, vol. 2, edited by B. G. Reed, G. M. Beschner, and J. Mondanaro, pp. 213–246. DHHS Publication No. (ADM) 82–1219. Washington, DC: U.S. Government Printing Office.

Evans, S. H., and D. F. Dansereau. 1991. Knowledge Maps as Tools for Thinking and Communication. In *Enhancing Learning and Thinking*, edited by R. F. Mulcahy, R. Short, and J. Andrews, pp. 97–120. Westport, CT: Praeger Publishers.

Finney, J. W., and R. H. Moos. 1986. Matching Patients with Treatments: Conceptual and Methodological Issues. *Journal of Studies on Alcohol*, 47, 122–134.

Gerstein, D. R., and H. J. Harwood (eds.). 1990. *Treating Drug Problems: A Study of the Evolution, Effectiveness, and Financing of Public and Private Drug Treatment Systems*, vol. 1. Washington, DC: National Academy Press.

Grabowski, J., M. L. Stitzer, and J. E. Henningfield (eds.). 1984. *Behavioral Intervention Techniques in Drug Abuse Treatment*. NIDA Research Monograph No. 46, DHHS Publication No. (ADM) 84–1282. Washington, DC: U.S. Government Printing Office.

Hawkins, J. D., and R. F. Catalano. 1985. Aftercare in Drug Abuse Treatment. *International Journal of the Addictions*, 20 (6, 7), 917–945.

Hubbard, R. L., M. E. Marsden, J. V. Rachal, H. J. Harwood, E. R. Cavanaugh, and H. M. Ginzburg. 1989. *Drug Abuse Treatment: A National Study of Effectiveness*. Chapel Hill: University of North Carolina Press.

Janz, N. K., and M. H. Becker. 1984. The Health Belief Model: A Decade Later. *Health Education Quarterly*, 11(1), 1–47.

Knight, K., and D. D. Simpson. 1992. Assessment of Mapping as a Psychoeducational Tool for Relapse Prevention Training with Drug Addicted Probationers. Unpublished manuscript. Fort Worth: Texas Christian University, Institute of Behavioral Research.

Lambiotte, J. G., D. F. Dansereau, D. R. Cross, and S. B. Reynolds. 1989. Multirelational Semantic Maps. *Educational Psychology Review*, 1(4), 331–367.

Marlatt, G. A., and W. H. George. 1984. Relapse Preventions: Introduction and Overview of the Model. *British Journal of the Addictions*, 79, 261–273.

Marlatt, G. A., and J. R. Gordon. 1980. Determinants of Relapse: Implications for the Maintenance of Behavior Change. In *Behavioral Medicine: Changing Health*

Lifestyles, edited by P. A. Davidson and S. M. Davidson, pp. 410–452. New York: Brunner/Mazel.

McAuliffe, W. E., and R. S. Ashery. 1992. Implementation Issues and Techniques in Randomized Trials of Outpatient Psychosocial Treatments for Drug Abusers: II. Clinical and Administrative Issues. *American Journal of Drug and Alcohol Abuse*, 18(4).

McLellan, A. T. 1986. "Psychiatric Severity" as a Predictor of Outcome from Substance Abuse Treatment. In *Psychopathology and Addictive Disorders*, edited by R. E. Meyer, pp. 95–135. New York: Guilford Press.

McLellan, A. T., G. E. Luborsky, G. E. Woody, and C. P. O'Brien. 1980. An Improved Diagnostic Evaluation Instrument for Substance Abuse Patients: The Addiction Severity Index. *Journal of Nervous and Mental Disease*, 168(1), 26–33.

Office of Technology Assessment, U.S. Congress. 1988. *How Effective Is AIDS Education?* Washington, DC: U.S. Government Printing Office.

Pickens, R. W., C. G. Leukefeld, and C. R. Schuster (eds.). 1991. *Improving Drug Abuse Treatment*. NIDA Research Monograph No. 106, DHHS Publication No. (ADM) 91–1754. Washington, DC: U.S. Government Printing Office.

Platt, J. J., S. D. Husband, and D. Taube. 1990–1991. Major Psychotherapeutic Modalities for Heroin Addiction: A Brief Overview. *International Journal of the Addictions*, 25(12A), 1453–1477.

Platt, J. J., and D. S. Metzger. 1987. Cognitive Interpersonal Problem-Solving Skills and the Maintenance of Treatment Success in Heroin Addicts. *Psychology of Addictive Behaviors*, 1(1), 5–13.

Platt, J. J., D. O. Taube, D. S. Metzger, and M. J. Duome. 1988. Training in Interpersonal Problem Solving. *Journal of Cognitive Psychotherapy: An International Quarterly*, 2(1), 5–34.

Rawson, R. A. 1990–1991. Chemical Dependency Treatment: The Integration of the Alcoholism and Drug Addiction/Use Treatment Systems. *International Journal of the Addictions*, 25(12A), 1515–1536.

Rowan-Szal, G. A., D. D. Simpson, and M. L. Holcom. 1992. Using Contingency Management to Improve Drug Abuse Treatment Compliance. Unpublished manuscript. Fort Worth: Texas Christian University, Institute of Behavioral Research.

Simpson, D. D. 1979. The Relation of Time Spent in Drug Abuse Treatment to Posttreatment Outcome. *American Journal of Psychiatry*, 136(11), 1449–1453.

Simpson, D. D. 1981. Treatment for Drug Abuse: Follow-up Outcomes and Length of Time Spent. *Archives of General Psychiatry*, 38(8), 875–880.

Simpson, D. D., and S. B. Sells. 1982. Effectiveness of Treatment for Drug Abuse: An Overview of the DARP Research Program. *Advances in Alcohol and Substance Abuse Treatment*, 2(1), 7–29.

Simpson, D. D., and S. B. Sells. 1990. *Opioid Addiction and Treatment: A 12-Year Follow-up*. Melbourne, FL: Krieger Publishing Company.

Sorensen, J. L., and G. Bernal. 1987. *A Family Like Yours: Breaking the Patterns of Drug Abuse*. San Francisco: Harper & Row.

Tims, F. M., and C. G. Leukefeld (eds.). 1986. *Relapse and Recovery in Drug Abuse*. NIDA Research Monograph No. 72, DHHS Publication No. (ADM) 86–1473. Washington, DC: U.S. Government Printing Office.

Tims, F. M., and J. P. Ludford (eds.). 1984. *Drug Abuse Treatment Evaluation: Strategies, Progress, and Prospects*. NIDA Research Monograph No. 51, DHHS

Publication No. (ADM) 84–1349. Washington, DC: U.S. Government Printing Office.

Zackon, F., E. E. McAuliffe, and J. Ch'ien. 1985. *Addict Aftercare: Recovery Training and Self-Help*. DHHS Publication No. (ADM) 85–1341. Rockville, MD: National Institute on Drug Abuse.

13

Drug Abuse Day Treatment Using the Therapeutic Community Model

Joseph Guydish, Jesus Bucardo, Monica Chan, Ethan Nebelkopf, Alfonso Acampora, and David Werdegar

Drug abuse in the 1990s is epidemic, with as many as 5.5 million Americans in need of drug abuse treatment (Institute of Medicine, 1990). Treatment for the injection drug user subpopulation alone, estimated at 1.2 million, would require a ten-fold increase in current treatment resources (Presidential Commission, 1988). Moreover, the epidemic is embedded in a matrix of health, policy, and social issues. The deinstitutionalization of health services since the 1970s has increased the number of dually diagnosed clients entering drug treatment; economic forces have yielded a growing cohort of homeless substance abusers; and the Human Immunodeficiency Virus (HIV) has infiltrated communities of injection drug users, their sexual partners, and their children. These and other issues highlight the magnitude and complexity of the drug abuse epidemic and the challenges confronting drug abuse treatment. Responding to these needs requires increased availability of drug treatment, enhancement of existing resources, and the development of innovative treatment strategies.

This chapter describes an intensive drug abuse day treatment program modeled on the therapeutic community. The program was designed to augment preexisting drug treatment services in the San Francisco community, expand the availability of drug treatment, and respond to some of the limitations of urban drug treatment systems. To develop a rationale for the drug abuse day treatment model, we first review existing drug treatment modalities and the application of the day treatment model in other areas. We then describe an intensive drug abuse day treatment program developed by Walden House, Inc., a San Francisco community-based organization experienced in drug abuse treatment. Finally, we discuss some general issues that have arisen in the course of our work, including acceptance of the day treatment program, the need for special services targeting women with children, and collaboration between clinical and research staff.

DRUG TREATMENT MODALITIES

The traditional armament of drug abuse treatment includes four modalities. These are commonly described as chemical dependency programs, methadone maintenance, therapeutic communities (TC), and outpatient drug-free (OPDF) programs. Chemical dependency programs are based on a twenty-eight-day inpatient model, generally supported by employer-sponsored health insurance that includes drug treatment benefits (Institute of Medicine, 1990). Although vital in promoting the health and welfare of the work force, such programs have little impact on uninsured and unemployed drug abusers who seek publicity supported drug treatment.

Methadone maintenance has demonstrated efficacy in reducing opiate dependency, reducing criminal behavior, and improving occupational status. For polydrug users and drug users seeking treatment with little or no history of opiate use, however, methadone maintenance has limited value. The recent surge in crack cocaine use in many urban areas illustrates the need for alternatives to methadone maintenance, which confers no benefit to the crack user. In San Francisco, for example, treatment admissions for crack cocaine increased 125 percent from 1986 to 1989 (Abramowitz et al., 1991).

The TC is an intensive residential treatment where the community acts as a surrogate family, becoming a major force in the treatment process. This modality originated in programs such as Synanon in California and Daytop Village in New York. The TC treatment model is long term, usually twelve to eighteen months, with cost per bed averaging between $7,000 and $9,000 per year (Hubbard et al., 1989: 64–68). The cost, duration, and intensity of TC treatment translate into limited availability. In San Francisco, TCs accounted for only 3 percent of all county-supported drug treatment admissions from 1987 to 1990. Conversely, the high demand for TC treatment generates preadmission waiting periods, sometimes as long as two to three months.

OPDF programs range in scope from two hours per month to six hours per day, differ in target populations, and vary widely in length and type of treatment provided. Perhaps due to the range of programs included under OPDF, some authors have commented that this model suffers a lack of clarity and definition (Tims and Holland, 1984). Consequently, the OPDF modality may best be characterized by what it is not: it is generally not pharmacologically based, and it is not a twenty-four-hour intervention.

Drug abuse day treatment programs are accurately described as OPDF programs within the drug treatment nomenclature. However, unlike outpatient programs that rely on weekly individual or group counseling, day treatment usually involves more intense client participation at least several times per week.

THE DAY TREATMENT MODEL

Widespread dissatisfaction with the conditions in public mental hospitals led the U.S. Congress, in 1955, to establish the Joint Commission on Mental Illness and Health. One change recommended by the commission was a shift from the existing policy of long-term inpatient custodial care for the mentally ill to alternative community-based models of care. This principle was formulated as national policy in the Mental Retardation Facilities and Community Mental Health Centers Act of 1963 (Braun et al., 1981). This policy of "deinstitutionalization" required that many hospitalized mentally ill be transferred to nonhospital settings, and intensive treatment alternatives needed to be available to forestall or avoid rehospitalization. Day treatment or "partial hospitalization" was developed as one alternative, and these programs grew in number to become a mainstay of community mental health services in the United States (Schinnar et al., 1990). Day treatment programs later expanded in scope to include not only the chronic mentally ill but also acutely ill patients (Creed, Black, and Anthony, 1989) and special populations such as children and adolescents (Doan and Petti, 1990). Although much of the available literature concerns psychiatric day treatment programs in the United States and the United Kingdom, such programs have also been implemented in Canada (Levitt, Hogan, and Buckosky, 1990) and parts of Europe (Volovik and Zachepitskii, 1986; Dabrowski and Stanczak, 1988; Schene, van Lieshout, and Mastboom, 1988).

Day treatment has also found wide application in the area of adult day care as an alternative to residential custodial care models. A national survey of adult day care categorized programs according to patient population and program affiliations: Auspice Model I programs were affiliated with nursing homes or rehabilitation hospitals; Auspice Model II programs were affiliated with general hospital or social service agencies; and Special Purpose programs were tailored to particular disabled populations such as veterans or the mentally ill. While many of the programs surveyed targeted the frail elderly, the proportion of otherwise disabled but nonelderly participants ranged from 15 percent to 31 percent (Weissert et al., 1990). Geriatric day hospitals have been used in the United Kingdom since the 1960s (Barker and McCarthy, 1989), and in the United States, they increased in number from 10 in 1972 to over 1,000 in 1982 (Eagle et al., 1987).

Although day treatment programs were used in the treatment of alcohol problems as early as 1956 (Fox and Lowe, 1967), the development of alcohol-related day treatment programs has lagged far behind the explosive growth of day treatment in psychiatric and geriatric care. As in the areas of mental health and adult day care, alcohol-related day treatment programs provide an alternative to more costly inpatient programs and provide greater therapeutic support than traditional outpatient programs (Bensinger and Pilkington, 1983; Collins, Watson, and Zrimec, 1980). In one randomized clinical trial comparing day treatment and residential modalities, no differences were found at a twelve-month followup for drinking behavior, legal involvement, or employment status (McLachlan and Stein, 1982).

Day treatment programs targeting more general substance abuse problems and polydrug abuse are underreported and infrequently studied, and there is a distinct paucity of literature concerning day treatment approaches to drug abuse (Feigelman, 1987; Feigelman, Hyman, and Amann, 1988; Feigelman et al., 1990). The application of an intensive day treatment model to the problems of drug abuse is compelling for several reasons. It is a nonspecific treatment in terms of drug of choice and can be applied to treatment populations having multiple addictions. Its demonstrated usefulness in mental health care confers credibility for extending the model to a drug use population with ever increasing proportions of dual diagnosis patients. In terms of intensity, cost, and duration of treatment, it represents a midlevel intervention between the residential TC and the traditional outpatient model. Adequately staffed, an intensive day treatment program provides a unique point of access to treatment for drug users and an opportunity to improve services in the community by providing triage and referral. The following section describes a drug abuse day treatment program operated by Walden House, Inc., a community-based drug treatment agency in San Francisco. This program was instituted in 1989 to respond to some of the shortcomings of existing drug treatment modalities and to capitalize on the strengths of the day treatment model.

DAY TREATMENT PROGRAM

Program Development and Philosophy

Generally, drug users are incapable of breaking the pernicious cycle of chemical dependency on their own, resulting in enduring high-risk practices and protracted exposure to their many deleterious effects. Prolonged preadmission waiting periods often discourage those in need of treatment. Few residential programs offer alternatives to this delay, and, as a result, potential clients may discontinue seeking admission. In response to this problem, a preadmission outpatient program was developed by Walden House to support prospective clients. The preadmission program both accelerated the start of treatment and challenged applicants by making the process of demonstrating commitment to treatment more demanding. Periodic, sometimes erratic, phone contacts were no longer sufficient to avoid being dropped from the residential waiting list. Regular attendance at outpatient support counseling became a requirement. The positive response to the program led to the development of a structured day treatment service.

The involvement of experienced TC staff was instrumental in developing the day treatment program and in adapting its curriculum to a nonresidential setting. Several modifications to the traditional Walden House residential TC were necessary, especially in administrative procedures, client documentation, and treatment phases. In addition, adaptations were made to the duration of treatment and client functions. Finally, a realistic balance between privileges and sanctions was sought, whereby the rewarding effect of the former and the therapeutic impact of the latter could both be preserved.

For some clients, day treatment continues to serve as orientation and preparation for later entry into the residential TC. However, many clients now participate in day treatment with no expectation of entry into residential treatment. The principal exception is clients who are mandated to residential treatment as a condition of parole or in lieu of prison time.

Walden House operates on a "family concept" in which staff and residents relate to one another in mutually supportive ways. Counselors are seen as role models. Substance abuse is considered, in part, to be a disease of isolation. It is believed that involvement in behaviors associated with addiction is more prevalent among those lacking functional social support. There is an emphasis on mutual help and the belief that each client has the potential for growth and change. Clients are encouraged to help each other work through problems, not validate them. Consequently, they become part of a functional TC "family" that fosters growth and provides effective, recovery-oriented support.

The program combines traditional clinical treatment with a therapeutic model. Counseling is aimed at eradicating drug-taking behavior and developing self-awareness, self-esteem, discipline, and appropriate expression of feelings in a nondestructive way. The main goal of treatment is for the individual to achieve significant behavior modification and permanent lifestyle change. Recovery is considered a lifelong process, a continuum that begins with abstinence, attempts to reactivate an interrupted maturation process, and leads to physical, psychological, and social health and well-being.

Program Description

Program Facility and Staff. The day treatment program is located at a separate project site, with "community," counseling, education, support, and administrative space. Staff characteristics are similar in both the residential and day treatment programs; most are graduates of the Walden House residential program and have gained some clinical experience through an apprenticeship under the guidance of senior treatment staff. However, there has been an increase in the number of professional therapists providing clinical services throughout the organization.

Client Characteristics. In Fiscal Year 1991, there were 452 day treatment admissions, of which 135 were referred to residential treatment; 33 percent were women, 75 percent were between twenty-six and forty years of age, 51 percent were African-American, and 35 percent were white. Crack cocaine was the primary drug of choice for 40 percent, injected heroin for 23 percent, and amphetamines for 9 percent. Average program census was 43 clients, and the mean retention in treatment was 35 days.

Table 13.1
Services Provided to Day Treatment Program Participants

CATEGORY	SERVICES
I. Social Services Advocacy	Medical and mental health screening and referral; HIV-related services; Legal Support; Social Services advocacy (food stamps, AFDC, SSI, Medical, etc.).
II. Family Services	Child custody and reunification assistance; Family Therapy; Couples Therapy; Parenting Classes; Walden Society Meetings (family and friends of WH system-wide clients)
III. Educational and Vocational Services	Educational Services: GED high school equivalency diploma classes, phase 3 or higher. Vocational Services: Job search workshops, resume writing and interview skills, phase 4 or higher.
IV. Minority Services	Level 1: in-house cultural-specific groups. Level 2: community-based groups.
V. Community Outreach	Specialized services and participation in community and neighborhood enhancement projects.

An estimated 80 percent of all clients requesting treatment in the Walden House system have some sort of legal involvement. These clients are encouraged to take action to clear their problems prior to admission. One-third of all potential clients are referred for psychological evaluation, and about 65 percent of these are found to have an additional psychiatric diagnosis, such as depression or psychosis. Walden House has several treatment slots designated specifically for dual diagnostic clients; however, those requiring psychiatric care must be stabilized prior to admission.

The Day Treatment Model. The day treatment program is best described as a nonresidential TC, as it relies on an effective therapeutic community atmosphere and employs as a model the daytime activities of the adult residential program. Services are provided seven days a week. As in the residential program, the phase system is the mainstay of the treatment and moves clients from dependency to self-reliance. Participation in groups is given considerable attention, and structured activities make up a substantial part of the daily schedule. Specific groups fall into five general categories: support groups, therapeutic groups, educational groups, recovery groups, and legal groups. Supportive services include: individual and family counseling, crisis counseling, social services advocacy, and recreational and social activities (see Table 13.1). When appropriate, participation in self-help groups such as Alcoholics Anonymous and Narcotics Anonymous is recommended as part of the individualized treatment plan.

Table 13.2
Phase System and Day Treatment Program Characteristics

RESIDENTIAL		DAY TREATMENT		
PHASE	Months	PHASE	Months	ACTIVITIES
I. Orientation	1-3	Orientation	1	Initial assessment/ Treatment Plan, Attend 6 days + 2 evenings/ wk., abstinence, autobiography, increase behavioral awareness, NA/ AA
II. Therapeutic Community	4-10	Day Treatment*	2-6	Mos. 2-3: develop long -term plan, attend structured activities, apply for phase II privileges. Participate as big brother/sister for new clients Mos. 4-6: problem-solving skills, outside social activities, take leadership with new clients, increase AA/NA participation
III. Re-entry	11-12	Re-entry*	7-12	Mos. 7-9: Resocialization treatment plan, vocational rehab., support system community service, outside activities, bank account, personal budget Mos. 10-12: working or in school, develop aftercare treatment plan, 25 hrs. extramural community service COMPLETION
IV. Aftercare/ Relapse Prev.	13-18	Aftercare/ Relapse Prev.	13-18	Mos. 13-18: 1 year clean, met legal commitments, strong outside support system, secure living situation GRADUATION

* = Day Treatment and Re-entry Phases are subdivided in two phases, giving Day Treatment a six phase system.

Phase System. The residential phase system (see Table 13.2) was modified for use in day treatment, and both programs include equivalent and parallel phases. At each successive phase, clients assume additional responsibilities for themselves and the community. For movement to the next phase, clients must write and submit a proposal, which is reviewed by a Clinical Committee that decides on advancement. Each phase has specific requirements that must be completed before advancement.

Phase 1 (Orientation): The first thirty days of treatment comprise an orientation to the therapeutic community and completion of client assessment. The objectives are for clients to form a bond with the treatment setting and to begin learning to take responsibility for their actions and behaviors. Daily program attendance is required, participation in groups begins, and clients are assigned a "big brother/sister" (an upper-phase client who serves as a role model).

Phase 2 (Day Treatment I): In this phase, two to three months in duration, a long-term treatment plan is developed. Clients gain privileges and may participate in the Core Group, a governing body that assists in peer review and the planning of special client events. They may also serve as a "big brother/sister" for new clients.

Phase 3 (Day Treatment II): During this phase, about three months in duration, participation in groups increases and involvement in extracurricular activities begins (e.g., NA, AA, community service projects). The planning process for the reentry phases begins with school or a job search.

Phase 4 (Reentry I): The client's treatment plan is revised so that resocialization and development of an outside support system are now priorities. Attendance in school, training, or employment begins. If appropriate, group participation can be reduced in accordance with the client's clinical needs.

Phase 5 (Reentry II) and completion of treatment: During this phase, the final phase of formal treatment, the client is either in school or working. Twenty-five hours of community service are required, and preparations for completion of treatment begin. Completion of treatment occurs at the end of Phase 5, after the client has satisfied the following requirements:

1. One year of abstinence (clean and sober).
2. Full-time employment (part-time if attending school).
3. An established bank account and savings.
4. Completion of a minimum of forty hours community volunteer work.
5. A stabilized living environment.

A ceremony and certificate of treatment completion are extended to individuals who have reached this milestone in their recovery process. The ceremony serves to reinforce the significance of this event, for many their first major accomplishment.

Phase 6 (after-care) and graduation: This is a six-month after-care program following completion of treatment. Individual and group counseling regarding specific issues such as financial, employment, and educational matters is provided. There is a focus on peer-bonding and support to aid in the resocialization and continuing recovery processes. Completion of Phase 6 leads to graduation from the Walden House Day Treatment Program.

OBSERVATIONS ABOUT DAY TREATMENT

The Walden House Day Treatment Program is now in its third year of operation and has developed from simply providing preadmission outpatient counseling to a fully structured day treatment program modeled on the therapeutic community. The development and evolution of the program have involved substantial challenge, change, and learning. In this final section we describe three issues faced in our work related to day treatment: the acceptance of this program by clients and staff, the need for special services targeting women with children, and collaboration between clinical and research staff in community-based settings.

Acceptance by Staff and Clients

Reactions to the day treatment program, from both clients and staff, have been mixed. Day treatment has had to compete with the tradition and reputation of the residential TC, which for years has been the backbone of the Walden House system. Such reaction is not exclusive to this project. Herz et al. (1971) encountered a similar phenomenon, where staff members of an inpatient mental health program voiced apprehension toward a plan to place mental health patients in day care. While apprehension diminished as day care experience was gained, the researchers found that the staff continued to prefer a traditional inpatient modality.

Strategies to modify such resistance are necessary if innovative interventions are to be evaluated fairly. One strategy would be the creation of a program similar to the Residential Counselor Training Program, which trains select graduates of the TC to be counselors. Training day treatment graduates would produce a cadre of counselors fully invested in the program and able to assist in the further development and adaptation of day treatment. A second strategy would be targeting recruitment of day treatment clients. Because the agency is known for its residential programs, individuals referred for treatment may be better candidates for residential than for day treatment. Outreach activities alerting referral sources and the community at large about the availability of a new type of program may translate into referrals of clients for whom day treatment is the most appropriate treatment condition.

Special Services for Women with Children

The issue of child care is a serious complication for drug users entering treatment, especially for women who must also provide for and care for children. Early in the development of the program questions arose concerning the child care needs of the treatment population, how the lack of child care acts as a barrier to treatment, and how the presence of children in the facility affects the quality of treatment for mothers. As the day treatment program matures, it places increasing demands on the clients. Children within the facility require parental attention, and parental involvement in treatment activities is correspondingly reduced. Moreover, the needs of the children are not limited to child care per se. These children often present developmental or behavioral problems or learning disabilities, possibly as a result of chaotic living environments or perinatal exposure to drugs, and they may require specialized therapeutic care. While we have not arrived at suitable answers to the questions presented, our impression is that drug abuse day treatment should include a child care component that offers basic therapeutic services.

Collaboration Between Clinical and Research Staff

One of the research goals is to evaluate the effectiveness of the day treatment program, requiring that clinical and research staff work together closely throughout the project. The success of any collaboration between a community-based organization and a university research team hinges on the level and quality of communication. A clear definition of objectives is important for guiding the project through the many changes and modifications necessary over time. Firm leadership and an executive commitment to both research and treatment goals are critical ingredients in successful collaboration.

One characteristic that makes our collaboration interesting and rewarding is that both clinical and research teams benefit from the development of the day treatment program, as well as from the experience and knowledge gained from each other. As research team members have become more invested in the clinical program, they have developed a strong respect for its integrity. Likewise, as clinicians and other treatment staff have become more interested in the research goals, they have become some of the project's strongest allies.

ACKNOWLEDGMENTS

This work was supported by grant number R18 DA06979 from the National Institute on Drug Abuse and by contract number T32 MH19105 from the National Institute of Mental Health.

The authors gratefully acknowledge the staff and clients of the Walden House Day Treatment Program for their patience and persistence in educating us about the complexities of drug abuse treatment. We also thank members of the Day Treatment Evaluation Project writing group for their review and comments on earlier drafts of this chapter.

REFERENCES

Abramowitz, A., J. Guydish, W. Woods, and W. Clark. 1991. *Five Year Trends in Crack Use in an AIDS Epicenter: San Francisco, 1986–1990*. Poster presentation, VII International Conference on AIDS (June 16–21, Florence, Italy, Abstract W.C. 3294).

Barker, L. C., and S. T. McCarthy. 1989. Geriatric Day Hospitals: Consultant and Community Units Compared. *Age and Ageing*, 18, 364–370.

Bensinger, A., and C. F. Pilkington. 1983. An Alternative Method in the Treatment of Alcoholism: The United Technologies Corporation Day Treatment Program. *Journal of Occupational Medicine*, 25, 300–303.

Braun, P., G. Kochansky, R. Shapiro, S. Greenberg, J. Gudeman, S. Johnson, and M. Shore. 1981. Overview: Deinstitutionalization of Psychiatric Patients, A Critical Review of Outcome Studies. *American Journal of Psychiatry*, 138, 736–749.

Chaisson, R. E., A. R. Moss, R. Onishi, D. Osmond, and J. R. Carlson. 1987. Human Immunodeficiency Virus Infection in Heterosexual Intravenous Drug Users in San Francisco. *American Journal of Public Health*, 77, 166–173.

Collins, G. B., E. Watson, and G. L. Zrimec. 1980. A Hospital Day Care Program for Alcoholics. *General Hospital Psychiatry*, 2, 20–22.

Creed, F., D. Black, and P. Anthony. 1989. Day-Hospital and Community Treatment for Acute Psychiatric Illness: A Critical Appraisal. *British Journal of Psychiatry*, 154, 300–310.

Dabrowski, S., and T. Stanczak. 1988. Treatment, Care, and Rehabilitation of the Chronic Mentally Ill in Poland. *Hospital and Community Psychiatry*, 39, 657–661.

De Leon, G. 1985. The Therapeutic Community: Status and Evolution. *International Journal of the Addictions*, 20 (6, 7), 823–844.

DesJarlais, D. C., and S. R. Friedman. 1989. AIDS and IV Drug Use. *Science* (Perspective), 245, 578–580.

Doan, R., and T. A. Petti. 1990. Patient Assessment and Treatment Planning in Child and Adolescent Partial Hospital Programs. *Community Mental Health Journal*, 26, 297–308.

Eagle, D. J., G. Guyatt, C. Patterson, and I. Turpie. 1987. Day Hospitals' Cost and Effectiveness: A Summary. *The Gerontologist*, 27, 735–740.

Feigelman, W. 1987. Day-Care Treatment for Multiple Drug Abusing Adolescents: Social Factors Linked with Completing Treatment. *Journal of Psychoactive Drugs*, 19, 335–344.

Feigelman, W., M. M. Hyman, and K. Amann. 1988. Day-Care Treatment for Youth Multiple Drug Abuse: A Six-Year Follow-up Study. *Journal of Psychoactive Drugs*, 20, 385–395.

Feigelman, W., M. M. Hyman, K. Amann, and B. Feigelman. 1990. Correlates of Persisting Drug Use among Former Youth Multiple Drug Abuse Patients. *Journal of Psychoactive Drugs*, 22, 63–75.

Fox, V., and G. D. Lowe. 1967. Day-Hospital Treatment of the Alcoholic Patient. *Quarterly Journal of Studies on Alcohol*, 29, 634–641.

Herz, M. I., J. Endicott, R. L. Spitzer, and A. Mesnikoff. 1971. Day Versus Inpatient Hospitalization: A Controlled Study. *American Journal of Psychiatry* (127), 1371–1382.

Hubbard, R. L., M. E. Marsden, J. V. Rachal, H. J. Harwood, E. R. Cavanaugh, and H. M. Ginzburg. 1989. *Drug Abuse Treatment: A National Study of Effectiveness*. Chapel Hill: University of North Carolina Press.

Institute of Medicine. 1990. *Treating Drug Problems*. Washington, DC: National Academy Press.

Levitt, A. J., T. P. Hogan, and C. M. Buckosky. 1990. Quality of Life in Chronically Ill Patients in Day Treatment. *Psychological Medicine*, 20, 703–710.

McLachlan, J.F.C., and R. L. Stein. 1982. Evaluation of a Day Clinic for Alcoholics. *Journal of Studies on Alcohol*, 43, 261–272.

National Commission on AIDS. 1991. *Report: The Twin Epidemics of Substance Abuse and HIV*, July. Washington, DC.

Presidential Commission on the Human Immunodeficiency Virus Epidemic. 1988. *Report of the Presidential Commission on the HIV Epidemic*. Washington, DC: U.S. Government Printing Office.

Schene, A. H., P.A.H. van Lieshout, and J.C.M. Mastboom. 1988. Different Types of Partial Hospitalization Programs: Results of a Nationwide Survey in the Netherlands. *Acta Psychiatrica Scandinavia*, 78, 515–522.

Schinnar, A. P., E. Kamis-Gould, N. Delucia, and A. B. Rothbard. 1990. Organizational Determinants of Efficacy and Effectiveness in Mental Health Partial Care Programs. *HSR: Health Services Research*, 22, 387–420.

Tims, F. M., and S. Holland. 1984. A Treatment Evaluation Agenda: Discussion and Recommendations. In *Drug Abuse Treatment Evaluation: Strategies, Progress, and Prospects*, edited by F. M. Tims and J. P. Ludford, pp. 167–174. NIDA Research Monograph No. 51, DHHS Publication No. (ADM) 84–1349. Rockville, MD: National Institute on Drug Abuse.

Volovik, V. M., and R. A. Zachepitskii. 1986. Treatment, Care, and Rehabilitation of the Chronic Mentally Ill in the U.S.S.R. *Hospital and Community Psychiatry*, 37, 280–282.

Weissert, W., J. Elston, E. Bolda, W. Zelman, E. Mutran, and A. Mangum. 1990. *Adult Day Care: Findings from a National Survey*. Baltimore, MD: Johns Hopkins University Press.

14

The Comprehensive Vocational Enhancement Program: A Research/Demonstration Project

Paula H. Kleinman, Holly Robinson, Paul Engelhart, Irv Finkelstein, Bradley Turner, Martin Lesser, and Robert B. Millman

The Comprehensive Vocational Enhancement Program (CVEP) is a nine-level vocational rehabilitation intervention designed specifically for recovering substance abusers in methadone treatment. The program addresses the entire range of vocational problems seen in recovering substance abusers, from assessing job-related needs and interests to clarifying educational and occupational goals and, finally, to securing necessary occupational, job behavior, and placement skills. The program described in this chapter is currently being implemented in a New York City methadone maintenance treatment program. The setting lends itself to evaluation because the clinic in which the CVEP is being implemented is one of two treatment clinics under the supervision of one director, located in similar neighborhoods, and with similar client bodies and counseling staffs.

The quasi-experimental design for the assessment of CVEP involves comparison of the outcomes of clients who receive traditional methadone treatment plus CVEP with those of clients who receive traditional methadone treatment only. Outcome criteria include: (1) treatment retention and utilization of clinical services, (2) drug use, (3) AIDS risk behaviors, (4) employment, (5) criminal behavior, and (6) psychological well-being.

This chapter focuses on the design and implementation stages of the project. The results of the formal evaluation will be presented in later work.

RATIONALE AND PREVIOUS RESEARCH

Heroin addicts are likely to have handicaps that extend beyond the immediate effects of their addiction. Those obstacles may include: low level of formal education; criminal involvement; unstable and inconsistent employment history; psychological disabilities such as severe depression and personality disorders; use of alcohol, cocaine, and other mood-altering drugs; and impaired interpersonal skills. In New York City in the 1990s these problems are compounded by the high levels of homelessness, AIDS, mental illness, and racial discrimination, which afflict the populations from which most urban addicts are drawn. In light of these difficulties, methadone treatment programs must provide services that extend beyond the mere provision of methadone, a medication that blocks heroin craving but does not address other problems.

Vocational rehabilitation is the process by which a disabled individual prepares for and secures employment. The rehabilitation process enhances an individual's ability to succeed at work. This process is not simply a consequence of or an adjunct to treatment but is a treatment in itself (Hersey, Rosenthal, and Goldberg, 1975). Vocational rehabilitation is seen as a key component of an effective methadone treatment regimen for a variety of reasons. Employment is a critical alternative to drug use. Society depends on the worker's participation and ability to be independent and productive. Employment offers a direct path out of the drug subculture by providing a stable, predictable source of income that does not depend on crime or prostitution. In addition, it provides the worker with an opportunity to develop meaningful and continuous relationships with non-drug-using persons. Work also significantly reduces the amount of time available for "hanging out," a large amount of which, in itself, may be associated with substance use.

Work gives people a sense of personal power and control. Because a negative self-image is a critical factor in the development and persistence of substance abuse, provision of skills and abilities leading to employment undercuts one of the conditions leading to addiction. The short-term, concrete activities of educational and vocational rehabilitation, and the clear reinforcements that accompany employment, serve as excellent builders of a positive view of self.

A nationwide survey of drug treatment programs reviewed thirty services that might be offered and found that vocational services were one of only three that contributed significantly to improved patient outcomes (Hubbard, 1981). Persons in the methadone treatment themselves appear to recognize the importance of work in their own rehabilitation. As part of the above-mentioned nationwide survey, vocational services were identified by clients as one of the most important of their needs that were unmet by their treatment program (Craddock et al., 1982).

Systematic attempts to implement and evaluate vocational rehabilitation services within methadone treatment programs are rare, in spite of their great potential value. An early study that looked at the effects of vocational rehabilitation versus psychotherapy on the self-esteem of unemployed and unskilled black clients found that, after a two-month treatment period, only members of the vocational rehabilitation group showed significant improvement on attitudinal measures associated with positive self-concept and perceptions of others (Brewington et al., 1987).

Job-search and interviewing skills were provided, as part of an experimental design, to a relatively small group (thirty) of methadone clients by means of a twelve-hour "Job Seekers' Workshop" (Hall et al., 1981). Outcomes after three months were compared with those of a control group of thirty clients who had not attended the workshop. Trends in the data suggested that those in the intervention group were more likely to have jobs three months following the intervention.

An interpersonal cognitive solving approach focused specifically on employment issues was developed by Platt and his colleagues (Platt and Metzger, 1987). This was a ten-week intervention delivered in group sessions, which focused on barriers to job participation and utilization of a variety of resources to overcome them. Unemployed methadone clients were randomly assigned to intervention and control groups. Treated clients were significantly more likely than controls to be employed at the six-month followup but were similar in terms of employment at the twelve-month followup period. The authors speculate that training in specific techniques related to job maintenance may be necessary.

A third study investigated the effects of the placement in a methadone clinic of a full-time vocational integrator. The task of the integrator was to train staff in vocational rehabilitation but not to work directly with clients. It was found that vocational activities increased as a result of the presence of the integrator, but there was no effect on client vocational status (Arella et al., 1990).

ADDRESSING CLIENT NEEDS

In general, methadone clients who attémpt to enter the job market face major barriers: unfocused or naive employment goals, limited interpersonal and communication skills, inconsistent or nonexistent work records, negative work experiences, criminal convictions, insufficient educational skills, lack of marketable job skills, and inappropriate stress-coping techniques.

Select characteristics of clients upon entry into the CVEP study show the deficits that need to be addressed in order to improve chances of successful entry into the labor market. Two-fifths (41 percent) used intravenous drugs before the age of eighteen, and 72 percent used them by twenty-one years of age. This early onset of substance abuse and addiction is likely to have impaired many aspects of clients' lives, including their physical, social, psychological, educational, and occupational functioning. As evidence of these impairments, upon entry into the study, almost one-half (47 percent) had less than twelve years of education, only 30 percent of clients had been regularly employed in full-time jobs in the past three years, and almost two-thirds (63 percent) had been convicted of a crime and had spent some time in jail.

To realistically address these multiple and enmeshed needs, the vocational rehabilitation intervention was designed as a long-term program that allowed for gradual progress. Flexibility was built in so that individual needs could be accommodated and temporary setbacks could be incorporated into the overall goal of employment. At the same time, the intervention needed to meet the four basic goals of vocational counseling in general: (1) developing a positive self-concept, (2) obtaining occupational information, (3) finding a way to express oneself in occupational terms, and (4) learning job-seeking skills (Reichman, Levy, and Herrington, 1979).

CVEP: THE STRUCTURE AND CONTENT OF THE NINE-LEVEL PROGRAM

The presence of an on-site vocational rehabilitation component in a methadone treatment program communicates support, hope, and high expectations to clients. Such a component delivers the message that clients attending the clinic have greater responsibilities than simply picking up their medication and not loitering around the facility. It indicates to clients that there are staff, procedures, and resources to support them in the transition to work. Its presence is a statement of the belief that clients can achieve some control over their environment and have a life characterized by fulfilling endeavors.

The CVEP program is structured into nine sequenced levels of activities (see Figure 14.1). The client's progress through the levels is facilitated through individual and group counseling sessions. However, because there has been some resistance to groups in methadone programs, most of the work with CVEP clients is accomplished in individual sessions with one of the two vocational rehabilitation counselors.

Level I: Orientation

Key activities in Level I include the completion of a full vocational history, assessment of reading and math levels, and identification of "prevocational concerns" (e.g., needs for a home, child care, or medical or legal services).

In this level, the program makes use of two structured, self-administered instruments, the Self-Directed Search and the Career Assessment Interest Inventory. Once the client has completed these instruments, the counselor is able to focus future sessions and activities on areas in which the client has indicated interest. Clients also complete Tests of Adult Basic Education in order to determine functional reading and math levels. Because functional performance levels may not be as high as would be indicated by the last grade completed, actual performance level is critical in helping the vocational counselor to recommend educational remediation or to make vocational planning more realistic.

In cooperation with the primary counselor, the vocational counselor also addresses a variety of prevocational concerns. These concerns often represent overwhelming obstacles, which need to be addressed before attention can be

Figure 14.1
The Comprehensive Vocational Enhancement Program

LEVEL I: Orientation (2 months)

- -Assessment of math & reading levels
- -Completion & interpretation of Self-Directed Search & Career Assessment Inventory
- -Counseling addressing pre-vocational issues: physical health, living situation

---

LEVEL II: Educational Remediation (2 months)

- -Attendance at necessary remediation services
- -Counseling addressing pre-vocational issues: daycare, income

---

LEVEL III: Aptitude Assessment (1 month)

- -Vocational aptitude battery
- -Continuation in necessary remediation services
- -Counseling addressing social skills: appropriate assertiveness

---

LEVEL IV: World of Work Exposure (3 months)

- -Adkins Life Skills Series
- -Occupational exploration homework
- -Continuation in necessary remediation services
- -Counseling addressing mental health concerns

LEVEL V: Work Adjustment (2 months)

- -Participation in part time, temp. or volunteer work experience
- -Continuation in necessary remediation services
- -Counseling addressing adjustment and career planning

LEVEL VI: Occupational Skills Training (6 months)

- -Attendance requirement at specific training program
- -Counseling addressing adjustment & career planning

LEVEL VII: Job Hunting and Placement (1 month)

- -Daily job-hunting steps
- - Counseling addressing frustration-coping and maintaining motivation

---

LEVEL VIII: Employment Establishment (12 months)

- -Counseling addressing adjustment & upgrading

LEVEL IX: Graduation (1 month)

- -Exit counseling session addressing support resources

focused on higher level training or employment concerns. In order to address these concerns, the counselor makes referrals, which enable the client to secure necessary services.

The client's attendance and punctuality at scheduled sessions are monitored, beginning at this level. This information serves as a significant behavioral indication of client motivation, resistance, and underlying problems.

An important underlying theme in Level I is the development of a good working relationship between the vocational counselor and the client. By the time the client has completed Level I, a high level of rapport, necessary for completion of future work together, has generally been established.

Level II: Educational Remediation

At Level II, the client continues to work with the vocational counselor to clarify occupational goals and steps to take in vocational planning. If the client's educational functioning level does not match his or her expressed employment goals, on-site remediation tutoring sessions can begin. Counseling sessions address hygiene and dress, budgeting, day care, and necessary prevocational issues. Where appropriate, the relationship between these concerns and the client's readiness to work is clarified with the client.

Level III: Aptitude Assessment

The client continues regular educational remediation if necessary and vocational counseling sessions. The client is referred out for further assessment by the Diagnostic Vocational Evaluation (DVE) or another appropriate occupational aptitude battery. DVE results are interpreted and reviewed with the client, and based on this additional information, the vocational treatment plan may be refined or changed. Counseling continues to address occupational exploration. The client's attendance and punctuality at clinic appointments are assessed, and these behaviors are addressed as they relate to work.

Level IV: World of Work Exposure

The vocational counselor works more intensely with the client on the development of employment readiness skills. Because many recovering persons have nonexistent or poor work records and references, they require special assistance in addressing the fears and anxieties associated with entering or returning to the work world. Specifically, they need help in organizing a job search, completing applications, evaluating their job-hunting steps, presenting their background in interviews, understanding employer expectations, and holding onto jobs once they are acquired (Beale, 1988). The Adkins Life Skills Program, which was designed by Columbia University's Institute for Life Coping Skills, has been utilized in CVEP to help meet these needs (Adkins, 1984). The Adkins workbooks, videotapes, and other materials are used in conjunction with role-playing exercises designed by the vocational counselors implementing CVEP. This is the first in a series of ongoing vocational group sessions.

Level V: Work Adjustment

The client is encouraged to participate in part-time, temporary, or volunteer work experience. Sessions address further preparation for occupational skills training, adjustment to work, socializing with work peers, and stress reduction techniques. The General Equivalency Diploma (GED) examination is taken at this level by clients who are judged to be prepared to pass it.

Level VI: Occupational Skills Training

The key activity at this level is to attend a specific training program in order to acquire a marketable skill. At the clinic, individual and group sessions continue to address issues that affect constructive adjustment to employment. These include areas such as coping with stresses that arise in training or on the job, developing relationships with supervisors and coworkers, assertiveness, conflict resolution, and dealing with the loss of welfare payments and entitlements.

Level VII: Job Hunting and Placement

Sessions at this level are designed to support the client in job-hunting efforts. The client is encouraged to use a variety of community resources, including networking. A client's job-hunting steps are monitored and evaluated, and counseling supports the client in maintaining motivation and dealing with the frustration that arises when initial efforts do not result in job offers.

Level VIII: Employment Establishment

At this level, the many adjustments that need to be made in a new job are addressed. These include continued focusing on relationships with supervisors, coworkers, and family members and job performance expectations. Once the client has made the initial adjustment to work successfully, counseling helps the client to look at the possibilities for upgrading his or her job level and for career planning.

Level IX: Graduation

The vocational counselor provides closure to group and individual counseling sessions. The client's outstanding concerns are addressed, and appropriate support resources are identified.

THE CLIENT'S PROGRESS THROUGH CVEP

CVEP is designed to take into account the realistic needs of both higher functioning and lower functioning clients. The program goal for higher functioning clients is to move from unemployment or underemployment (part-time, temporary, or off-the-books jobs) to skills training and competitive employment. For lower functioning clients, the immediate goals are to solve some of the pressing prevocational issues that interfere with employment-relevant activities and also to help them become more aware of their need to address basic issues in their primary therapy before they can effectively attempt employment-related steps. For all participants, the goals of the program are to address deficits and obstacles that limit the ability to work, to develop an understanding of their interests and abilities, and to develop or build upon job-relevant skills.

Clients have thirty months to participate in CVEP. Although guidelines for the amount of time appropriate to completion of each of the nine levels have been established, these guidelines are not rigid. Some of the counseling topics overlap with each other, and certain tasks may be taken out of sequence to meet the needs of an individual client. A client may stay in a given level for a much longer time than usual or, occasionally, for a shorter period than prescribed, depending on his or her particular needs and aptitudes.

Progress through CVEP is coordinated with the client's primary therapist. A client will not be allowed to move to a higher level until the tasks of the earlier one have been completed. For example, as a general practice, a client is not referred for skills training until he or she has completed the occupational interest and aptitude testing, which help the individual to determine a realistic employment goal. In addition, urines are tested randomly for indications of drug use as part of the clinic's general policy. The inability to provide a pattern of ''clean'' urines may indicate that the client is inappropriately managing stress; the client will, therefore, not be allowed to progress to higher CVEP levels until a pattern of clean urines is reestablished. Reciprocally, the client's vocational behaviors serve as additional evidence upon which the primary therapists can evaluate overall clinical progress. Progress in CVEP may contribute to the granting of increased clinic privileges, such as reduced medication pickup schedule and earlier medication hours.

Resources in the larger community are utilized. Efforts are made by the vocational counselors to research and identify specialized resources appropriate to the wide variety of client needs. Linkages are made with agencies providing temporary shelter, showers, clothing, food, unemployment insurance advocacy, AIDS support groups, psychiatric services, long-term educational remediation, and short-term occupational training. An effective liaison has been established with New York State's Office of Vocational and Educational Services for Individuals with Disabilities (VESID), and as a result specialized aptitude assessment and skills training have been made available to selected clients when needed.

The following is an excerpt from the case study of ''Juanita,'' which illustrates the creative identification and use of community resources to meet a set of specific client needs:

Juanita is a bright, forty-one-year-old, divorced, Hispanic woman who lives with her five-year-old daughter. Her work history includes a number of unrelated jobs, gaps in employment, and periods of underemployment. At the time of her initial contact with CVEP she was unemployed. Aptitude testing showed a high level of mechanical ability. To help her break her previous pattern of accepting any job that became available when she was out of work, and to make her more competitive in a weak New York City economy, the vocational counselor referred her to a competitive six-week training program for nontraditional employment for women. During the time that she was in this program, Juanita was denied unemployment benefits. The counselor referred her both to a clinic that provided free legal services (which eventually assisted her in establishing her right to unemployment benefits) and to a special welfare program that paid a child-care stipend for mothers in training. Juanita successfully completed the training program, applied for and was offered jobs by two Fortune 500 companies, and accepted one of them.

IMPLEMENTATION OF CVEP

The project has been remarkably successful in attracting clients to the CVEP intervention. As of February 29, 1992 (approximately 30 months after the date of the first client's admission to CVEP), 221 clients had kept at least one appointment with a CVEP counselor. Of those who have attended at least one session, 40 percent have remained in treatment for seven sessions or more. Reasons for this success in program implementation are explored below.

Staff Characteristics

The program is delivered by two additional full-time vocational counselors, supervised by an experienced vocational rehabilitation expert. The fact that there are two vocational counselors means that they are able to support each other in maintaining a high level of enthusiasm. The fact that they are full-time staff means that the client can be seen when he or she is motivated; in fact, many unscheduled sessions have been conducted.

The caliber and attitude of the staff implementing the intervention are critical to CVEP. Although recruitment to the vocational program was slow initially, the number of people accepting the enhanced treatment has increased as the staff has become known to the patients. The vocational counselors have expressed their personal interest in clients by advocating for whatever clients need, whether it is considered technically "vocational" or not. The vocational rehabilitation counselors engage clients around their immediate needs, such as a place to sleep, legal assistance, health programs, and newspaper reading and comprehension, and then draw a connection with the vocational rehabilitation process where appropriate.

The formal qualifications of the two vocational counselors include previous experience in vocational rehabilitation, as well as work with recovering substance abusers specifically. It is important, also, that one of the vocational counselors has expertise as an educational remediation specialist so that basic tutoring can be provided on-site at the methadone clinic. This means that clients do not have to go to an outside agency for educational services until they have overcome their initial anxieties and self-esteem issues in a familiar setting.

Program Characteristics

It has been noted in past studies that there is often staff resistance to integrating vocational rehabilitation into treatment facilities (Brewington et al., 1987). By contrast, the regular clinic staff have generally accepted the CVEP vocational counselors. This is probably related to a number of factors. Initially, presentations were made to the full clinic staff to orient them to CVEP and to the research component of the project. Questions and concerns of staff members were fully addressed by project staff.

In addition, the active support of the director of the methadone treatment program was clear from the outset, as evidenced by a number of actions. Even though space in the clinic was scarce, he provided a separate office to each of the two vocational counselors. From the time of the first client's admission to CVEP, the vocational counselors were included in all staff meetings, and their opinions were given the same bearing and respect as those of the primary counselors. These steps gave the clear message that the enhanced program had the full support and approval of the director. This in turn facilitated full and open communication between primary counselors and vocational counselors regarding those clients who were seen by both of them.

There has been a therapeutic benefit resulting from the structural separation between the role of the primary counselor and that of the vocational counselor. Because the primary counselors bear the responsibility for monitoring clients' drug use and adherence to clinic rules, the vocational counselors are not seen in the punitive role by the clients. This makes the vocational counselors less threatening and more approachable.

Other Factors

Some of the staff resistance to vocational rehabilitation, noted above, may relate to differences between the psychotherapeutic model and the vocational rehabilitation model. Vocational rehabilitation is often misunderstood by clinical professionals who have been trained in different academic and therapeutic disciplines. In the case of the CVEP program, the training and interests of the vocational counselors and supervisor resulted in the integration of a psychotherapeutic model with a vocational rehabilitation model. This may have contributed to acceptance of the CVEP by regular clinical staff. In addition, the inclusion of the psychotherapeutic model in the CVEP approach means that early in the vocational rehabilitation process, the client can be assisted with anxieties and interpersonal difficulties that might otherwise be an obstacle to his or her progression in the program.

As noted earlier, communication between primary and vocational counselors is good. Boundary struggles, which might have made the client the pawn of disputes between staff members, have been avoided. In some cases, clients have been able to establish a better relationship with the vocational counselor than with the primary counselor. In those instances, they have been assisted by the CVEP staff to work more effectively with their primary counselor, resulting in a higher level of overall service to the client.

A CASE HISTORY

"Harmon" is a thirty-nine-year-old, white, single male who had been in the methadone program for a year at the time of his first contact with the CVEP program. At that time, the longest he had been drug free in the past twenty years was three months. He was primarily addicted to heroin but listed cocaine as a secondary addiction. His family of origin is very large, with thirteen siblings, all of whom use drugs. His father was an alcoholic who died when Harmon was twelve. He lived with his mother and two brothers and described his family relationships as "strained."

His work history is primarily in unskilled positions. He said he lost all of these jobs either directly or indirectly because of drug use. At the time of first contact with CVEP he had been unemployed for six years and had been supported by public assistance, his family, and street peddling.

Early in treatment, Harmon was described by his primary counselor as uncooperative, deceitful, disturbed, and "sometimes hostile." He did not keep counseling appointments and, by his own admission, had a poor relationship with his primary counselor.

At the time of his enrollment in CVEP, he stated that his goals were to get his GED, to find a new career, and to "live like a normal person my age," including having his own apartment. He had no clear idea of the kind of career in which he would be interested. Harmon also said that he would really like to learn to spell better since he feels "stupid" when he has to communicate in writing and that this affects his self-esteem.

After academic testing revealed a reading grade level of 7.8 and a math grade level of 9.7, he was referred for inhouse tutoring. After having five weeks of "clean" urines, he was referred for a DVE, which indicated that he was appropriate for a trades occupation that he was considering, but which also revealed some difficulty in concentrating and following instructions. By the time several months had passed, his GED tutor and the vocational counselor noticed that Harmon was extremely sensitive to environmental stresses that impaired his ability to concentrate, thereby affecting his vocational and treatment performance.

As an intermediate training step, he was referred to VESID for further evaluation. The VESID evaluation confirmed that "anxiety and depression . . . result in concentration difficulty and his not functioning up to his level of potential." Harmon was referred to a community mental health center for private therapy, which he has continued to attend weekly, and which he describes as being a good experience.

Throughout this period, the vocational counselor encouraged him to speak with his primary counselor for concrete services, and he began to meet with her for weekly counseling sessions. He continued to attend the weekly vocational/educational support group, to attend tutoring twice weekly, and to meet weekly with the vocational counselor. He also started to attend an inhouse Narcotics Anonymous (NA) group. His motivation and fortitude were noticed by clinic staff and by his primary counselor. He was rewarded for this progress with earned clinic privileges—namely, a reduced pickup schedule and reduced dosage.

Through contact with his cousin he secured a job as a construction laborer one year after initial contact with CVEP and quickly advanced to crew foreman. He arranged with his employer to have Thursday mornings off so he could attend tutoring, private therapy, and meet with the vocational counselor. In the following six months he remained employed, appeared to be in better spirits than previously and to have improved his ability to concentrate. He had abstained from all illicit drug use for a period of several months.

Seventeen months after his initial contact with CVEP, Harmon was detoxified from methadone. Prior to his departure from the methadone program and CVEP, an after-care program was designed with the cooperation of his treatment counselor in order to help him deal with the ongoing stresses and changes in his life, and referrals were made to community GED programs. He later moved out of his mother's house, got married, and became a partner in the business in which he was first employed. There are still a number of unresolved issues, however. He has not yet completed his GED and is still vulnerable to the stresses created by his social and physical environments and relationships. Hopefully, with the skills he learned in the CVEP and the larger methadone treatment program, and with the careful discharge planning that occurred, he will be able to continue to grow, adapt, and achieve his goals.

REFERENCES

Adkins, W. 1984. Life Skills Education: A Video-Based Counseling/Learning System. In *Teaching Psychological Skills: Models for Giving Psychology Away*, edited by D. Larson, pp. 44–68. Monterey, CA: Brooks/Cole.

Arella, L. R., S. Deren, J. Randell, and V. Brewington. 1990. Increasing Utilization of Vocational Services in Methadone Maintenance Treatment Programs: Results of a One-Year Intervention. *Journal of Applied Rehabilitation Counseling*, 21(2), 45–57.

Beale, A. 1988. A Replicable Program for Teaching Job Interview Skills to Recovering

Substance Abusers. *Journal of Applied Rehabilitation Counseling*, 19(Spring), 47–49.

Brewington, V., L. R. Arella, S. Deren, and J. Randell. 1987. Obstacles to the Utilization of Vocational Services: An Analysis of the Literature. *International Journal of the Addictions*, 22(11), 1091–1118.

Craddock, S. G., R. Hubbard, R. Bray, E. Cavanaugh, and J. V. Rachal. 1982. *Client Characteristics, Behaviors, and In-Treatment Outcomes: 1980 TOPS Admission Cohort*. Contract No. 271793511. Rockville, MD: National Institute on Drug Abuse.

Hall, S., P. Loeb, K. Coyne, and J. Cooper. 1981. Increasing Employment in Ex-Heroin Addicts: I and II. *Behavior Therapy*, 12, 443–460.

Hersey, B., R. Rosenthal, and I. Goldberg. 1975. *The Addict and Ex-Addict in the World of Work: Job-Finding Experiences and Performance in Employment*. Springfield, VA: National Technical Information Service.

Hubbard, R. 1981. *Employment Services in Drug Treatment Programs*. Rockville, MD: National Institute on Drug Abuse.

Platt, J. J., and D. S. Metzger. 1987. Cognitive Interpersonal Problem-Solving Skills and the Maintenance of Treatment Success in Heroin Addicts. *Psychology of Addictive Behaviors*, 1(1), 5–13.

Reichman, W., M. Levy, and S. Herrington. 1979. Vocational Counseling in Early Sobriety. *Labor Management Alcoholism Journal*, 8(March-April), 192–197.

15

St. Louis's Efforts to Reduce the Spread of AIDS

Linda B. Cottler, Wilson M. Compton III, Rumi K. Price, Audrey M. Shillington, Daniel J. Claverie, Jane E. Works, Douglas E. Mager, Dian Sharma, and Oval Miller

In response to the local St. Louis AIDS crisis, Washington University School of Medicine investigators proposed a treatment demonstration project entitled St. Louis's Effort to Reduce the Spread of AIDS among Injection Drug Users (IDUs)—ERSA. This areawide project, which was funded in 1989 by the National Institute on Drug Abuse (NIDA), is aimed at reducing the spread of HIV while improving drug treatment among the city's most vulnerable population.

The advantages of doing a longitudinal study of treatment outcomes in St. Louis were evident. First, when the study began, the cumulative incidence of AIDS cases was low presumably because St. Louis was at an early stage of the AIDS epidemic. Second, the number of treatment slots provided by the Missouri Division of Alcohol and Drugs was inadequate to treat the estimated 8,000 IDUs in the area. Third, AIDS intervention and educational efforts at the treatment centers needed enhancement. Finally, a group of investigators, treatment providers, and the health department were committed to changing the status quo.

As of November 1991, 14.5 percent of the reported AIDS cases in St. Louis were attributable to injection drug use (St. Louis Health Department, 1991) compared to a rate of 25 percent nationwide. In St. Louis, the rate of HIV infection among IDUs is also low (about 3 percent) compared to rates of 50 percent to 60 percent in the New York City and New Jersey areas (Cottler et al., forthcoming). However, the rate of high-risk behavior (such as unprotected sex with multiple partners and needle sharing) among St. Louis's IDU population is comparable to rates in other cities with high HIV infection rates. Because the rate of HIV infection can increase dramatically in a short time, as seen in New York City, where the rate rose from 0 percent in 1978 to 56 percent in 1984

(Novick et al., 1986); Scotland (Robertson et al., 1986); Italy (Amgarano et al., 1985); and Spain (Lange et al., 1987), we evaluate our status as one of either a continuing low prevalence area or as a time bomb waiting to go off.

Blacks account for 12 percent of the U.S. population, yet the Centers for Disease Control report that 80 percent of heterosexual men and women with AIDS are black or Hispanic. In St. Louis, 17.3 percent of the metropolitan area's population is black; yet 27 percent of the AIDS cases are among blacks (St. Louis Health Department, 1991). Thus, culturally specific interventions and education are primary needs for this population. Efforts such as these have become the hallmark of the ERSA project.

ERSA was jointly proposed by investigators from Washington University School of Medicine, drug-free and methadone providers from two treatment programs, and the Health Commissioner of St. Louis. This study represents the first areawide collaborative effort of such a multi-disciplinary team. St. Louis has several needs that the ERSA project has proposed to fill: too few drug abuse treatment slots, inadequate HIV prevention efforts among drug abusers, and no street outreach efforts targeted at the most vulnerable, underserved population.

ERSA GOALS

The primary objectives of the ERSA study are to attract IDUs to enter treatment, to improve drug-free and methadone maintenance treatment at two city programs, and to educate persons about how to change high-risk behaviors. For evaluation purposes, we are enlisting IDUs not entering treatment from a community street outreach program; this is one of the most unique aspects of this project.

The following are the specific aims of the project:

Aim 1: To develop a community/street outreach program aimed at attracting substance abusers into treatment and providing primary and secondary prevention.

Aim 2: To establish 100 additional treatment slots for methadone treatment and 200 drug-free treatment slots for persons located in the inner-city St. Louis area and to enhance existing treatment protocols of two programs.

Aim 3: To recruit index subjects for a longitudinal study to (a) evaluate improvements in the programs and (b) compare the efficacy of drug-free treatment versus methadone maintenance, a culturally specific program versus a racially generic program, and after-care versus no after-care.

Aim 4: To identify individual characteristics that predict changes in outcomes among individuals regardless of treatment program. These characteristics may include family history, psychiatric symptoms (both past and current), patterns of symptoms of abuse of and dependence on drugs and alcohol, high-risk sexual behaviors, knowledge of HIV transmission, and needle-sharing behavior.

To achieve these goals, we settled on a research methodology that utilized the strengths of our areawide network. The focal point of the research quickly became the community outreach program, which functioned as a triage unit.

SUBJECT RECRUITMENT

Community Outreach

The ERSA project took advantage of the St. Louis Public Health Department's newly proposed street outreach program called the Community Outreach for Risk Education (CORR) program. CORR was just getting underway as the city's first and only program to educate high-risk populations about risk for HIV infection and safer sex practices. ERSA proposed to expand and enhance this program rather than create a new and competing outreach program.

The main component of this expansion was the establishment of an outreach storefront. For months there were negotiations with the comptroller of the city of St. Louis over location of this outreach office. Some aldermen and civic leaders prevented the outreach office from opening "in their backyards." However, in July 1990, the St. Louis Public Health Department, with funding from this demonstration project, rented and furnished two fixed office spaces in areas of the city that were determined to be at high risk for substance abuse—that is, areas with drug arrests, prostitutes, and high rates of AIDS. The storefront operation is named HealthStreet; it serves as home base for outreach workers and provides a site for various public health screening measures.

At the grand opening of HealthStreet, state and local government officials, community leaders, public health officials, and the Washington University research team officially introduced community outreach efforts to the media and the public. Shortly after the opening, several activities occurred which brought positive public attention to HealthStreet and its outreach efforts. First, it served as the host site for a three-day training session given by the Association for Drug Abuse Prevention and Treatment (ADAPT). It also increased its publicity campaign for free drug treatment with doorknob tags and flyers in neighborhoods with high rates of drug use. In addition, the St. Louis Police Department began to distribute to its patrolmen information regarding free drug treatment so they could disseminate this information to the public. A brief videotaped presentation of HealthStreet's activities was also included for a period of time on the police department's morning roll call program as a regular feature.

Once the HealthStreet operation was under way, community health outreach workers (CHOWs) were hired. They underwent orientation to the ERSA project goals, trained in outreach techniques, and began working the streets of St. Louis to identify persons in need of drug treatment. In general, CHOWs approach persons and engage them in conversation about AIDS and drug use. Where appropriate, they encourage persons to accept referral to HealthStreet and give them a Priority Health Referral Appointment Slip, which helps the counselors at HealthStreet identify potential clients for drug treatment.

Figure 15.1 illustrates the ERSA subject flow chart. There are two sources of referrals to HealthStreet: self-referrals (walk-ins) and CHOW referrals. Walk-ins come to HealthStreet after stumbling onto it or after learning about it through tabloids, newspapers, radio, or television. HealthStreet is advertised by the media as a ''mini-health department'' that provides free health services to the public in addition to drug abuse screening. The Health Department, taking advantage of the primary prevention opportunity, provides other health services through HealthStreet free of charge. These services include flu shots and screening for diabetes, high blood pressure, and chronic obstructive pulmonary disease.

Everyone arriving at HealthStreet sees an information specialist who completes an intake form. The intake form asks the reason for the visit to HealthStreet, the source of referral, problems the subject would like to discuss, and socio-demographic information. A series of health questions are then asked including medical history and services desired. For evaluation purposes, both the services rendered and requested are recorded.

The next intake questions focus on history of current drug use defined as use within the past twelve months on a regular basis. As shown in Figure 15.1, persons who are not current users are ineligible for the ERSA project. If eligible, they are informed briefly about the ERSA project and are told about free drug treatment. If a subject is interested in treatment, an appointment with either the drug-free or methadone treatment program is made, depending on the history and type of drug used. Eligible persons who do not want treatment are recruited for the comparison sample. Persons who wish to participate in the study in either the treated or comparison sample are asked to complete a future contact form to facilitate study enrollment and tracing by Washington University staff.

Baseline interviews for the ERSA study are done by Washington University staff and may be done at HealthStreet immediately following intake. Interviewing HealthStreet clients as soon as possible is important because persons may desire treatment when in crisis but change their minds when the crisis subsides; also, rapid recruitment increases the likelihood that people will continue to participate in the study. Conducting a baseline interview with everyone who comes to HealthStreet allows us to follow people whether or not they actually enter treatment. As shown in Figure 15.1, persons requesting treatment are considered part of the treatment group if they enter treatment within thirty days and stay at least seven days. Desisters, those who do not enter treatment within thirty days of their HealthStreet debut or enter but stay less than seven days, are placed in the comparison group.

Drug Treatment Program Admissions

In addition to HealthStreet funneling potential clients to drug-free or methadone programs, the programs themselves admit persons to our study directly and

Figure 15.1
ERSA Subject Flow Chart

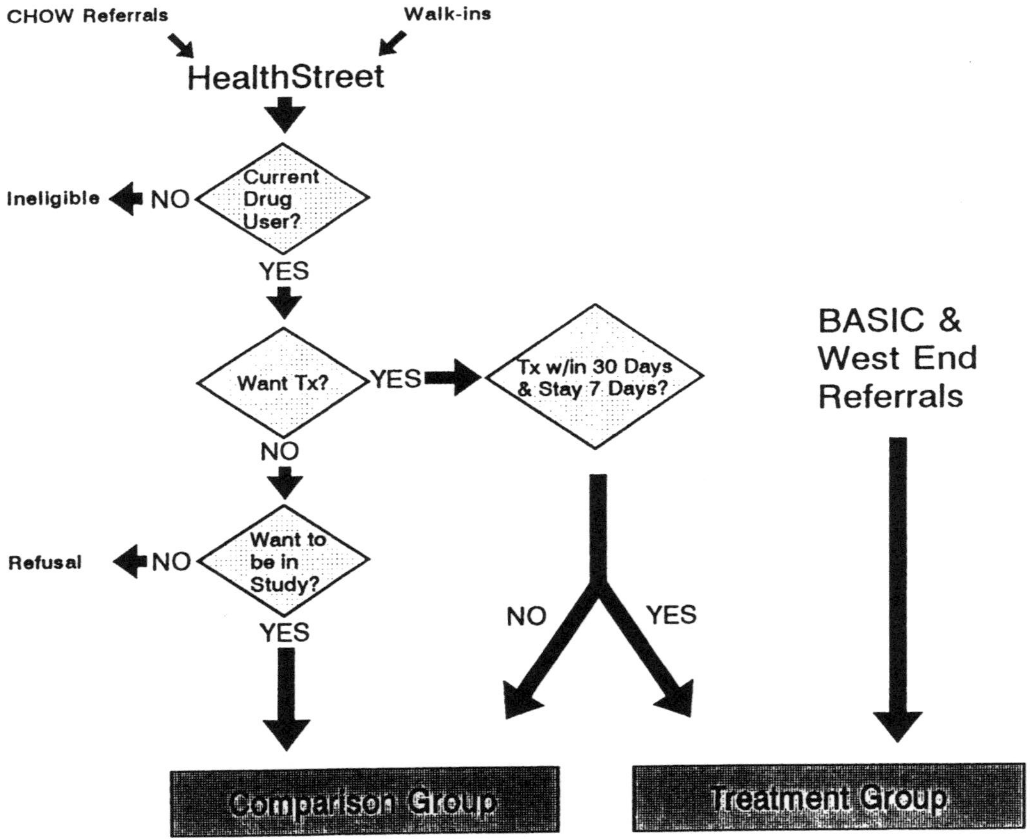

thus into the treatment group. The two programs were chosen for study because of client characteristics, census, and their eagerness to enhance their substance abuse treatment protocols. The programs draw clients from similar parts of the metropolitan area, and the majority of clients are black. The major difference in these outpatient programs is that one is a methadone treatment program (West End Clinic) and the other is a drug-free treatment program (Black Alcohol/Drug Service Information Center—BASIC).

TREATMENT PROGRAMS

West End Clinic

The West End Clinic is a branch of St. Louis Comprehensive Health Center, a fully accredited primary health care facility, which serves the residents of St. Louis. Established in 1984, West End Clinic is located in a blighted area of the city. It is the largest state-funded program for methadone detoxification and maintenance in the city and currently serves approximately 190 outpatients. West End's usual treatment protocol includes individualized treatment; Hepatitis B, syphilis, and HIV antibody testing; and a physical exam conducted by a staff physician. Three types of outpatient treatment are offered: (a) outpatient methadone maintenance of unspecified duration (largest proportion of admissions), (b) methadone detoxification lasting 21 days, and (c) drug-free treatment. However, at any one time, only 2 to 3 clients are enrolled in the drug-free program. Finally, an important component of the usual treatment protocol is random urine screening performed once a month or on an ad lib basis, such as after a client misses a methadone dose for 2 consecutive days, after receiving a vacation privilege, or at the counselor's request.

With the start of the ERSA program, certain improvements and additions were initiated in the West End protocol. First, the ERSA project was funded to add 100 methadone treatment slots. Other changes include increased and enhanced individual and family counseling. This is done through intensive care-management techniques where one counselor is assigned to the ERSA subjects, thereby increasing the intensity and consistency of counseling. ERSA subjects in treatment at West End receive 1 hour of individual counseling weekly and 2- to 3-hour sessions of group counseling monthly. Thus, individual counseling increased by 1 session a month. Group counseling, while not increased, was enhanced by the inclusion of such topics as improving job-seeking and employability skills, interpersonal relations skill-building, and HIV/AIDS risk reduction. Another important change was the initiation of a child care program stocked with age-appropriate toys and books, which allows parents to bring children to the clinic during counseling appointments, thus eliminating one barrier to care. Further, West End's existing AIDS education program for clients and their families and significant others was expanded to include group discussions and individual sessions focusing on risk reduction. Finally, the decor was changed with the purchase of desks, chairs, and greenery to enhance the image of the center.

BASIC

BASIC was developed in 1983 to provide community education, intervention, and support services for minority clients with substance use disorders. In 1986, it developed into an outpatient drug-free treatment program. This program was selected for the study because of its culturally specific program, a program developed to make counseling, treatment, and after-care more relevant to and effective for blacks. Located in the inner city of St. Louis, BASIC's census in 1989, when the proposal was submitted, was 130, with a waiting list of 265 persons. The composition of admissions has consistently been 98 percent black.

Prior to treatment at BASIC, clients must be drug free for at least ten days. This requirement is waived if the client has received at least three days of inpatient detoxification. During this initial period, each client is evaluated through a computer-assisted health assessment, which attempts to assess DSM-III-R (American Psychiatric Association, 1987) substance use and dependence criteria, criminal behavior, previous substance abuse treatment, and stress-related factors. This assessment is used to develop an individualized treatment and after-care plan. ERSA treatment involves four to six months of drug-free treatment, which utilizes a multi-disciplinary approach and incorporates principles of recovery similar to the twelve steps of Alcoholics Anonymous (AA). Specifically, exclusive of any participation in AA or Narcotics Anonymous (NA), BASIC's clients receive one hour of individual counseling and five hours of group counseling each week while also attending a ninety-minute substance abuse educational lecture each week. Clients who are unemployed are required to file for state vocational rehabilitation services or submit two employment applications a day until they have secured employment.

The essential focus of treatment at BASIC is on the area of emotional pain, which generally hinders recovery for black clients and is not usually addressed by racially or culturally generic treatment programs. Specifically, clients explore and learn to cope with black racial self-hatred, black double consciousness, and overreliance on culturally determined defense mechanisms.

One unique aspect of this program is the after-care. Clients who successfully complete their outpatient treatment graduate to BASIC's fourteen-week after-care program, which includes attendance at a weekly three-hour counselor-facilitated group session and, as needed, individual counseling sessions. Treatment graduates meet individually with their counselors to assess sobriety three and six months after graduation.

Throughout the course of treatment at BASIC, vigorous attempts are made to engage the client's family and social network in the treatment process. Additionally, there are many structured, chemical-free experiences available, such as skating parties, a bowling league, a client newspaper, as well as scholarship and feed-the-hungry drives.

The ERSA project has made possible several important enhancements to the program. One improvement is the expansion of services and space; another is the implementation of urine and HIV antibody testing to validate self-reports of drug and HIV status. Additionally, ERSA provides a much needed Child Activity Center to help parents attending counseling and educational sessions. This has proven to be very important to the program and has benefited not only ERSA enrollees but all other persons enrolled in treatment. With the beginning of on-site child care, BASIC has reported a sharp and sustained increase in the number of counseling appointments kept, especially among female clients with children.

LONGITUDINAL ASSESSMENT

As discussed above, the ERSA treatment is provided by the two treatment programs. The ERSA evaluation component, consisting of sampling, data collection, urine and blood collection, and testing and data analysis, is carried out by the Washington University investigators and staff.

Followup of Study Subjects

In addition to a baseline assessment, subjects are interviewed at three, six, nine, twelve, and eighteen months to determine changes in behaviors. In order to accomplish this, extensive followup efforts begin with letters being sent to each subject three weeks prior to their interviews to remind them that a member of the research team will be calling them. Alternatively, the person can phone the research team. The contact tracing is further facilitated by the future contacts form completed on each subject during the baseline interview. With this, the team records the telephone numbers and addresses of persons who can serve as alternate contacts—usually relatives and friends, frequently parole officers, and occasionally social workers and employers. A number of other sources are used to trace and locate subjects: local and long-distance telephone directory assistance, commercial criss-cross directories, voter and post office records, corrections and motor vehicle registration departments' records, vital statistics bureaus, and commercial credit bureau databases. A history of the effort expended tracing and contacting subjects throughout the duration of the study is maintained on each subject on a record of contacts form.

Subject Retention and Attrition

No subject is dropped from the protocol once he or she has completed a baseline interview. If a subject misses any of the followups, fresh efforts are made to secure cooperation for the next followup. Among the Washington University staff are several highly experienced interviewers who have extensive experience in tracking and locating subjects as well as converting refusals to agreements.

The date for all other followup interviews is established at the time of the baseline interview. As a target date approaches, a six-week window of opportunity for completing the interview opens. This includes three weeks after the target date. To augment the number of followups completed at twelve months, the window stays open seven weeks beyond the established followup interview date. For the final eighteen-month interview, the window is open from three weeks before the target date until interview completion or until completion is determined impossible at any level of effort.

Remuneration

Payment to subjects minimizes self-selection bias and encourages participation. Although some research centers pay more, our experience indicates that remuneration of $10 for each completed research assessment is sufficient. Because cash payments may be coercive or may be used to purchase drugs, ERSA subjects are compensated with gift certificates for food (not food stamps) redeemable at a major grocery market chain in St. Louis. Treatment subjects who complete their course of treatment as evidenced by graduation to after-care (after four to six months of treatment at BASIC) or completion of scheduled methadone detoxification (after twelve months at West End) receive an additional $15 in certificates as a bonus. All subjects receive a bonus of $15 in certificates for participating in the eighteen-month followup.

Explanation of the Study

ERSA treatment center staff are involved only in identifying eligible subjects and in introducing Washington University interviewers to potential subjects. An explanation of the study procedures and discussion of the informed consent are the responsibility of the Washington University interviewer.

OUTCOME MEASURES

To achieve our goal of identifying characteristics that predict changes in outcomes among individuals, we incorporated structured, standardized assessments into our protocol. All data collected are protected by an Alcohol, Drug Abuse, and Mental Health Administration (ADAMHA) Certificate of Confidentiality, and an individual's results are not shared with treatment personnel.

DIS-III-R

Written at the request of the National Institute of Mental Health (NIMH) Division of Biometry and Epidemiology, the Diagnostic Interview Schedule

(DIS, Robins et al., 1981) has been a popular diagnostic instrument for psychiatric epidemiologic research since 1980. Psychiatric symptoms are assessed on a lifetime and current basis according to DSM-III and III-R criteria. The DIS assesses approximately forty psychiatric disorders, including affective disorders, schizophrenia, somatization, anxiety, and antisocial personality disorders. With the DIS, it will be possible to examine comorbidity of substance use with other psychiatric disorders and to determine the effect that this comorbidity has on subsequent remission and relapse.

WHO/ADAMHA CIDI–Substance Abuse Module and Treatment Modules

Although the DIS-III-R contains questions necessary to make DSM-III and III-R substance abuse and dependence diagnoses, the instrument does not obtain detailed information on the severity, recency, and onset of injection substance use or the onset of each positive symptom attributed to substance use. Written in collaboration with researchers at the World Health Organization (WHO) and ADAMHA, the Composite International Diagnostic Interview (CIDI)–Substance Abuse Module (SAM) is an assessment tool for use in epidemiological studies (Robins, Cottler, and Babor, 1989; Cottler, Robins, and Helzer, 1989). It is highly structured and ascertains information on use of alcohol, tobacco, sedatives, opioids, cocaine, other stimulants, minor tranquilizers, PCP, other hallucinogens, cannabis, and inhalants. In addition to substance use, the SAM obtains information on the course of substance use, age of onset and recency of each positive symptom, duration of use, recency of use, route of administration, and information on quantity and frequency. For each substance used, a detailed history of treatment and attitudes toward treatment, and DSM-III, III-R, ICD–10, and proposed DSM-IV criteria are covered.

NIDA AIDS Initial Assessment Questionnaire

The AIDS Initial Assessment Questionnaire, developed by NIDA's Community Research Branch in 1988, includes questions on high-risk sexual behaviors (number of partners, use of condoms) and needle use behavior (frequency of injection, cleaning habits, number of needle-sharing partners). It also includes questions concerning attitudes toward the AIDS epidemic and knowledge of HIV infection.

Family History Screener and Pedigree

The Family History Screener and Pedigree is used to assess the familial prevalence of major psychiatric disorders among the subject's first-degree relatives. This instrument records each subject's pedigree and assesses psychiatric disorders including substance abuse and dependence.

Sociodemographic Factors

Each of the instruments described above contains some sociodemographic information to make available data on age, race, gender, marital history, number of children, occupation, health care utilization, education, income, and geographic mobility.

HIV Testing

A unique component of the ERSA demonstration project is the inclusion of HIV testing. ERSA interviewers are trained to perform phlebotomy, which is done only in conjunction with pre- and posttest HIV counseling. This counseling focuses on the reduction of HIV risk behaviors. Counseling and blood drawing are performed subsequent to the baseline interview to minimize the possibility of retrospective recall bias among persons who know their HIV status. This is necessary because persons who are HIV positive may think harder than others about the risk factors that have led to their contracting the virus. HIV testing is done with counseling again at the twelve-month followup.

The interviewers give their names and the ERSA phone number to subjects at the close of the pretest HIV counseling after blood has been drawn. Subjects are asked at that time to schedule an appointment at least two weeks later for posttest counseling with their interviewer. (Two weeks is required by the study to allow for completion of laboratory HIV testing.) Preferably, treatment subjects' appointments are piggybacked onto other treatment appointments to increase the likelihood of completing posttest counseling. All tested subjects are advised also of a weekly two-hour session at HealthStreet for receiving their test results. Furthermore, other sites are used for posttest counseling if necessary, such as the Department of Psychiatry or a place chosen by the subject. Blood test results are never given over the telephone nor are they given to anyone other than the subject. To protect confidentiality, pre- and posttest counseling is done by Washington University study personnel; the treatment staff do not have access to test results. If subjects wish to inform their treatment counselors about their HIV status, it is their decision. Because subjects may use posttest counseling to present other related issues and concerns, the Washington University staff are prepared to handle such situations.

All HIV antibody tests are performed at the Washington University Core Retrovirology Laboratory. HIV antibodies are detected using a licensed ELISA (enzyme-linked immunosorbent assay) kit. A sample that is ELISA positive on first testing is retested. If the second ELISA test is negative, the sample is tested a third time. If the third ELISA is positive, it is classified as ELISA positive; if negative, it is considered negative. The presence of HIV antibodies in all reproducible ELISA positive samples is confirmed by Western blot. The Western blots are also performed in the Core Retrovirology Lab using commercially available materials. The presence of two of the following three bands are required for a blot to be considered positive: p24, gp41, gp120/160. Western blots are preserved (and photographed if necessary) in case confirmatory readings are desired at a later date. Anyone found to be positive is offered the chance to participate in the AIDS Clinical Trials protocols. Samples are stored indefinitely in a sera bank at −70 degrees Centigrade for possible future analysis.

Urine Drug Screening

Drug screening is done by Barnes Hospital, part of Washington University Medical School. The urines are tested for barbiturates, methadone, propoxyphene, methaqualone, benzodiazepines, phenothiazines, cocaine metabolites, PCP, cannabinols, amphetamines, and opiates. All positives are confirmed by either gas chromatography or gas chromatography/mass spectometry (GC/MS). Because of the expense, screenings are done at three, nine, twelve, and eighteen months. Supervision of urine collection is done by a person of the same gender. Results of the urine screening are not given to the treatment center or to the subjects themselves.

SELECTION AND TRAINING OF INTERVIEWERS

Our site, experienced with the St. Louis Epidemiologic Catchment Area survey, has extensive experience choosing, training, and monitoring sensitive and reliable interviewers. A seven- to ten-day training program is necessary to train interviewers on the correct administration of the interviews, as well as proper completion of administrative, locating, and tracking forms. Each interviewer is supervised in administration of one or two taped interviews on pilot subjects. Thereafter, every tenth interview is taped and reviewed to assure interview quality. Ongoing editing and cleaning of data are completed with computer data entry programs after manual editing. A field editor meets weekly with interviewers to review performance, accuracy, and concerns regarding study subjects. Independent interview validation is conducted for each interviewer every month.

OBSTACLES

State and local government policies and procedures markedly slowed the project's startup at HealthStreet and West End. Although the Public Health Department was able to find qualified staff for HealthStreet, the search for these workers took considerably longer than expected. The Public Health Department was also impeded in establishing its storefronts because the leases had to be approved by City Hall. These approvals were delayed because of reluctance to lease properties in the areas targeted by the department for the very reasons that the areas were targeted. In addition, all HealthStreet purchases over $200 were subject to a lengthy bid process, delaying startup substantially. Also, it was rumored that a ward alderman blocked the location of a storefront in his ward because he was uneasy about the clientele it would attract. Once these problems were managed, initiation of HealthStreet moved swiftly.

Washington University had difficulties as well. It had to gain the trust of the treatment centers, which had no previous experience with us. Relationships were facilitated on both sides with the help of concerned leaders from national, state, and local levels. Special efforts were made to hire a culturally diverse staff. Gaining the trust of the treatment centers and working with a culturally diverse staff to improve drug treatment and reduce the spread of HIV has been one of the most enlightening and satisfying components of the ERSA project for all of us.

SUMMARY

In response to St. Louis's unique situation—currently low prevalence but at a potentially explosive state in the AIDS epidemic—the Washington University School of Medicine investigators proposed an areawide treatment demonstration project—ERSA. This project is aimed at reducing the spread of HIV among drug-abusing populations and the wider heterosexual populations by increasing and improving drug treatment in the most vulnerable inner-city area.

The ERSA project has allowed a multi-disciplinary team to collaborate on ways to improve drug treatment, increase treatment availability to susceptible populations, and initiate outreach efforts. These collaborative endeavors have been among the most worthwhile for all team members. Researchers from Washington University have come to acknowledge their role as guests in the treatment centers. Similarly, the treatment providers have come to appreciate the value of participating in research.

The ERSA project has significantly enhanced HIV prevention efforts in the city of St. Louis. Treatment availability has improved, treatment programs have been enhanced, and outreach has become an integral part of the city's public health strategy to help its most underserved population. Efforts to ensure the continuation of this areawide collaboration are currently under way.

ACKNOWLEDGMENTS

The authors acknowledge the contributions of Myrtle Davis, Wardell Carter, Pamela Byes, and the treatment staff of West End; Oval Miller, Deborah Pratt, and the counselors at BASIC; Health Commissioner Dian Sharma; Don Cuvo and William Dotson of St. Louis Public Health Department; HealthStreet staff; ERSA interviewers; and ERSA participants. We also acknowledge the technical assistance of Jeanette Haynes and Greg Asmus.

REFERENCES

American Psychiatric Association (APA). 1987. *Diagnostic and Statistical Manual of Mental Disorders*. Washington, DC: APA.

Amgarano, G., G. Pastore, L. Monno, T. Santantonio, N. Luchena, and O. Schiraldi. 1985. Rapid Spread of HTLV-III Infection among Drug Addicts in Italy. *Lancet*, 2, 1032.

Cottler, L. B., W. M. Compton, R. K. Price, R. W. Pearl, G. A. Storch, and S. Keating. 1992. *Low Rates of HIV Infection among Substance Abusers Reporting High Risk Behavior: Trend or Time Bomb?* NIDA Research Monograph No. 119 on 1991 Annual Meetings of College on Problems of Drug Dependence, DHHS Publication No. (ADM) 92–1888. Washington, DC: U.S. Government Printing Office.

Cottler, L. B., L. N. Robins, and J. E. Helzer. 1989. The Reliability of the CIDI-SAM: A New Comprehensive Substance Abuse Interview. *British Journal of Addiction*, 84, 801–814.

Lange, W. R., R. J. Primm, F. S. Tennant, J. T. Payte, and C. M. Luney. 1987. *The Geographic Distribution of HIV Antibodies in Parenteral Drug Abusers*. Presented at the Third International Conference on AIDS (June, Stockholm, Sweden).

Novick, D. M., M. J. Kreek, D. C. DesJarlais, T. J. Spira, E. T. Khuri, J. Ragurath, V. S. Kalyanaraman, A. M. Gelb, and A. Miescher. 1986. Antibody to LAV, the Putative Agent of AIDS in Parenteral Drug Abusers and Methadone-Maintained Patients. Therapeutic, Historical and Ethnic Aspects. In *Problems of Drug Dependence 1985*, edited by L. S. Harris, NIDA Research Monograph, DHHS Publication No. (ADM) 86–01448. Washington, DC: 67: 318–320.

Robertson, J. R., A.B.V. Bucknall, P. D. Welsby, J.J.K. Roberts, J. M. Inglis, J. F. Peutherer, and R. P. Brettle. 1986. Epidemic of AIDS Related Virus (HTLV-III/LAV) Infection among Intravenous Drug Abusers. *British Medical Journal*, 192, 527–529.

Robins, L., L. B. Cottler, and T. Babor. 1989. *The Composite International Diagnostic Interview–Substance Abuse Module*, 4th edition (1983–1987, 1988). St. Louis: Department of Psychiatry, Washington University.

Robins, L. N., J. E. Helzer, J. Croughan, and K. S. Ratcliff. 1981. National Institute of Mental Health Diagnostic Interview Schedule. *Archives of General Psychiatry*, 38, 381–389.

St. Louis Health Department. 1991.

St. Louis Health Department. May 1991.

Index

About the Editors and Contributors

JAMES A. INCIARDI is the director of the Center for Drug and Alcohol Studies at the University of Delaware and a professor in the university's Department of Sociology and Criminal Justice. He received his Ph.D. in sociology at New York University and has extensive research, field, teaching, and clinical experience in the areas of criminal justice, drug abuse, and criminology. He has been director of the National Center for the Study of Acute Drug Reactions at the University of Miami School of Medicine, vice president of the Washington, DC-based Resource Planning Corporation, and associate director of research for both the New York State Narcotic Addiction Control Commission and the Metropolitan Dade County (Florida) Comprehensive Drug Program. Dr. Inciardi has done extensive consulting work both nationally and internationally and has published more than 130 articles, chapters, and books in the areas of criminal justice, substance abuse, history, folklore, criminology, medicine, law, public policy, and AIDS. In addition to teaching criminal justice at the University of Delaware, Dr. Inciardi is also the PI of two large, federally funded drug treatment programs designed for criminal justice populations.

FRANK M. TIMS is deputy chief, Treatment Research Branch, National Institute on Drug Abuse. He received his Ph.D. in sociology in 1980 from the American University and has written and lectured widely on problems of drug abuse and dependence. Among his recent NIDA research monographs are *Relapse and Recovery in Drug Abuse*, *Drug Abuse Treatment in Prisons and Jails*, and *Compulsory Treatment of Drug Abuse*, each in collaboration with Dr. Carl Leukefeld. He was recently a member of a NIDA delegation to Eastern Europe to assess the scope of drug problems and research collaboration opportunities in that region. He also recently received the Administrator's Award for Meritorious Achievement, the highest civilian award of the U.S. Alcohol, Drug Abuse, and Mental Health Administration, for scientific leadership and outstanding contributions.

BENNETT W. FLETCHER has been with the National Institute on Drug Abuse since 1987. During that time, Dr. Fletcher's primary work has been in developing large-scale longitudinal drug treatment evaluation research. These include the Drug Abuse Treatment Outcome Study (DATOS), begun in 1989 to evaluate treatment outcomes for clients in five treatment modalities, and parallel studies designed around the DATOS core, such as the Drug Abuse Treatment Outcome Study of Adolescents (DATOS-A), begun in 1990. Prior to joining NIDA, Dr. Fletcher was with Texas Christian University's Institute of Behavioral Research, where he worked on projects to estimate the prevalence of heroin and cocaine use, to study the relationships between neighborhood characteristics and use of illicit drugs, and to evaluate modes of treatment for substance abusers.

ALFONSO ACAMPORA is the chief executive officer of Walden House, Inc., the largest publicly funded substance abuse program in San Francisco. He has worked in the field of substance abuse since 1966. Acampora is one of the cofounders of the Delancey Street Foundation and has been the driving force behind the development of the Walden House program for seventeen of its twenty years. He founded California Therapeutic Communities, was its president for five years, and now operates in the capacity of government liaison for that organization. He is on the executive board of Therapeutic Communities of America and on the Executive Council and International Organizing Committee of the World Federation of Therapeutic Communities. His knowledge of substance abuse is all encompassing, and he stands ready to serve in any capacity to help this nation win the war on drugs.

M. DOUGLAS ANGLIN is the director of the Drug Abuse Research Center and adjunct associate professor of Medical Psychology, Neuropsychiatric Institute, UCLA. He is principal investigator for the Enhanced Methadone Maintenance project.

PETER J. BOKOS has served as president and chief executive officer of Interventions since the corporation's inception in 1974. Prior to joining Interventions, Dr. Bokos spent three years as director of development, Illinois Drug Abuse Program, Illinois Department of Mental Health and Developmental Disabilities. For two years, he served as director of educational programs, University of Chicago, Department of Psychiatry, Drug Abuse Program. He has served on numerous committees and commissions. He is past president of the Illinois Alcohol and Drug Dependency Association and chairs the treatment committee.

Dr. Bokos holds degrees in psychology (B.S., M.Ed.) and public administration (Ph.D.) and has over twenty professional publications.

JOSEPH V. BRADY is professor of behavioral biology and of neuroscience at the Johns Hopkins University School of Medicine where he has served on the faculty since 1967. He is also the president and chairman of the Board of Trustees of the Institutes for Behavior Resources, a nonprofit human service, educational, and scientific organization with research and service programs in the District of Columbia and Baltimore. Dr. Brady received his Ph.D. from the University of Chicago in 1951 and directed a research program in behavior analysis and behavioral pharmacology at the Walter Reed Institute of Research in Washington, DC until his move to Johns Hopkins in Baltimore. He has served as chairman of the Committee on Problems of Drug Dependence (CPDD) and as president of the Behavioral Pharmacology Society. He is presently a member of the National Academy of Sciences Committee on Toxicology and chairman of the National Institute on Drug Abuse Clinical and Behavioral Initial Review Committee (Study Section).

JESUS BUCARDO is a postdoctoral scholar at the Center for AIDS Prevention Studies, University of California, San Francisco. His clinical emphasis has been in primary care and preventive medicine. Before coming to UCSF he worked five years in substance abuse and HIV treatment and prevention in San Diego. Past research includes seroepidemiology of malaria and HIV prevalence, and epidemiology of sexual and drug use practices among high-risk populations. Current research emphasis includes HIV transmission and risk behavior among injection drug users, substance abuse treatment research, and HIV risk and prevention issues among U.S. Hispanics.

MONICA CHAN serves as research analyst for the Drug Abuse Day Treatment Evaluation Project. She completed graduate studies in business administration, specializing in strategic planning, at the University of Michigan in 1986. Chan has worked in both the nonprofit and private sectors in research and management capacities. Past experience in nonprofit organizations includes program evaluation and marketing planning, cost analyses, program satisfaction evaluation and modification, and community networking. Her current interests in substance abuse treatment are in the areas of relapse prevention and family and social relationships.

LOIS R. CHATHAM became a senior research scientist in the Texas Christian University's Institute of Behavioral Research in 1989. She came to TCU from the U.S. Department of Health and Human Services where she was a member of the Senior Executive Service. She has extensive experience as a senior manager of federally sponsored programs in the fields of alcohol, drug abuse, and mental health. As a member of the staff of the National Institute on Drug Abuse she managed and evaluated the first nationwide network of addiction treatment programs. While working for the National Institute on Alcohol Abuse and Alcoholism, she directed the Divisions of Extramural and Basic Research and the Division of Special Treatment and Rehabilitation. She received her Ph.D. in clinical psychology in 1960 from the University of Houston. Dr. Chatham has received numerous national awards for her contributions to the field of substance abuse and citations for contributions to the understanding of women's health issues.

DANIEL J. CLAVERIE, a lifelong resident of St. Louis, is coordinator of the ERSA Project. He came to the project from the field of public health. Throughout the 1980s he worked in the St. Louis area as a field epidemiologist in communicable disease control for the City Health Department and later as AIDS surveillance coordinator for the joint city-county AIDS public health program. During the heroin epidemic of the early 1970s he counseled participants in the federally funded Treatment Alternatives to Street Crime (TASC) Program in St. Louis. He has a bachelor's degree in psychology and a master's degree in counseling from the University of Missouri–St. Louis.

PHYLLIS COLE is the program manager for the Weekend Intervention Program at Wright State University School of Medicine.

WILSON M. COMPTON III finished his psychiatry residency training in 1990 and has been on the faculty of Washington University since that time. He is currently instructor in psychiatry at Washington University School of Medicine and coinvestigator of St. Louis's Effort to Reduce the Spread of AIDS (ERSA) program. Dr. Compton's research interest has been the cultural and sociodemographic correlates of psychiatric disorder. His interest in substance abuse follows these same lines of inquiry. Recently he has focused on the comorbidity of psychiatric disorders, especially the relationship of substance-use disorders and non-substance-use disorders.

LINDA B. COTTLER, principal investigator (PI) of the ERSA project and assistant professor of epidemiology in psychiatry, is a psychiatric epidemiologist whose research has focused on substance abuse, high-risk behaviors, and comorbidity of these behaviors with psychiatric disorders. She completed training as a registered nurse in 1972, earned a masters in public health degree in 1980, and Ph.D. in sociology from Washington University in 1987. Dr. Cottler is the PI of several NIDA-funded grants that focus on seroprevalence of HIV among substance abusers, reliability of substance abuse criteria, and treatment evaluation.

GEORGE DE LEON received his doctorate in psychology from Columbia University. Currently he is director of the Center for Therapeutic Community

Research at the National Development and Research Institutes, Inc. (NDRI). He is also research associate professor of psychiatry at New York University. He is a member of the Extramural Scientific Advisory Board of the National Institute on Drug Abuse. His numerous publications and papers address scientific treatment and policy issues in the areas of substance abuse.

PAUL ENGELHART has worked in the field of substance abuse since the early 1980s. He is currently director of education for the National Association on Drug Abuse Problems, having previously worked for the Nassau County Department of Drug and Alcohol Addiction. He has an M.S. in rehabilitation counseling and an M.A. in pastoral counseling, as well as certification as a rehabilitation counselor, employee assistance professional, and national counselor. He is on the faculty of Molloy College's Alcoholism and Drug Addiction Counselor Education Program.

IRV FINKELSTEIN has been the director of the Greenwich House Methadone Treatment Programs since 1984. He has been in the social work field since 1978, and served for several years as director of social services for the Educational Alliance. He is currently a board member and is past chairman of the New York State Committee of Methadone Program Administrators.

JAMES FISHER is the research director of the Enhanced Treatment Through Induction and Case Management Project. He is a doctoral candidate in population and development at the University of North Carolina, Chapel Hill.

RAY FROST is research director at Marathon, Inc., where he serves as site coordinator of the NIDA study AIDS Prevention, Four Residential Treatment Models (grant number R01DA06151).

FRANCES GARFIELD is a research associate at Spectrum Addiction Services, Inc., where she is the on-site project director for the NIDA study AIDS Prevention, Four Residential Treatment Models (grant number R01DA06151).

CHRISTINE GRELLA is an assistant research psychologist at the Drug Abuse Research Center at UCLA. Her research interests include evaluation of alcohol, drug and mental health treatment programs, with a focus on special populations such as women, the homeless, and the dually diagnosed.

BENJAMIN GROSS was vice president of development at Argus Community, Inc., during the inception of Harbor House as well as this research project and contributed significantly to the development of both. He is currently pursuing a masters degree in public health at Columbia University.

ELENA GUAGENTI-TAX is the director of research and program evaluation at Argus Community, Inc., and co-principal investigator of this study. She was an assistant professor at Fordham University School of Social Work, where she taught methods of research and statistics, and program evaluation. Her interests are in drug treatment research and treatment retention.

JOSEPH GUYDISH completed doctoral training in clinical psychology at Washington State University in 1987, and completed the M.P.H. program at the University of California–Berkeley School of Public Health in 1990. Currently he is project director for the Drug Abuse Day Treatment Evaluation Project and assistant clinical professor of medicine. His clinical specialty is in behavioral medicine, and areas of research include substance abuse treatment, evaluation of community-based service organizations, HIV-related risk behavior among injection drug users, and the effectiveness of needle exchange.

ROBERT HILTON has been a clinician and program design specialist in the field of therapeutic community treatment since the 1970s and is a founding board member of Community Studies Institute, Inc. (CSI), in New York City. He is currently the primary service provider in the subcontract between CSI and National Development and Research Institutes, Inc. (NDRI). It is through this contract that Hilton provides clinical design, staff training and supervision, and technical assistance to the Therapeutic Community Methods in Methadone Maintenance (Passages) project.

RITA HINDIN is a senior research fellow and adjunct assistant professor in the Department of Biostatistics and Epidemiology at the University of Massachusetts/Amherst School of Public Health. She is the research coordinator on the study described herein. She is also the principal/co-principal investigator on two evaluation studies for the city of Springfield, Massachusetts, under their Office of Substance Abuse Prevention (OSAP) Community Partnership grant.

STEPHEN D. HUSBAND is an assistant professor of mental health sciences at the Hahnemann University School of Medicine, Division of Addiction Research and Treatment. He received his doctorate in clinical psychology from Hahnemann University. His research interests include the application of problem-solving skills training and cognitive-behavioral therapeutic approaches in the treatment of addicted populations.

MARTIN Y. IGUCHI is an assistant professor of mental health sciences at Hahnemann University School of Medicine, where he is a member of the Division of Addiction Research and Treatment. He received his doctorate in experimental psychology from Boston University and his postdoctoral training at Johns Hopkins University School of Medicine, Department of Psychiatry and Behavioral Science, Behavioral Pharmacology Research Unit. Dr. Iguchi is the PI of a

NIDA treatment demonstration grant entitled Methadone Treatment: Behavioral/Pharmacological Variables. He conducts research on behavioral treatment methods, AIDS risk behaviors, and pharmacological interventions.

HOWARD ISENBERG is project director of NorthEast Treatment (NET) Centers, Lower Kensington Environmental Center (LKEC, Delaware), Inc., Non-Residential Treatment Services, Delaware. He has a master's degree in counseling with an emphasis on marriage, family, and child counseling. He is currently managing a network of outpatient, intensive inpatient, and community support programs for the treatment of alcohol and drug dependence. These programs include the Assertive Community Treatment Program; the Continuing Care Unit and the Women's Intensive Outpatient Program, both offender-dedicated substance abuse treatment programs located in the NET Counseling Center; and Foundations: Intensive Outpatient Program, a shelter-based program for homeless men and women with substance abuse problems in Wilmington, Delaware. His consultant and training work includes the development of case management strategies and treatment efforts to promote effective treatment for drug-involved offenders. He has served as director of an adolescent self-contained residential treatment program for substance abusers and as a therapist in an outpatient mental health clinic.

GEORGE W. JOE originally joined the Institute of Behavioral Research (IBR) at TCU in 1969, after he received his doctorate in Research Design and Educational Measurement from the University of Georgia. In 1983 he became a research scientist in the Behavioral Research Program at Texas A&M University, and in 1989 he moved back to TCU to help reestablish the IBR. His research has focused on the etiology of drug abuse, components of the treatment process, the use of toxicant inhalants, statistical methodology, and psychometric theory. As a senior statistician for the IBR, he has extensive experience in the application of univariate and multivariate statistical methods and in analytic modeling of data. He also is experienced in questionnaire development, sample selection, and survey research. He has published approximately fifty articles or chapters in books and professional journals.

PAULA H. KLEINMAN is assistant professor of sociology, Department of Public Health, Cornell University Medical College, and the research director of the Comprehensive Vocational Enhancement Program. She has conducted research on substance abuse issues as a principal investigator, co-principal investigator, or project director since the 1970s. Her areas of study include the effectiveness of methadone maintenance treatment; the relationship between school problems, marijuana use, and multiple substance use among adolescents; knowledge about and behavior affecting the spread of AIDS among intravenous drug abusers; and the efficacy of therapy in treating cocaine abuse. Dr. Kleinman has published widely in sociological and substance abuse journals on these and related topics.

R. J. LAMB is an associate professor of Mental Health Sciences at Hahnemann University School of Medicine, where he is a member of the Division of Addiction Research and Treatment. He received his doctorate in pharmacology from the University of Arkansas for Medical Sciences. He received postdoctoral training at the Johns Hopkins University School of Medicine's Division of Behavioral Biology and at the Clinical Pharmacology Branch of the National Institute on Drug Abuse's Addiction Research Center. He conducts behavioral pharmacological research into both the basis and treatment of drug addiction.

MARTIN LESSER is director, Division of Biostatistics at North Shore University Hospital and associate professor of Biostatistics, Department of Public Health, Cornell University Medical College. He holds Ph.D. and M.S. degrees in mathematical statistics from Rutgers University and a B.A. in mathematics from Cornell University. His areas of statistical applications are in clinical trials, clinical epidemiology, epidemiology, and diagnosis and screening. Dr. Lesser has coauthored over eighty-five papers in the medical and statistical literature; he has coauthored two book chapters, one on design and analysis of clinical studies in cancer research and the other dealing with statistical issues in diagnostic testing and screening.

BENJAMIN F. LEWIS is the director of research at Spectrum Addiction Services, Inc., where he is the principal investigator on NIDA research studies including AIDS Educational Interventions for IVDUs (grant number R01DA04508), "Comprehensive Surveillance of HIV among IVDUs—Greater Worcester, MA (grant number R01DA5615), and AIDS Prevention, Four Residential Models (grant number R01DA06151). Dr. Lewis is also on the faculty at the University of Massachusetts/Amherst School of Public Health.

BRUCE G. LINK is a research scientist at the Epidemiology Mental Disorders Research Department and an associate professor of public health at Columbia University. He has researched and published extensively on aspects of labeling theory, help-seeking, and service delivery.

DOROTHY LOCKWOOD is an associate scientist with the Center for Drug and Alcohol Studies. She is the project director for the NIDA-funded therapeutic community/work release project. She is also part of the research team evaluating two OSAP community-based prevention demonstration grants. She also conducts program evaluations of various juvenile and adult offender programs. She serves on several state level committees that develop and assess policies and plans for the state criminal and juvenile justice systems. Prior to joining the center, Lockwood was a research specialist at the Delaware Council on Crime and Justice where she conducted policy-oriented research on both the adult and juvenile justice systems and evaluations of state-operated offender programs. She has presented papers as well as published articles and book chapters on drug treatment for offenders, therapeutic communities, women and drug use, and substance abuse. Her research interests include juvenile delinquency, women and drug abuse, drug abuse treatment, community-based substance abuse prevention, and criminal justice policy.

JAMES F. MADDUX graduated from the University of Georgia School of Medicine in 1941. After completing an internship, he served in the commissioned corps of the Public Health Service from 1942 into 1969. Most of his career in the Public Health Service was devoted to clinical psychiatry and mental health administration. He acquired special experience in treatment of narcotic addiction at two large Public Health Service hospitals located at Lexington, Kentucky, and Fort Worth, Texas. From 1969 to the present, Dr. Maddux has served as professor of psychiatry at the University of Texas Health Science Center at San Antonio, where his teaching, research, and clinical work have been concentrated on substance abuse. Now partially retired, he continues to be active in clinical research on methadone maintenance. Dr. Maddux is the author or coauthor of fifty-two articles and one book.

DOUGLAS E. MAGER is a statistical data analyst in the Department of Psychiatry at Washington University School of Medicine. He has gained extensive experience in data management at all levels, from acquisition to cleaning and analysis. Recently, he has been specializing in epidemiologic data gathered in three ongoing, federally funded research grants. He is also involved in the training of visiting research in the DIS data input, cleaning, and scoring algorithms. He has an undergraduate degree in mathematics and is currently involved in graduate study in statistics at Southern Illinois University.

KEAN MANTIUS is a research associate with the Enhanced Methadone Maintenance project as well as psychotherapist specializing in recovery from addiction, a consultant in research writing and editing, and a teacher of communication.

STEVEN S. MARTIN is an associate scientist with the Center for Drug and Alcohol Studies in the Department of Sociology and Criminal Justice at the University of Delaware. He has a Master of Science degree from the London School of Economics and M.A. in sociology from the University of Michigan. He is co-PI and project director on the Assertive Community Treatment Project reported on in this book. He previously worked as field director of a NIDA study of adolescents at Baylor College of Medicine in Houston, then as a scientific analyst at the NIDA-sponsored Center for Prevention Research at the University of Kentucky. He has taught criminology at the University of Delaware. Besides his work in Delaware, he is a consultant to NIDA on the National Household Survey on Drug Abuse and continues a working association with the Kentucky Prevention Center. He has coauthored a number of articles in the areas of survey research, attitudes and behavior, delinquency, and substance abuse.

JANE McCUSKER is professor of epidemiology and director of the AIDS Research Unit in the School of Public Health, University of Massachusetts, Amherst. She is principal investigator of the evaluation team for Project IMPACT and is involved in other AIDS prevention research in Massachusetts.

CHERYL L. MEJTA holds a doctorate in psychology from the Illinois Institute of Technology. She serves as a research consultant with Interventions. In addition, she is the chairperson of the Division of Health and Human Services and professor of Alcoholism and Drug Abuse Sciences at Governors State University. Previously, she has been employed as a research associate (assistant professor) in the Department of Psychiatry at the University of Chicago and research psychologist with Community Corrections Drug Abuse Programs. She has numerous professional publications and presentations.

JUDITH MICKENBERG has served as the Interventions Case Management Study supervisor for two years. She holds a masters degree in social welfare from the University of Wisconsin–Milwaukee. She has worked as a social worker in a variety of positions since 1973.

MARK L. MILLER is currently a compensation analyst in the Human Resources Services Department at Stanford University. His doctoral training and research interests are in social psychology and industrial/organizational psychology.

OVAL MILLER is executive director of Black Alcohol/Drug Service Information Center, Inc. (BASIC), which he founded in 1983. He began his substance abuse training at St. John's Mercy Hospital in 1981. He also completed a one-year internship at the Minnesota Institute on Black Chemical Abuse in 1982. He is past recipient of the Helen B. Madden Award for outstanding achievement in the field of alcoholism from the National Council on Alcoholism and Drug Abuse. He is a graduate of Leadership St. Louis, Class of 1986/1987. Miller is president of the St. Louis Chapter of the National Black Alcohol and Drug Council.

ROBERT B. MILLMAN is the Saul P. Steinberg Distinguished Professor of Psychiatry and Public Health at Cornell University Medical College and acting chair of the Department of Public Health at Cornell University Medical College. He is the principal investigator of CVEP. He has been renowned in the substance abuse field since 1967 and is currently the director of Alcohol and Substance Abuse Services for the Payne Whitney Psychiatric Clinic of the New York Hospital, the projector director of the Adolescent Development Program at New York Hospital–Cornell University Medical College, the medical director of the Employee Development Center of Cornell University Medical College, and the director of the Midtown Center for Treatment and Research of Cornell University

Medical College. Dr. Millman has served as consultant to numerous governmental and foundation committees on substance abuse affairs and has written over 100 book chapters, scientific papers, and reviews.

ROBERT L. MONKS has served at Interventions, a Chicago-based drug treatment program, as director of administrative services for three years and director of research for two. Dr. Monks was a faculty member and administrator at Loyola University for thirteen years. Prior to employment at Loyola, he was a school administrator in Indiana for eleven years. He has authored sixteen professional publications and has been special education hearing officer for the state of Illinois since 1982.

ETHAN NEBELKOPF is director of training at Walden House, Inc. A pioneer in applying personal growth and holistic methods in treating addicts and their families, Dr. Nebelkopf has written several books including *The Herbal Connection: Drug Abuse and Holistic Health*. He has practiced in San Francisco, Oakland, and San Diego, California, and Eugene, Oregon, since 1967. Ethan has also conducted professional training at universities and clinics, including the University of Humanistic Studies, San Diego State University, Berkeley Holistic Health Center, National Holistic Institute, Medicine Wheel, White Cird Clinic, and the World Federation of Therapeutic Communities. His work has been featured in *Well Being*, *Psychology Today*, and the *International Journal of the Addictions*. As president of the California Association of Drug Programs and Professionals, he serves on the Coalition on Professional Standards and the Licensing and Certification Committee of the State Department of Alcohol and Drugs.

BERT PEPPER is a clinical psychiatrist, trained in epidemiology, who has been studying the dually diagnosed since 1978. He is the executive director of the Information Exchange on Young Adult Chronic Patients, Inc.; clinical professor of psychiatry at New York University; and director of the Consultation Service of the American Psychiatric Association. He was part of the team that conducted staff training at Harbor House and serves as the psychiatric consultant and trainer.

JEROME J. PLATT is professor of mental health sciences at Hahnemann University School of Medicine, where he is director of the Division of Addiction Research and Treatment. He earned his doctorate in experimental psychology from the University of Georgia. Dr. Platt also received postdoctoral training in behavior therapy with Dr. Joseph Wolpe at Temple University School of Medicine and Eastern Pennsylvania Psychiatric Institute. He conducts research into the social and psychological bases of addiction; one of his main areas of focus has been interpersonal cognitive problem-solving skills in the assessment and treatment of substance abusers.

RUMI K. PRICE is currently research instructor of epidemiology in psychiatry, Washington University School of Medicine, and coinvestigator of ERSA. She obtained her Ph.D. in sociology from the University of California, Berkeley, and a masters degree in psychiatric epidemiology from Washington University School of Medicine in 1991. Her areas of interest encompass psychiatric and social factors influencing prognosis and treatment outcome of drug abuse, such as premorbid behavioral disorders, psychiatric comorbidity, peer selection, and influences (social networks).

MICHAEL RAHAV is the principal investigator of a NIDA-funded treatment demonstration project and an adjunct assistant professor at New York University. He is a sociologist trained in psychiatric epidemiology and has published numerous articles in a variety of fields.

RICHARD C. RAPP is a clinical social worker, case manager/advocate supervisor, and project director of the Enhanced Treatment Through Induction and Case Management Project.

RICHARD RASKIN is a research scientist for the study on dually diagnosed men. He has a masters in social work from Fordham University and has worked in research and clinical settings in the areas of substance abuse treatment and prevention since 1982.

JAMES RIVERA is a research psychologist for the study on dually diagnosed men. He has recently completed a postdoctoral fellowship in behavioral treatment approaches for the persistently mentally ill at the Albert Einstein College of Medicine. His training has been in planning and evaluating service delivery for this population.

HOLLY ROBINSON is the project manager for the CVEP project. She has worked in the drug treatment community since 1972 and has special expertise in vocational rehabilitation as a counselor and a consultant. She has managed and led training programs for recovering substance abusers and drug treatment staff, including several courses offered by the New York State Division of Substance Abuse Services. She has also served as an investigator and advisor on several research studies addressing substance abuse treatment and vocational rehabilitation.

STANLEY SACKS received his Ph.D. in psychology from the University of Houston. He is currently deputy director of the NIDA-funded Center for Therapeutic Community Research at National Development and Research Institutes, Inc. His current work focuses upon the development and evaluation of modified therapeutic communities for methadone and mentally ill chemical abusing clients. Dr. Sacks has directed mental health programs, conducted evaluation studies of enuresis, and provided organizational consultation to several human services agencies. He has maintained a private practice since the early 1970s.

DIAN SHARMA is currently the Health Commissioner for the city of St. Louis. Prior to this appointment, Dr. Sharma was the epidemiologist and director of Communicable Disease Control for St. Louis County. She earned a master of science degree in bacteriology from Wagner University in New York and a Ph.D. in Microbiology and Immunology from Rutgers University in 1978. She conducted research as assistant professor at California State University in Los Angeles following graduation. Dr. Sharma began her career in St. Louis as laboratory administrator at Bethesda Hospital and Eye Institute. She conducted research and pursued teaching at St. Louis University Medical School for several years.

AUDREY M. SHILLINGTON is presently working in the Department of Psychiatry at Washington University's Medical School. She is a National Institute of Mental Health (NIMH) postdoctoral trainee studying in the area of epidemiology. Her areas of study are the mental health issues of alcohol and drug abuse and dependence, as well as risk factors for and prevention of HIV and AIDS. She graduated from Drury College with dual majors in history and psychology and for a few years was a Peace Corps volunteer in Benin, West Africa. Upon her return to the United States she started and completed her masters degree and Ph.D. at the George Warren Brown School of Social Work, Washington University in St. Louis, Missouri.

HARVEY A. SIEGAL is the director of substance abuse intervention programs at Wright State University's School of Medicine and principal investigator of the Enhanced Treatment Through Induction and Case Management Project.

D. DWAYNE SIMPSON originally joined the faculty of the Institute of Behavioral Research at TCU in 1970, after receiving his Ph.D. in experimental psychology at TCU. He moved to Texas A&M University in 1982 where he was professor of psychology and director of the Behavioral Research Program. He returned to TCU as director of the IBR and professor of psychology in 1989. The etiology of substance abuse, the long-term course of drug addiction careers, and the effectiveness of drug abuse prevention and treatment efforts have been the principal interests addressed by Dr. Simpson's research. He is experienced in establishing large-scale data and management information systems, performing program evaluations of health services delivery agencies, and conducting longitudinal research. He has published over 125 articles on these subjects in books and professional journals. His work and consultation with state, national, and international agencies concerned with drug and alcohol issues have been recognized through research awards and grant support.

ELMER L. STRUENING is the director of the Epidemiology Mental Disorders Research Department and the Community Support System Evaluation Program of the New York State Psychiatric Institute. He has published extensively in the field of evaluation research.

ELIZABETH L. STURZ is founder, president, and chief executive officer of Argus Community, Inc. She has developed a number of innovative programs for substance abusers and high-risk populations and has published three books on related subjects.

BRADLEY TURNER is currently employed as a vocational rehabilitation counselor with the National Association on Drug Abuse Problems (NADAP). He has worked with the employment-related issues of youth, the elderly, low-income, disabled, and substance abusing populations since the early 1980s. He is currently a master's degree student at the Columbia University School of Social Work, studying counseling and administration in the area of workplace-based social work/employee assistance.

JOSEPH H. WAGNER is a research assistant on the Enhanced Treatment Through Induction and Case Management Project. He holds a masters degree of epidemiology from Tulane University.

DAVID WERDEGAR currently holds the position of professor of Community Medicine at the University of California, San Francisco, where he is principal investigator for the Drug Abuse Day Treatment Project. In addition, Dr. Werdegar has been appointed by the governor to the post of director of the Office of State Health Planning and Development. Dr. Werdegar has long been active in community medicine. He served as director of the San Francisco Health Department from 1985 to 1990, a period in which the city experienced major epidemics of AIDS and substance abuse as well as inadequate access to health care. Addressing such issues amplified his interest in innovative approaches to substance abuse treatment and rehabilitation and AIDS prevention education. Other related interests include the relationship of health services to community needs, the organization of health services, and health team approaches to primary care and prevention.

JANE E. WORKS is a research coordinator in the department of psychiatry at Washington University School of Medicine. She is experienced in coordinating psychiatric research projects, developing and pretesting standardized instruments and related instructional materials, training and supervising interviewers in administering instruments, and editing and cleaning project data. She completed her undergraduate degree in social and behavioral sciences at Webster University in St. Louis and her masters degree in education from the University of Missouri–St. Louis. Before working in psychiatric research, she spent several years in the area of special education.

www.ingramcontent.com/pod-product-compliance
Ingram Content Group UK Ltd.
Pitfield, Milton Keynes, MK11 3LW, UK
UKHW020803290926
15470UKWH00003B/926

9 780313 284229